Paula McCullough

CCEA GCSE LEARNING FOR LIFE & WORK

Revised Specification

COLOURPOINT EDUCATIONAL

ISBN: 978 1 78073 212 1

First Edition
First Impression

Layout and design: April Sky Design
Printed by: GPS Colour Graphics Ltd, Belfast

Page 189 constitutes an extension of this copyright page.

Colourpoint Educational
An imprint of Colourpoint Creative Ltd
Colourpoint House
Jubilee Business Park
21 Jubilee Road
Newtownards
County Down
Northern Ireland
BT23 4YH

Tel: 028 9182 0505
E-mail: sales@colourpoint.co.uk
Website: www.colourpoint.co.uk

The Author

Paula McCullough has over 30 years of teaching experience in Northern Ireland, including Learning for Life and Work at KS3 and GCSE level. She currently teaches at Methodist College Belfast, where she is the Co-ordinator for Citizenship. Paula is also the author of the 'Learning for Life and Work in Close-up' series of books for KS3 level.

Acknowledgements

Once again, it has been a pleasure to work with Colourpoint Educational. Thanks are due especially to Rachel Allen, Education Editor, for supporting me through the process of revising this GCSE LLW series.

Publisher's Note

This book has been written to help students preparing for the GCSE Level Learning for Life and Work specification from CCEA. While Colourpoint Educational and the author have taken every care in its production, we are not able to guarantee that the book is completely error-free. Additionally, while the book has been written to closely match the CCEA specification, it is the responsibility of each candidate to satisfy themselves that they have fully met the requirements of the CCEA specification prior to sitting an exam set by that body. For this reason, and because specifications change with time, we strongly advise every candidate to avail of a qualified teacher and to check the contents of the most recent specification for themselves prior to the exam. Colourpoint Creative Ltd therefore cannot be held responsible for any errors or omissions in this book or any consequences thereof.

Contents

Introduction

Exercises

Activity

These exercises are designed to improve skills such as the use of ICT, thinking, problem solving, decision making and being creative.

Teamwork

These exercises are designed to encourage group participation and debate. They aim to improve skills such as communication and working with others.

Further thinking

These extended exercises are designed to encourage research and wider learning. They aim to improve skills such as the use of ICT, managing information, thinking, problem solving and decision making.

Think about

These exercises are designed to encourage personal reflection on a topic or issue studied.

Assessment for learning

These are examples of the types of questions that could be found on a GCSE exam paper. They aim to test knowledge, understanding and evaluation skills. This book uses the following colour code to identify the assessment objectives for GCSE LLW:

Communicating knowledge and understanding

These questions usually begin with the following command words:

- Write down…
- Name…

They require a short answer, which might be a word, phrase, name or sentence. They are worth 1 mark.

Applying knowledge and understanding

These questions usually begin with the following command words:

- Describe one/two…
- Explain one/two…

They require a slightly longer answer, where a point is made followed by a short description or explanation. They are worth 2 marks (if one point with development is needed) or 4 marks (if two points with development are needed).

Analysing and evaluating information, making judgements and presenting conclusions

There are three types of longer questions in this section:

1. Source-based questions
These questions include the command word 'analyse'.

They require a paragraph answer and expect students to use the information provided plus their own knowledge. It is important to use the source to *support* their answer, not just restate the information in the source. The questions are worth 6 marks.

2. Discussion questions
These questions begin with the command word 'Discuss'.

They require a paragraph answer using knowledge and understanding relevant to the question as the basis for discussion. Students should aim to make at least two developed points in their arguments. These questions are worth 6 marks.

3. Evaluation through extended writing
These questions include the command word 'Evaluate'.

They require an extended answer that identifies and comments on issues relevant to the question. Evaluation questions must also have a conclusion at the end of the answer, linking to the points made previously in the answer. The questions are worth 10 marks.

Assessment

CCEA GCSE Learning for Life and Work is assessed through three external written examinations and a controlled assessment task.

UNIT 1: Citizenship	1 hour examination	20%
UNIT 2: Personal Development	1 hour examination	20%
UNIT 3: Employability	1 hour examination	20%
UNIT 4: Controlled Assessment	Investigation task from either Unit 1, 2 or 3	40%

CHAPTER 1A
Diversity and Inclusion: Challenges and Opportunities

Chapter Summary

In this chapter you will be studying:

- **The benefits and challenges associated with expressions of cultural identity.**
- **The influences on a young person's sense of cultural identity.**
- **The causes and consequences of prejudice and discrimination.**
- **The benefits and challenges of immigration.**
- **The causes and consequences of conflict at local, national and global levels.**
- **Ways to resolve conflict peacefully.**
- **Ways to promote inclusion in society.**

Cultural identity

Cultural identity is the sense of belonging to a group. There are many different types of group that someone can relate to, such as race, religion, nationality, language, gender, age and social class. Cultural identity is important as people like to feel that they can identify with others or share a common background.

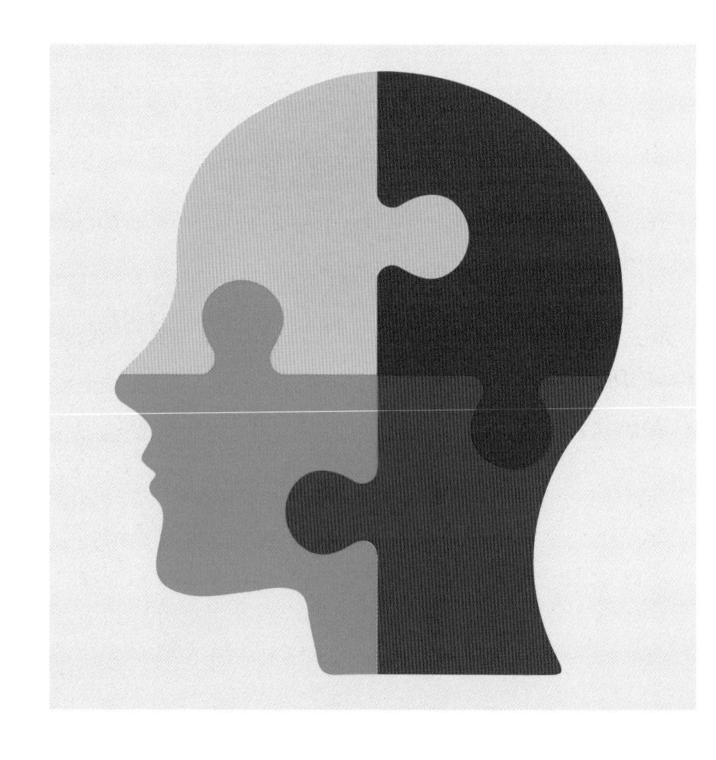

Influences on a young person's cultural identity

Cultural identity doesn't just involve belonging to one group. Most people will identify with a variety of groups and there are many different factors that can influence a person's cultural identity.

INFLUENCES ON CULTURAL IDENTITY

Family – Children usually develop their sense of self from their families. Parents, grandparents and other adults have an important influence on a child's social development and knowing right from wrong.

Religion – A person's religion can influence their behaviour and moral values, as well as the food they eat and the way they dress. Often this influence comes from a young person's family, but not always.

Friends – Outside of the family, friends and peers often have the most influence on a young person's beliefs and values, especially throughout their adolescence and teenage years.

Nationality – Identifying with an ethnic group can influence many young people's language, beliefs and political views. National identity can be particularly influential if a young person belongs to a minority group.

School – Most children and young people spend a significant amount of their time in education. A school can give a sense of belonging and identity, especially if it identifies with a particular group or religion.

Sexuality – A young person's sexual orientation can influence their values, beliefs, behaviour, relationships and friendship groups.

Think about

What things have an influence on your identity, beliefs and values? Have these influences changed as you have grown older? If so, in what way?

Expressions of cultural identity

Many people consider it important to show their cultural identity. If this is done in a positive way, it can create a strong sense of identity and belonging with a particular group. It can also be an effective way of showing others in the community something of their background and traditions. People express their cultural identity in many different ways. Here are some examples:

- **Music and dance** – Many people in Northern Ireland enjoy traditional Irish music and dance as a way of showing cultural identity. Dance is important for people of many different ethnic backgrounds. The Indian Community Centre in Belfast organises displays of traditional Indian dance for visiting school children and members of the public.
- **Food** – Some foods have a connection with religious worship or celebrations. For example, for Hindus, food is an important part of temple worship and sweet treats called Prasad (meaning 'edible gift') are given to worshippers at festival times.
- **Clothes** – Many people choose to express their cultural identity through their clothing. Some will express themselves daily, others only on special occasions, such as at a wedding. For some, it is also an important religious obligation, such as a Muslim woman wearing a hijab or a Sikh man wearing a turban.
- **Language** – For many people, language is an important way of showing cultural identity. For example, in Northern Ireland, many children are educated through Irish and the Ulster-Scots Agency promotes the use of Ulster-Scots as a living language. For Muslims, Arabic is an essential part of their religious identity, as all worship is carried out in this language.
- **Lifestyle** – All families have different ways of doing things. Cultural differences in lifestyle can include the food that is eaten, what languages are spoken at home and the activities that families take part in.
- **Sport** – Sport may be used as an expression of cultural or social identity. For example, Gaelic

football, hurling, camogie, rugby and soccer may all be identified with different cultural groups. Sport can also unite different cultural groups when a local person or team is competing at national or global level.

- **Political symbols** – Some cultural groups choose to express their political beliefs by displaying political symbols. In Northern Ireland, this includes the display of flags, paintings and murals.

Celebrating cultural identity

Joining in with a festival or celebration can be fun and interesting, as well as being a good way to break down barriers and increase understanding. Here are some examples of how cultural identity can be celebrated in a positive way:

- **St Patrick's Day** – This is a cultural and religious celebration held on 17th March to remember St Patrick, the patron saint of Ireland. In many parts of Ireland, and even worldwide, the day is celebrated with processions and parades.
- **Twelfth of July** – Some people in the Protestant community celebrate the Twelfth with marches led by bands. This marks the victory of King William of Orange at the Battle of the Boyne.
- **Belfast Mela** – is a unique summer festival, held in Botanic Gardens in Belfast. This Indian celebration has become a large multi-cultural event, and it attracts tens of thousands of people from all communities living in Northern Ireland.
- **Chinese Welfare Association** – promotes the largest Chinese New Year celebrations annually and the Dragonboat Festival. These events are enjoyed by all communities.
- **Belfast Pride Festival** – This is one of the largest festivals in Northern Ireland and it is a cross-community event. It is both a celebration of the LGBTQ+ community and a protest to demand equality for LGBTQ+ people in Northern Ireland.

Activity

Produce a diversity calendar listing the celebrations of various cultural groups. You will find there are a lot of events happening so you might need to limit the number of groups you decide to include.

St Patrick's Day parade in Dublin

Twelfth of July Parade, Belfast

Chinese New Year

Belfast Pride Festival

Think about

- What is your cultural identity?
- Do you identify with more than one cultural group?
- What influences your cultural identity?

Activity

'Just a minute'

Take it in turns to speak for one minute. Your topic is how the group you identify with expresses cultural identity. Only positive methods are allowed!

Benefits of expressing cultural identity

There are benefits to the whole community when cultural identity is expressed in a positive way, for example:

- **Sense of belonging** – Cultural identity can provide a sense of belonging to a particular group. This can help to form stronger relationships with others and offer a network of support.
- **Promoting mutual understanding** – Making the effort to learn about another person's customs, lifestyle and religious beliefs can lead to more tolerant attitudes.
- **Multiculturalism** – Different cultural groups bring their own traditions, language and beliefs. For example, if a community is made up of people from different cultural backgrounds, then there will be a wider variety of food, entertainment and shops available to cater for them. Expressions of cultural identity can lead to a more interesting and diverse society.

Activity

Organise an assembly celebrating different cultural groups living in the local community or in Northern Ireland today. You might decide to make this a lunchtime event and have some food available from the different groups represented.

Challenges of expressing cultural identity

Some expressions of cultural identity don't always lead to a positive outcome, for example:

- **Isolation and exclusion** – Expressions of cultural identity can make some individuals feel isolated if they are not part of that cultural group. Sometimes cultural identity is used to threaten or intimidate others, and so increases the feelings of exclusion.
- **Division and conflict** – Sometimes having a strong cultural identity can make it difficult for people to relate to other cultural groups. This can lead to division in the community between people of different cultural identities. In a divided community, the mutual understanding and respect needed between different groups is often lacking. In a situation such as this, conflict is more likely to arise and can be more difficult to resolve. The result is even greater division and mistrust, resulting in prejudice and stereotyping. Sectarianism and racism quickly develop in situations such as these. This is shown in the following diagram:

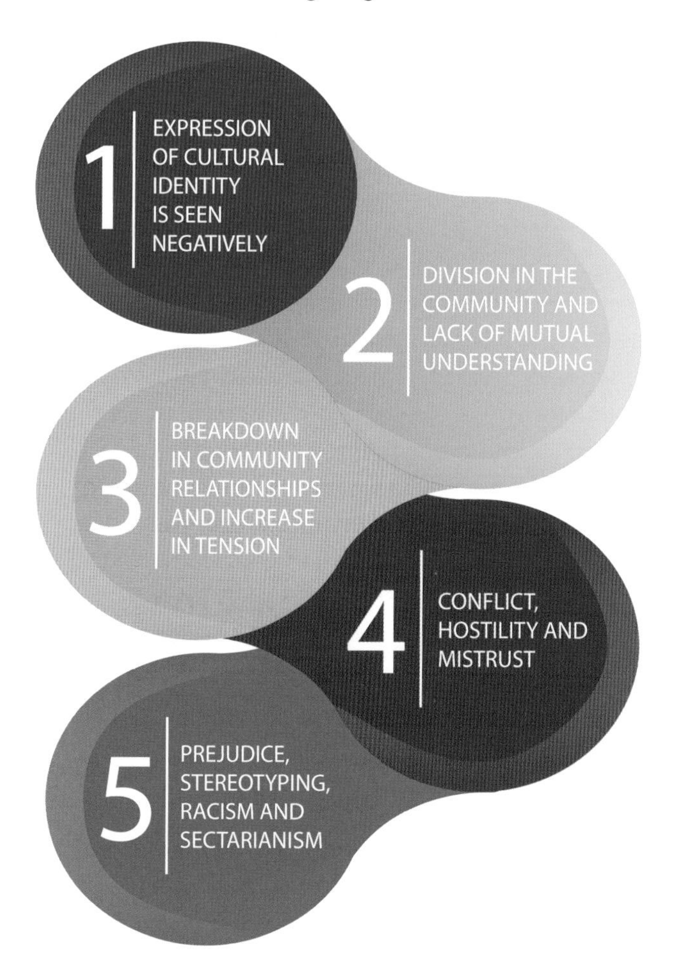

Division in Northern Ireland

Northern Ireland has traditionally been seen as two distinct groups defined by religion and politics. Members of one group tend to consider themselves Protestant and British, either 'Unionist' or 'Loyalist'. Members of the other group tend to consider themselves Catholic and Irish, either 'Nationalist' or 'Republican'. Particularly during the Troubles, displays of cultural identity often caused conflict in the community.

Causes of prejudice and discrimination in society

Prejudice

The word 'prejudice' literally means to 'pre-judge' someone. It is when someone makes up their mind about a person, or group of people, without knowing anything about them. Prejudice is therefore a judgement based on ignorance. Prejudice concerns a person's thoughts rather than their actions.

Where does prejudice come from?

- **It is a natural instinct** – People tend to feel safe with others who are from a similar background and share the same views. Therefore, anyone who is outside this group can appear strange or threatening.
- **It is learnt from an early age** – Children might develop racist or sectarian views because they learn them from their parents or the community they grow up in. As children grow older, their friends and peer group may influence their attitudes towards others.
- **It is the result of experience** – If a person receives bad treatment from someone from a different cultural group, this could make them think negatively of other people from the same background.
- **It is the result of strongly felt views** – Many people have firm opinions about politics or religion. Sometimes this can lead to intolerance of others who don't share their views. Some people feel it's important to express these opinions or even send out a message to anyone who doesn't share their views. This belief may be used to justify certain actions.

Discrimination

Discrimination occurs when a person puts their prejudiced thoughts into action. It involves treating a person or group of people less favourably because of culture, race, religion, gender, sexual orientation or disability. There are laws in place in our society to try to ensure that discrimination doesn't affect a person's right to be treated fairly in education, employment and society.

Racism

Racism is the belief that one race of people is superior or inferior to another (prejudice). As a person's race might influence their skin colour, language, nationality and culture, racism can involve discrimination because of any of these factors. Racial harassment is a form of racism. It can involve verbal abuse, graffiti and damage to property.

Sectarianism

Sectarianism is the belief that one religious or political group (or sect) is superior or inferior to another (prejudice). It involves a dislike of the other group and discrimination against them. Sectarian tensions can be seen between some Sunni Muslims and Shi'a Muslims, or some Catholic and Protestant groups in Northern Ireland.

Sexism

Sexism is discrimination based on a person's gender. It is often caused by stereotyped views about the different roles of men and women, or the belief that one gender is superior or inferior to the other.

Activity

Stereotyping

A stereotype is a crude mental picture that a person might have of someone from another culture. Like prejudice, stereotypes are usually based on ignorance. If you assume that everyone in a particular cultural group is the same, then you probably don't know many people from that group!

- Write (or draw) a stereotyped view of yourself.
- This means you have to imagine that everyone with the same first name as you is exactly the same – likes and dislikes, physical characteristics, character, abilities, and so on. For example, 'All people called Sean are good at football, have blond hair and hate Brussels sprouts.'
- Compare your stereotype with others in your class – especially those who have the same name as you! What does this show about stereotypes?

Think about

Have you ever been a situation where you or someone you know felt discriminated against? How did this make you feel?

Consequences of prejudice and discrimination on society

Prejudice and discrimination can have a negative effect on individuals. It can lead to people feeling:

- marginalised, isolated and alone, with no one to support them.
- frightened in their own community.
- undervalued by the society in which they live.
- stressed and anxious.

Discrimination can have a negative impact on an individual's employment, accommodation and the contribution they can make to society. It can also affect their right to a relationship, such as marriage, or to raise a family. All of these things can have a negative effect on an individual's health and well-being.

Prejudice and discrimination don't just affect the individual discriminated against, they affect society as a whole. A society is supposed to be a group of people living and working together. However, in a society where prejudice and discrimination are tolerated, certain groups may be more vulnerable to abuse (for example, because of their race, gender or sexual orientation). They might also be denied equal protection under the law and feel excluded by society. This all leads to an atmosphere of distrust and intolerance, prevents people from living peacefully alongside each other, and stops society from working as it should.

Teamwork

Working in a group:

- Choose either racism or sectarianism.
- Discuss the causes and consequences of this belief for the whole of society and for individual people.
- Produce two spider diagrams on a large sheet of paper, one for causes and one for consequences.

Immigration

Migration is the movement of people from one country to another. Immigration is when people move into a country from another country. This can be permanent or temporary, and take place over long or short distances.

Reasons for immigration

People immigrate for a variety of economic, social, political and environmental reasons. Some people choose to immigrate, while others are forced to do so.

- **Economic** – Many people choose to immigrate to another country for financial reasons. This might be an exciting new job opportunity or pay rise.
- **Social** – Many people move country to ensure a better life for themselves and their family. This might be the chance of a better education for their children, improved healthcare, a higher standard of living or the chance to experience living in a different culture, perhaps with a more pleasant climate.
- **Safety** – Some people are forced to leave their home country as they fear for their safety and that of their family. They may be escaping from political unrest, conflict, war or a situation where they face persecution for their beliefs or cultural background.
- **Environmental** – Some people are forced to leave their home due to natural disasters, such as hurricanes or earthquakes. Perhaps rebuilding their home and way of life in their home country is impossible or too daunting.

Benefits of immigration

If cultural diversity is celebrated in a positive way, then this will create many benefits for the whole of society. Here are some examples:

- **Understanding other cultures** – Living beside, working with or going to the same school as people from different backgrounds can bring an understanding of different cultures that doesn't come from watching television or reading a book! This understanding is important today, as people are far more likely than in the past to have contact with people from different cultures and beliefs.
- **Sense of community spirit** – Shared cultural experiences can be a very effective way of creating community spirit. Some of the examples on pages 7 and 8 are excellent ways of doing this.
- **Economic benefit** – Many of the people who immigrate to another country want a better life for themselves and their families, and they are determined to work hard to achieve this. These immigrants often ease work and skills shortages in their destination country. Some set up their own businesses, boosting the economy and creating more jobs for the local community.

Think about

Can you think of any other ways that society could benefit if immigrants were welcomed and valued?

Challenges of immigration

Imagine that your family is moving to a country half way around the world that you know very little about. You may have to adjust to different circumstances.

- **Way of life and culture** – These might seem strange and confusing.
- **Food** – The ingredients for your favourite meal may not be available.
- **Climate** – This can be difficult to get used to, and will also affect what you wear – it may be too hot for your favourite jeans.
- **Language** – At first, you may not be able to read notices or understand what people are saying to you.

- **Accessing resources and public services** – Some simple and essential things such as registering with a doctor, enrolling children into a local school or finding a place to live can be very daunting if you are new to the country and trying to cope with language barriers at the same time.
- **Negative attitudes** – Perhaps the most difficult challenge is coping with some people's negative attitudes, such as prejudice, hostility or simply misunderstanding. This can lead to division in society and conflict can arise. The challenge for everyone in society is to try and be as well-informed and tolerant as possible towards people from different cultures.

Think about

Can you think of anything else you might have to adjust to?

Teamwork

Immigration is a controversial topic. Some people welcome immigrants, others oppose them.

- Working in a group, read the following opinions on immigrants.
- Individually, write down the comments that you agree with (if any).
- Taking it in turns, explain to the rest of the group why you agree with these comments.
- Are there any comments that no one agrees with? If so, discuss why people may have these views.
- Finally, evaluate the evidence to support each comment.

"Immigrants take our jobs. That's why so many people here are unemployed."

"They help with labour shortages, when the people here haven't filled the jobs."

"Many set up new businesses when they arrive here, which provides new jobs for local people."

"They're only come here to claim benefits."

"Many new arrivals don't qualify for state benefits."

"People usually move here to make a better life for themselves and their families. They are prepared to work hard to achieve this."

"They're putting pressure on our public services. Waiting lists in hospitals are going to get longer. I think local people should be treated first!"

"Many doctors, nurses and healthcare workers are immigrants because we have a shortage of skilled people to fill these posts. Without them, waiting lists would be even longer!"

Think about

Read the comments above again. Are any of these an example of a) stereotyping or b) discrimination?

How governments can support immigrants

When an immigrant arrives in a new country, particularly if they are an asylum seeker or refugee, they will have a number of urgent needs. Governments can support them by having policies which will:

- allow their situation and request for asylum to be assessed as quickly as possible.
- give access to suitable accommodation, which will be especially important for families with children.
- provide emergency cash payments.
- give access to emergency health care, if needed.

Once a family is settled, there will be additional ways that governments will need to support its new citizens:

- There will be a need for more permanent accommodation.
- The family will need to be registered with a local health centre.
- Children will need to be enrolled in a local school. They might also need additional support, such as help with learning a new language.
- Language classes for adults should also be provided.

The government needs to have laws in place to make sure that immigrants are protected from discrimination at all stages in their resettlement in their new country. In chapter 1C, you will learn about how the government is doing this in Northern Ireland.

An **immigrant** is a person who comes to live permanently in a foreign country.

A **refugee** is a person who has been forced to leave their country to escape war, persecution, or natural disaster.

An **asylum seeker** is someone whose claim for refugee status has not yet been determined. Not all asylum seekers are granted official refugee status.

Assessment for learning

1. Write down one reason for immigration. [1]
2. Name one type of prejudice. [1]
3. Describe two ways that people choose to express their cultural identity. [2]
4. Explain two positive impacts of immigration on society. [4]
5. Discuss some of the influences on a young person's cultural identity. [6]
6. Evaluate some of the ways that governments can support immigrants. [10]

Further thinking

- Use the Internet to find out more about immigration in Northern Ireland.
- After researching the facts, evaluate the impact that immigration has had in Northern Ireland.

Conflict

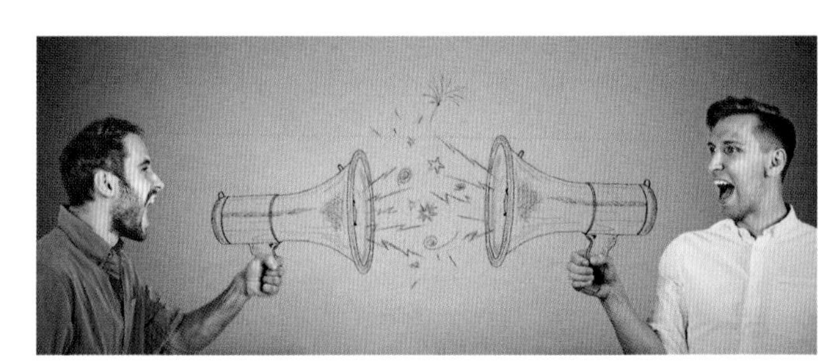

The causes of conflict

There are many sources of conflict within societies today – religion, culture, politics, race and social inequalities are just some examples. Conflict simply means a disagreement or difference. It sometimes occurs when different cultures come together, as they may not hold the same values or follow the same traditions. Conflicts can arise if a particular group feel that their rights are being overlooked or denied. This can create feelings of discontentment and tension in society. Poverty is also thought to be one of the main causes of conflict.

Many people experience conflict in their personal lives, perhaps with family members, neighbours or in the workplace. Personal conflict might arise from a lack of communication or struggling to see someone else's point of view.

Local conflict – This refers to conflict in the local community and usually involves a relatively small geographical area. Local residents may disagree with a decision that will affect their way of life, such as plans to construct a new road or to close a local hospital.

National conflict – This refers to conflict that can affect the whole country. National conflict can arise when government policies lead to people facing unemployment or a low standard of living. This can create feelings of discontentment and tension in society.

Global conflict – This refers to conflict between different nations, or between people and organisations in different states. Global conflict might result from an act of aggression from one country to another, perhaps with the intention of controlling a natural resource or invading territory.

The consequences of conflict

- **Conflict can lead to violence** – If a conflict is based on fear, then, for some, violence might be a first reaction. Violence has a negative impact on both individuals and the whole of society. Through examining the causes of conflict, it should be possible to work out a positive solution that does not involve violence.
- **Conflict can lead to unhealthy relationships** – This is particularly true when conflict is on a personal level, perhaps between work colleagues or family members. This may lead to someone feeling undervalued in the workplace or misunderstood at home.
- **Conflict can have a positive outcome** – Perhaps a problem is solved or a misunderstanding is sorted out. How the conflict is handled by everyone involved is important.

Resolving conflict

When differences of opinion, disputes and conflicts arise between groups of people, there are constructive ways of dealing with them. Some people seem to respond to any conflict or disagreement with violence and aggression, but this causes damage on both sides of the disagreement and does not resolve any issues.

Conflict resolution

The term conflict resolution refers to a range of methods for removing sources of conflict. These usually involve people talking to each other and working out a solution that is acceptable to everybody involved.

Many conflicts can be resolved successfully through informal discussion or **negotiation** by the people involved. If this does not happen for any reason, then mediation is the next stage. **Mediation** uses a third party (the mediator) to help two or more people or groups to communicate on a difficult issue.

Conflict resolution is a creative approach to problem solving in the local community, and it can also be effective on a global level if there are disputes to be resolved between nations. While violence offers a **destructive** response to conflict, conflict resolution is **constructive**.

Think about

Evaluate the role of mediation as a strategy for resolving conflict.

Peaceful resolution

Here are some of the ways that the global community can peacefully put pressure on groups or governments to end conflict:

- **Judicial system** – If a person feels that an injustice or criminal action has taken place towards them, they can report it to the police. It will then be dealt with through the legal system.
- **Sanctions** – A sanction is an official action taken against a country to force it to obey international law. A sanction usually involves stopping trade, so the country can't import any goods or sell its exports. Over a period of time, this will seriously damage a county's economy, so the leaders of the country will agree to act reasonably so the sanctions can be lifted.
- **Boycotts** – A boycott means a complete refusal to buy a product or take part in an activity as a way of registering a protest. In the past, some countries have boycotted the Olympic Games as a way of showing their disapproval of another country's actions. The biggest Olympic boycott ever was in 1980 when the games were held in Russia. A total of 61 countries did not compete in protest over the Russian invasion of Afghanistan.
- **International Human Rights Instruments** – These can be divided into two categories:

  1. Declarations (which *are not* legally binding)
  2. Conventions (which *are* legally binding)

  An example of a declaration is the Declaration on the Rights of the Child, and it describes how children ought to be treated. An example of a convention is the European Convention on Human Rights. This protects human rights and basic freedom in Europe.
- **The United Nations (UN)** – The United Nations was founded in 1945 after the Second World War. It aims to maintain international peace, develop friendly relations among nations and promote human rights. The United Nations also has a range of other functions, including disaster relief, encouraging sustainable development and protecting refugees.

Further thinking

- Use the Internet to find out more about the methods of non-violent action described in this section.
- Assess the effectiveness of each method in dealing with conflict.

Further thinking

Use the Internet to find examples of recent conflicts – one local, one national and one global.

For each example identify:

1. How the conflict started.
2. Who is involved in the conflict.
3. The different opinions each group or person represents.
4. The reasons for the conflict.
5. Ways in which the conflict could be resolved.

Consider all your examples. Are there any similarities between them?

Activity

Consider the situations on the page opposite and decide on a course of action from the list below:

- Sanctions
- Judicial action
- Mediation
- Boycott

Further thinking

You could also...

- Write a possible outcome for each of the first two situations.
- Use the Internet to find out more about the two historical examples.

Situation 1

Hilda lives in a Housing Executive apartment. There have recently been a number of complaints that Hilda's behaviour is starting to upset the other residents and the housing association says that she has to leave. Her doctor believes that dementia is the cause of this and he recommends that a care home might give Hilda the care she needs. Hilda refuses to leave her apartment.

How should the conflict be resolved?

Situation 2

Jim is a builder and he has to park his large van overnight in his driveway. New neighbours have recently moved in next door and they are constantly complaining that the van is spoiling their view. Jim has tried to ignore them rather than get into an argument. One morning, he discovered that the head lamps on his van were smashed. The man across the street says he saw Jim's neighbour on his driveway late the previous night.

What should Jim do?

Situation 3

In 1955, in the American town of Montgomery, a black woman called Rosa Parks was ordered to give up her seat on a bus to a white man. The action that followed started out as a campaign against the seating on the buses but developed into a nation-wide civil rights movement, led by Martin Luther King.

What course of action was originally taken in this historical example?
Was it successful?

Situation 4

From 1948 to 1994, South Africa had a policy called Apartheid. It meant that black people and white people were segregated (kept separate), with white people allocated better housing, healthcare and education. The United Nations condemned South Africa's policies and many countries throughout the world started to take action against South Africa.

How did the world community show disapproval of South Africa's actions?
Was this action effective?

Ways to promote inclusion in society

In this section we will be considering some of the ways in which society can be made more inclusive. Although there are laws making discrimination illegal, it's attitudes that need to change.

Promoting inclusion in schools

Schools can use a number of strategies to help everyone to feel that they are valued and belong. If children can learn tolerance and understanding, then there is hope that society will become more inclusive in the future. There are also a number of legal obligations on schools to meet particular needs, for example, if a student has a disability. Here are some of the ways that schools could promote inclusion:

- **Language** – Helping new arrivals with English should be a priority, so students don't feel isolated because of language barriers. If there's a significant number of students in the school with the same first language, then it might be possible to have a translator in school, even on a part-time basis. Some schools have a 'buddy' system where a pupil with the same first language can help a new arrival to settle in. Parents should not be overlooked. An inclusive school could aim to have important school documents translated for parents who don't have English as a first language.
- **The curriculum** – The school curriculum could cover human rights and issues relating to diversity and inclusion, through subjects such as Learning for Life and Work. A diversity calendar could be produced representing the religious traditions of all the pupils in the class. These festivals could be studied at the appropriate time of year as a way of encouraging inclusion. Younger pupils could listen to stories and sing songs from the various cultural traditions represented by their classmates.
- **Anti-bullying policy** – A school should have an effective anti-bullying policy that specifically addresses issues such as racism, sectarianism and homophobia.

Inclusion in the workplace

It is important that employees know their rights and are made aware of equality issues in the workplace. Discrimination in the workplace is illegal; every employee has to have equal opportunity for employment, promotion, holidays, etc. However, people need to be made aware of the relevant legislation and their rights as employees. They can then ensure that they are being treated fairly and treat others in the same way.

A more inclusive community

A tolerant and inclusive society allows people to live together in harmony. This starts at community level. Here are some of the ways that the community could promote inclusion:

- **Government laws and policies** – It is the responsibility of the government to put laws in place to make discrimination illegal. If someone feels they have been treated unfairly, whether at work or in society, the law should protect them. You will learn about some of these laws in more detail in chapter 1C. An important piece of legislation is Section 75 of the Northern Ireland Act 1998. It protects people from discrimination and promotes equality of opportunity and good relations in society.

- **Education** – The government is responsible for the curriculum taught in schools. It is important that pupils learn about the need for tolerance and respect for others. Schools are also expected to have an inclusive admissions policy that is inclusive and support arrangements for pupils who may need additional help.
- **Raising awareness** – The Equality Commission for Northern Ireland is concerned with inclusion in the whole of society. They organise campaigns to raise awareness and inform people of the law. Their current priorities include culture and identity issues for migrants and refugees, issues around sexual orientation and the low representation of women in politics. The Equality Commission for Northern Ireland also raises awareness about other issues, such as racism, homelessness and disability.
- **Local community groups** – Local groups play an important role in promoting inclusion in the community. Some receive government funding but many are charities or voluntary groups relying on funding from the public. For example, Disability Sports NI promotes inclusion for people with disabilities; Embrace NI is an inter-church group promoting positive attitudes towards refugees, immigrants and people from minority ethnic backgrounds.

Assessment for learning

1. Write down one cause of global conflict. [1]
2. Write down one cause of national conflict. [1]
3. Describe one role of the United Nations. [2]
4. Explain two ways of resolving conflict without using violence. [4]
5. Evaluate the role of schools in promoting equality and inclusion. [10]

CHAPTER 1B
Rights and Responsibilities: Local and Global Issues

Chapter Summary

In this chapter you will be studying:

- **The importance of human rights.**
- **The Universal Declaration of Human Rights (UDHR).**
- **The United Nations Convention on the Rights of the Child (UNCRC).**
- **Examples of human rights abuse: child and slave labour, child soldiers, sexual exploitation.**
- **Balancing protecting the human rights of the individual with those of society.**

Human rights

Why do we need human rights?

Human rights are defined as "The basic rights and freedoms that belong to every person in the world".[1] Some rights are concerned with physical needs, such as adequate housing and health care. Others emphasise the right of each citizen to have their own opinions and beliefs, and follow any lifestyle or religion. Human rights are a basic guarantee that each person can have a decent standard of living.

An awareness of human rights is vitally important. Many people in the world live in poverty, without access to clean water, adequate food or health care; others are tortured or imprisoned without trial because their government does not agree with their opinions.

In our society, there are people who face discrimination because of their gender, race or sexual orientation. We need human rights to ensure the fair and equal treatment of every citizen.

Further thinking

- Use the Internet to research the history of human rights.
- Produce a timeline of the important events in the history of human rights.

[1] Source: Equality and Human Rights Commission, www.equalityhumanrights.com

The Universal Declaration of Human Rights *(a summary)*

Everyone has the right to:

1. be born free and equal.
2. all human rights, no matter their race, gender, religion, etc.
3. life, freedom and safety.
4. freedom from slavery.
5. freedom from hurt and torture.
6. legal rights, regardless of where they are.
7. equality before the law.
8. ask for legal help if their rights are violated.
9. protection from unfair arrest, imprisonment or exile.
10. a fair and public trial.
11. presumed innocence until they are proven guilty.
12. privacy.
13. travel freely.
14. seek safety in another country.
15. a nationality and the freedom to change it.
16. marriage and a family.
17. own property and possessions.
18. freedom of thought, beliefs and religion.
19. freedom of opinion and expression.
20. peaceful public assembly.
21. choose and take part in the government of their country.
22. social security.
23. work in a safe environment, for fair pay and to join a trade union.
24. rest and leisure time.
25. an adequate standard of living and support if they are unable to work.
26. an education.
27. participate in culture, art and science.
28. a fair, free and just world.
29. respect and protect the rights of others.
30. protection of these human rights. No one can take them away.

Teamwork

Working in a group, discuss the following questions:

- Why it is it important that everyone should have human rights?
- If a country is ignoring human rights, should other countries intervene?

The importance of human rights

Participation rights

Some examples from the Universal Declaration of Human Rights (UDHR) include:

15. Everyone has a right to a nationality and the freedom to change it.

21. Everyone has a right to choose and take part in the government of their country.

Everyone in society has the right to take part in the government of their country, either by choosing politicians to represent them or being elected themselves. Elections should be held regularly and a person must be able to vote in secret. All votes should be equal. This right to participation should apply to someone wherever they choose to live.

A democracy is a form of government where the ordinary people can take part in the process of choosing who will rule them. If everyone has a vote, and people are free to vote as they choose, then the government that is elected will be the choice of the majority. A good democratic government will try to ensure that everybody is treated fairly, not just a privileged few.

Further thinking

Our country has a democratic government but there are other types of government in the world.

Choose one of the following countries and find out about its government. Use the bullet points to help you.

China *Saudi Arabia* *North Korea* *Brunei*

- What type of government does this country have?
- List two positives and two negatives of this type of government.
- Does this country have any human rights issues?

Protection rights

Some examples from the UDHR include:

3. Everyone has the right to life, freedom and safety.

7. Everyone has the right to equality before the law.

Having the right to life is the most basic and important right that a person can have. Most people would agree that every human being, regardless of their race, religion, sexuality, social class or political beliefs has the right to life – and to live in freedom and safety. It is the responsibility of local and national governments to provide safety and security in society for all citizens. The police and the courts can do this through the laws that are made and the way they are enforced. An effective legal system is one that protects people but does not deny anyone their basic right of freedom.

Survival rights

Some examples from the UDHR include:

5. Everyone has the right to freedom from hurt and torture.

25. Everyone has the right to an adequate standard of living and support if they are unable to work.

Having an adequate standard of living is one of the most basic human rights that everyone should receive. It includes access to clean drinking water, a sufficient amount of nutritious food, and somewhere clean and safe to live. Access to health care is also an essential right for survival. Governments should ensure that families can provide these essentials for their children so they can survive and develop into healthy adults.

Development rights

Some examples from the UDHR include:

24. Everyone has the right to rest and leisure time.

26. Everyone has the right to an education.

Everyone has the right to an education, which should be free and compulsory for childhood years. After this, technical and professional education should be generally available, and higher education equally accessible to everyone on the basis of merit.

Education is an important human right and it should also strengthen respect for human rights. At school, children should be taught to show respect for others, whatever their race, religion or nationality. Education should promote peace, tolerance and understanding.

Most governments are trying to increase their resources for education but in some poorer countries many parents either can't afford to pay for schooling or must send their children to work at a very young age. Some children can't receive an education because of discrimination based on gender, race or social class.

Activity

Look at the UDHR on page 21.

- What other articles could be considered participation, protection, survival or development rights?
- List the articles under each type and explain the reasons for your choice.

Children's rights

In 1990, the United Nations Convention on the Rights of the Child was produced. It recognises that children are particularly vulnerable and need special protection. It covers civil rights, health and welfare, education, family environment and leisure activities.

The UN Convention on the Rights of the Child

The convention gives children and young people over 40 rights. These include the right to:

- special protection and assistance.
- access to education and health care.
- the right to develop their personalities, abilities and talents to the fullest potential.
- grow up in an environment of love, happiness and understanding.
- be informed about their rights and how to achieve them.

All of the rights in the convention apply to all children and young people without discrimination.

Almost all countries in the world have agreed to adopt this convention. However, throughout the world, not all children receive their rights. They are denied an education, forced to work or fight as soldiers, live on the streets or suffer cruelty at the hands of adults.

Examples of human rights abuse

Child labour

All over the world, children are being denied their basic rights through child labour. Child labour is the exploitation of children through work that is harmful, illegal or interferes with their attendance at school. Some of the illegal activities that children might be forced to do include prostitution, pornography, armed conflict and drug trafficking. Children might be sold as slaves, by being forced into bonded labour, and spend their childhood working in factories, farms, homes and shops. All child labour is harmful and can cause mental, physical and emotional damage. Having to do difficult and often dangerous tasks in harsh working conditions can lead to a number of problems, such as malnutrition, depression and drug dependency. Child labour can also limit a child's education, impacting on their long-term opportunities.

One of the main reasons for child labour is poverty. Some parents can't afford to let their children attend school, even if education is free. They often have no choice but to send their children out to earn a wage from a very young wage.

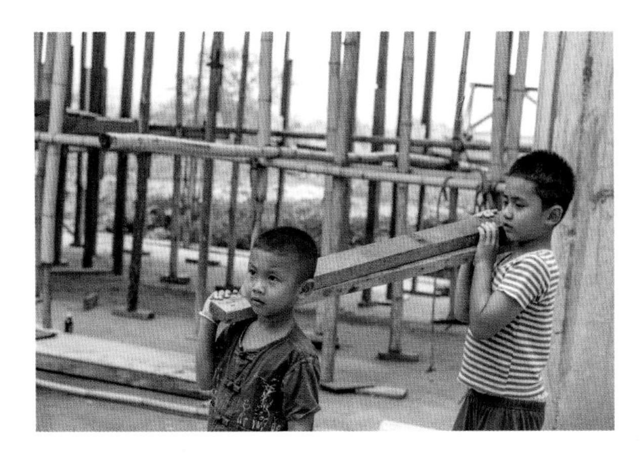

Think about

Do children have the right to work or the right to a childhood?

In the UK, young people have to be at least 14 years old before having a part-time job. However, in some parts of the world, children as young as 4 or 5 years old will work for many hours each day, just to help their family survive. In India, child labour is a serious problem. Many young children work in factories making many different products, including carpets, fireworks and glassware, as their small hands are suited to delicate tasks. However, some people say that if all child labour was banned, very poor families would suffer even greater hardship as they depend on their children's wages.

Slave labour

Forced labour, or slave labour, is a serious abuse of human rights that affects millions of people around the world. It is work that people are forced to do against their will. The victims are often threatened with violence or manipulated into thinking they have a dream job or life in an overseas country.

Slave labour can affect anyone, of any age, gender or nationality. However, it is usually the most vulnerable and excluded groups that are most at risk. Women and girls are more likely to be in forced labour than men and boys. Migrant workers are often the victims of slave labour as they may not speak the local language or have anyone to represent their rights. Forced labour also happens because of poverty. Sometimes a weak economy or government policies mean that there are very few jobs available and people are forced to work long hours, often in appalling conditions, in order to survive. Parents might even be forced to sell a child into slavery as they can't afford to feed everyone in the family.

Some of the areas where men, women and children may be victims of slave labour include:

- domestic work
- construction, mining and quarrying
- prostitution and sexual exploitation
- agriculture and fishing
- illegal activities

Human trafficking

Human trafficking involves the trade of people, mostly for the purpose of sexual slavery, forced labour, prostitution or being forced to perform criminal acts. Victims of trafficking can be very hard to detect and are often afraid or unable to seek help.

Child soldiers

International law prohibits young people under the age of 18 taking part in armed conflict, and the use of children under the age of 15 is considered a war crime. However, throughout the world many thousands of children – some as young as 9 or 10 years old – are given weapons and forced to fight for government armed forces or paramilitaries. Some children have witnessed their whole family being killed in conflict and see no alternative but to agree to fight. Child soldiers are frequently sent to the frontline of any fighting rather than risk the lives of trained, adult soldiers. Children are also used as spies, messengers, porters and servants. Girls are particularly at risk of rape and sexual abuse.

Sexual exploitation

Sexual exploitation is when an abuser uses their relationship or position of authority to take advantage of (exploit) someone and persuades them to take part in sexual activities. If that someone is under 18 years old, this is known as child abuse. Children who are being exploited may not know that what they are being asked to do is wrong. **Prostitution** is a form of sexual exploitation. It involves engaging in sexual activities in return for something beneficial, such as money, affection, drugs and alcohol, or somewhere to stay. Both sexual exploitation and prostitution are forms of sexual abuse. There is more information on sexual abuse on pages 106–109.

Balancing protecting the rights of the individual with those of society

Sometimes when a person claims a right, this can cause another person's right to be violated. This is why the rights of the individual have to be carefully balanced against the rights of society. Here are some issues to consider:

- **Does everyone have the right to freedom of speech?** Everyone is entitled to his or her own opinion. However, there is debate about whether freedom of speech should be limited in some cases. A person may have extreme racist views. Is it right for these views to be posted online, printed in a newspaper or heard on the radio if they could lead to hate crime? This would mean that another person's right to live in safety was being denied. It is necessary to balance which right is the most important.

- **Do criminals have rights?** A person who commits a crime and receives a prison sentence has their right to freedom limited. This is partly to keep society safe from the person who has committed an anti-social act and partly to serve as a punishment. There is divided opinion as to whether a criminal in prison should have other rights denied as well. For example, some people feel very angry when they hear that prisoners have more material goods than many people who are not in prison. However, a prisoner is still a human being and has to be treated with basic human dignity. A difficult question is should prisoners lose other rights as well as their right to freedom?
- **Is privacy more important than security?** Most people would agree that national security and crime prevention are important issues. However, there is growing concern that the price to be paid for this is an invasion of privacy. There are different opinions about the use of security cameras. They can deter crime and help identify offenders, but some people resent being 'spied on' whether they are in a shop, a waiting room or just walking in the street.

Think about

Look at the Universal Declaration of Human Rights on page 21 and answer the questions that follow:

- Which rights from the declaration might be denied if people don't have freedom of speech?
- On the other hand, which rights could be denied if everyone is allowed to express their views publicly?
- Can human rights change depending on the circumstances?

Activity

Read the case study below and answer the questions that follow:

- Which rights are being infringed or ignored?
- Do you think this denial of rights can be justified?

Case study

There is a US Naval base in Guantanamo Bay in Cuba. A detention centre there has been the cause of controversy since it opened in 2002. Following the threat of terrorist attacks, particularly by extremist groups such as al-Qaeda, the Guantanamo Bay centre has been used to detain those suspected of terrorism.

There have been serious concerns about the treatment of prisoners, many of whom have not been charged with any specific offence. By 2005 an estimated 600 prisoners had been detained without trial. Pictures were shown in the media of prisoners with hoods over their faces and wearing shackles on wrists and ankles. Newspaper reports made allegations of prisoners being tortured, beaten, deprived of sleep and exposed to extremes of temperature.

Human rights organisations have campaigned for many years to have the detention centre closed. Under international human rights law, everyone has the right to a fair trial and cannot be detained for long periods of time without charge. Torture and other forms of ill treatment, whether to punish, intimidate or obtain a confession, are a denial of a prisoner's basic human rights.

Others have justified the harsh treatment of these prisoners. In the war against terrorism, it is argued that such measures are undesirable but necessary.

In January 2009, President Obama announced that the Guantanamo Bay detention centre would be closed within a year. However, President Obama did not close the prison before leaving office and by January 2017, there were still 41 prisoners in the camp. President Trump has vowed to keep the prison open, claiming the methods it uses are effective.

Teamwork

Working in a group, discuss the following questions:

- Why do different cultures and countries have different ideas about human rights? Can you think of examples?
- If a country is ignoring human rights, should other countries intervene?
- Can you think of any examples, in the local community and worldwide, where human rights are being ignored?

Assessment for learning

1. Write down one protection right. [1]
2. Write down one development right. [1]
3. Describe two ways that children can have their rights abused. [4]
4. Explain two benefits of having participation rights. [4]
5. Using the information in the Source and your own knowledge, analyse some of the issues involved with limiting people's rights. [6]
6. Evaluate how the Universal Declaration of Human Rights can help people who are suffering from injustice. [10]

Source

In the UK, human rights are protected by the Human Rights Act 1998. However, sometimes the rights of one person conflict with the rights of another, or with the interest of the wider community. The rights of the individual have to be carefully balanced against the rights of society.

In certain circumstances, human rights can be limited, if there is good reason and it is justified in society. For example, it is the duty of the police to protect the public. This may involve searching a person's home, limiting that person's right to privacy, in order to obtain evidence. Rights may have to be restricted to protect other people's rights or the rights of the community. For example, the right to free speech may have to be restricted to protect someone else's right to feel included in society.

Some rights can never be restricted. These rights are absolute rights. They include the right not to be tortured or treated in a degrading way and the right to have religious or non-religious beliefs.

CHAPTER 1C
Government and Civil Society: Social Equality and Human Rights

Chapter Summary

In this chapter you will be studying:

- **Social responsibility of the government, politicians, MLAs, public representatives, media companies and young people.**
- **Ways in which these groups can support democracy, social justice, social equality and human rights.**
- **The role of the government in promoting social equality, social justice and human rights.**
- **Causes and consequences of social inequality and social injustice.**
- **The importance of Section 75 of the Northern Ireland Act 1998.**
- **The roles of the Equality Commission for Northern Ireland, the Northern Ireland Human Rights Commission, civil society and NGOs in safeguarding human rights.**

Social responsibility

What is social responsibility?

Social responsibility is when the government, groups and individuals in society act in a way that benefits everyone. There is the underlying idea that there is the obligation to behave in an ethical way, as no one should be disadvantaged. Social responsibility requires sensitivity towards people's different beliefs, backgrounds and lifestyle choices, and also takes environmental concerns into consideration.

Sometimes, individuals or groups in society may be marginalised or feel they are subjected to unequal treatment. Acting in a socially responsible way, whether it is a government passing laws, or individuals in their day-to-day treatment of colleagues and neighbours, can prevent this from happening and allow everyone to feel included. People who act in a socially responsible way show a genuine concern for the rights and well-being of others and want to make society better for everyone.

People from the following groups may feel they receive social inequality and/or exclusion from society:

- poor
- elderly
- homeless
- unemployed
- LGBTQ+ (lesbian, gay, bisexual, transgender, questioning and plus) community
- ethnic minorities
- disabled

Think about

Can you think of any other groups?

We will examine how the following groups of people can show social responsibility to support democracy, social justice, social equality and human rights:

The government

The Northern Ireland Act 1998 led to the formation of the Northern Ireland Assembly. The First Minister is a member of the largest party in the Assembly and the deputy First Minister is a member of the second largest. Usually one would represent a Unionist party and the other a Nationalist party. Under the original agreement, they were jointly responsible for the Office of the First Minister and deputy First Minister (OFMDFM) and shared responsibilities with each other. In 2016, it was renamed **The Executive Office**.

This office has many important duties, such as economic policy and improving public services. It also has the responsibility to tackle disadvantage, promote equality of opportunity and good relations, and tackle poverty and social exclusion. There is a focus on reducing poverty across all ages to improve children and young people's health, well-being and life opportunities, thereby breaking the long-term cycle of poverty. The Executive Office ensures that all areas of legislation and policy comply with the European Convention on Human Rights.

Politicians, MLAs and public representatives

Politicians in Northern Ireland include Members of the Legislative Assembly (MLAs), members of the UK parliament (MPs) and Members of the European Parliament (MEPs).[1] There are also councillors who represent their area at local level. These people all have a role to play in supporting social justice and social equality. They will support any policies put forward by the government or their particular party, but it is also important that they set a good example themselves. The public generally expect politicians to show honesty and integrity in their own lives and a genuine concern for others. There is public outcry and concern when politicians are reported to be dishonest, make unnecessary claims for expenses or put policies in place from which they benefit financially. Politicians have to be accountable to the public in the work they do and seen to be fair.

Organisations such as the National Health Service (NHS) and the Northern Ireland Housing Executive (NIHE) are also expected to show their social responsibility by spending money wisely and prioritising the needs of the people they are there to serve.

[1] Current at the time of writing.

The media

The media covers three main types of communication: print (newspapers and magazines), broadcasting (TV and radio) and the Internet. The media has a social responsibility to inform the public with truthful, well-researched and balanced material. It has an important role in educating people about social equality and human rights, and highlighting injustice. The media should be run independently of the government so it can hold the government to account and is not forced to portray what the authorities think people should hear.

Socially responsible media will also consider what news stories will contribute to the well-being of society, given that there is a limited amount of time and space. Often an item about a community initiative or a minority group may get overlooked in favour of a celebrity scandal. The media is a business, with fierce competition to present the stories that get the most readers or viewers, so this has to be balanced with responsible reporting.

Further thinking

Most of the world's largest media companies are controlled by a few people who represent the interests of a small minority.

- Use the Internet to find out who owns the largest media companies a) in the UK and b) in the world.
- Is the media these companies produce influenced by its owners' interests, opinions or beliefs? If so, do you think this is fair?

Teamwork

Working in a group, discuss the following opinions:

"The public has a right to know if a politician is dishonest or behaving immorally. The media should report on it."

"A lack of privacy is a small price for celebrities to pay for their fame and fortune."

"Everyone has a right to privacy, no matter who they are."

What do you think is more important – protecting the privacy of individuals or the right of the public to have access to information?

Young people

Young people have a very important role to play in supporting social equality and human rights. The next generation may have to deal with issues such as climate change, an aging population and economic uncertainty. Instead of being disinterested, various studies have shown that most young people are socially aware and want to take action on the problems facing their generation. Many young people are using social networking as an effective means of spreading information, starting a campaign or supporting a good cause.

Chapter 1E considers how young people can get involved in democracy in the local community and school, and show social responsibility through active participation, such as voluntary work.

Social inequality and social justice

Social inequality is the unequal distribution of resources, opportunities and rights across society. This leads to **social injustice**, when individuals or groups are unfairly disadvantaged.

Causes

There are many causes of social inequality and social injustice. Many of them are closely linked, which can make it especially difficult for a person to change their circumstances.

- **Unequal distribution of wealth** – Worldwide, the unequal distribution of wealth means that those born into wealth have more opportunities, can afford good housing, private healthcare and education. Those without are often disadvantaged.
- **Poor education** – Children from disadvantaged homes are more likely to find themselves in poorer school facilities or having to leave school early for economic reasons. This leads to fewer qualifications, which can make it more difficult to get well-paid jobs, and reduces opportunities.
- **Unemployment and low income** – Changing economic and employment patterns have led to cut backs and job losses in many sectors. As a result, people may have to face unemployment, which can have a devastating effect on a family's income. Job shortages, wage freezes and lower pay rises have led to some families having to survive on a very low income.
- **Government policies** – It is important for governments to prioritise spending, as public funds are not unlimited. However, when cut backs are made to benefits or essential services, such as public health care, this can lead to social injustice. It is often the people who are most in need that are most affected.

Further thinking

Use the Internet to research the distribution of wealth across the world.

- How much of the world's wealth is owned by the richest 1% of the world's population?
- Who are currently the top 5 richest people in the world? How much (approximately) do they own and how did they acquire their wealth?
- Do you think this distribution of wealth is fair?

Consequences

Social inequality and social injustice have a negative effect on both the individuals affected and society as a whole, as shown by the following examples:

- **Poverty** – Social inequality means that some groups of people are more likely to live in poverty than others, such as those who are unemployed or on a low income, disabled, homeless or from a cultural minority. There are two types of poverty: absolute and relative. With **absolute poverty**, a person does not have the basics needed for survival, such as adequate food, healthcare or shelter. In the UK, the most common form of poverty is **relative poverty**. This is where people don't have the resources to participate fully in society and have a standard of living much lower than average. They may be unable to afford many of the things people take for granted (such as having a car, the Internet, new clothes and holidays) or may even have to skip meals.

- **Poor health** – Social inequality means that some people, particularly those on a low income, may live in an unhealthy environment, eat a less nutritious diet, and face stress and anxiety about their circumstances. All this is damaging to their health. This in turn affects society, as the more people there are suffering from poor health, the more healthcare is needed to look after them.
- **Discrimination** – When people are denied access to the resources and opportunities available to others, because of culture, race, religion, gender, sexual orientation or disability, this is discrimination. For example, under Taliban control in Afghanistan, women were denied access to education and their freedom of travel was greatly restricted. These restrictions were not applied to men. This is **gender inequality**.
- **Marginalisation** – All people need to feel valued by the community in which they live. However, social inequality can make people feel isolated and marginalised from society. A society is a group of people living and working together. If some individuals, or groups of people, feel that they have been deliberately excluded then the society is not working as it should.

Further thinking

Use the Internet to research the following:

- Does living in a wealthy country affect a person's life expectancy (how long a person is expected to live)?
- If so, give some reasons why. If not, why not?

The role of government

The government has a key role to play in promoting social equality, social justice and human rights. This can be achieved in the following ways:

Legislation

Legislation is law that has been made by the government. There are various laws that promote social equality, social justice and human rights in Northern Ireland. Examples include:

- **The Northern Ireland Act (1998)** – **Section 75** of this important piece of legislation protects equal rights and ensures that the government promotes equality. There is more on this act on the following page.
- **The Sex Discrimination (Northern Ireland) Order 1976 (amended 1998)** – You cannot discriminate against someone because of their gender, marital/civil partner status, gender reassignment, pregnancy or maternity.
- **The Race Relations (Northern Ireland) Order 1997 (RRO)** – You cannot discriminate against someone because of their race, colour, ethnic group or nationality.
- **Disability Discrimination Act 1995 (DDA)** – You cannot discriminate against someone because they have a disability.
- **The Fair Employment and Treatment (Northern Ireland) Order 1998 (FETO)** – You cannot discriminate against someone because of their religious beliefs or political opinion.

These anti-discrimination laws make it illegal to treat someone less favourably in the workplace and in the community.

Teamwork

Working in a group, read the following examples and discuss the questions below:

- What type of discrimination has taken place in each scenario?
- Which do you think is the most serious?
- What law has been broken in each scenario?

In an interview for a promotion at work, Joanna is asked about her family arrangements. Her boss then assumes she would not be able to do the job properly as she has too many commitments at home.

A young Asian couple enquire about a flat for rent. They are told the flat has already been let. The landlord thinks some of the other tenants in the building would object to neighbours from an ethnic minority group.

A transport company needs to hire a lorry driver. They do not think a woman would fit in very well as all the other drivers are men. The job advertisement says that applicants must be over 5 foot 10 inches tall.

Sylvia uses a wheelchair. She and her partner go out to a busy restaurant without a reservation. There is one table available, but they are told the restaurant is fully booked, as there is concern that Sylvia's wheelchair will get in the way.

There is a lot of gossip in the office about whether the new clerical assistant is homosexual. He has been the victim of bad jokes and spiteful comments. Some of the men in the office are trying to avoid contact with him.

Policies

The Northern Ireland Assembly has a number of policies addressing equality, which are detailed on the Assembly website (www.niassembly.gov.uk). The purpose of policies is to outline the action that will be taken to make sure legislation is effective. Two current initiatives include:

- **Disability Action Plan 2016–21:** The focus of the plan is to promote positive attitudes from others and encourage people with disabilities to participate in public life.
- **Good Relations Action Plan 2016–21:** Under the Northern Ireland Act (1998), the Assembly must promote good relations between people of different religious belief, political opinion or racial group. This action plan sets out how the Assembly intends to fulfil this duty and it has been submitted to the Equality Commission for Northern Ireland.

Communication

It is important for the government to communicate with the public about their work, so people are well informed and can keep up to date with the latest news. The Northern Ireland Assembly does this in a number of ways and makes good use of social media in helping the public to stay in touch. Some examples include Twitter, Facebook, Instagram and videos on YouTube. In addition to social media, regular press releases are given to newspapers and broadcasting companies.

Education

The government has an important role in educating people about the need for social responsibility and also raising awareness on how they are taking action themselves. The Northern Ireland Assembly operates an Education Service, which is free to schools. They provide programmes and resources for teachers, young people or anyone who wants to learn about the work of the Assembly. The Education Service works with MLAs to engage with young people and help them to understand how the Assembly is relevant to them and how they can take part in the democratic process.

The government can also make funding available to organisations, such as the Northern Ireland Human Rights Commission and the Equality Commission for Northern Ireland, to develop educational resources for use in schools.

The Northern Ireland Act 1998

The Northern Ireland Act is a detailed Act of Parliament, covering the arrangements for the devolved rule of Northern Ireland. It is divided into 101 sections, and it is **Section 75** that deals with equal opportunities and the need to promote good community relations.

Section 75 of the Northern Ireland Act came into force on 1 January 2000 and it placed a legal obligation on public authorities to promote equality of opportunity:

- between persons of different religious belief, political opinion, racial group, age, marital status or sexual orientation.
- between men and women generally.
- between persons with a disability and persons without.
- between persons with dependants and persons without.

Legal obligation

An action that must be carried out or a service that must be provided, as there is a law in place to make sure this happens.

Public authority

This is a group or organisation, such as a local council or the Education Authority, that has been given official power to govern or administrate in the local community. This responsibility is usually given by the government.

In addition, public authorities are also required to promote good relations between people of different religious beliefs, political opinions and racial groups. Public authorities include groups such as the Northern Ireland Housing Executive (NIHE), the Education Authority, local councils, the National Health Service (NHS) and the Northern Ireland Civil Service.

Activity

- Use the 'Legislation' bullet points on page 31 to make your own list of the groups of people whose rights are protected under Section 75 of the Northern Ireland Act.
- How many different groups of people does this legislation protect?
- Do you think this list covers everyone who might face discrimination in society? If not, list any people/groups that are not covered.

Equality Commission for Northern Ireland

The Equality Commission is a non-departmental public body established by the Northern Ireland Act 1998. It aims to promote equality and good relations, and protect against discrimination on the grounds of age, disability, race, religion and political opinion, sex and sexual orientation. Its roles include:

- promoting equality of opportunity.
- working to eliminate unlawful discrimination and harassment.
- keeping relevant legislation under review.
- promoting good relations between persons of different racial groups and good disability practice.
- overseeing the effectiveness of statutory equality duties on public authorities.
- providing advice and support to individuals with potential complaints under the anti-discrimination legislation.
- providing guidance to employers and service providers about their obligations under the law and good practice.
- encouraging public authorities to promote equality of opportunity and address inequalities.
- ensuring that equality considerations are central to decision-making by focusing particular attention in a number of key public policy areas.

Information from: www.equalityni.org

Northern Ireland Human Rights Commission

The Northern Ireland Human Rights Commission (NIHRC) is an independent, statutory organisation. It is not an NGO (Non-Governmental Organisation), and not a government body. It was established on the basis of the Belfast (Good Friday) Agreement and created by Parliament through the Northern Ireland Act 1998, starting its work on 1 March 1999.

The NIHRC is recognised as a member of the worldwide network of National Human Rights Institutions. There are seven Commissioners (a full-time Chief Commissioner and six part-time Commissioners) appointed by the Secretary of State.

The NIHRC works to protect and promote the human rights of everyone in Northern Ireland. They do this by:

- providing advice on legislative bills introduced in the NI Assembly and on policy proposals made by Ministers in the NI Executive.
- providing advice to the UK government and Parliament on matters affecting human rights in NI.
- conducting investigations on systemic human rights issues. They can enter places of detention, and may compel individuals and agencies to give oral testimony or to produce documents.
- promoting understanding and awareness of the importance of human rights in NI by undertaking or supporting research and educational activities.
- providing legal advice and initiating strategic legal cases.

Information from: www.nihrc.org

Further thinking

Visit www.nihrc.org to find out which human rights issues the NIHRC is currently involved with.

Think about

- What role does the NIHRC play in relation to human rights in Northern Ireland?
- What are the main reasons for its effectiveness?

The role of civil society, including NGOs

There are a number of means by which society is kept running smoothly: the government makes laws to ensure good order in society and protect people's rights; there are businesses providing goods and services in return for money. However, there are many other groups that play a vital role in society but are not part of the government or primarily concerned with making a profit. Examples include:

- credit unions
- charities and NGOs (non-governmental organisations)
- housing associations
- religious/faith groups
- neighbourhood self-help schemes
- international agencies, such as the Red Cross or the United Nations

The term 'civil society' is used to describe these organisations. They help to look after people, protect their rights and improve health, education and living standards at home and overseas.

On a global scale, NGOs and charities have a very significant role to play. They are not operated by any government and provide assistance for little or no fee. They are usually funded by donations from the public and rely heavily on volunteer help. Following a natural disaster, such as a hurricane, earthquake or flood, groups like the Red Cross and Habitat for Humanity, help those who were affected to get back to normal. Examples in the local community include the Chinese Welfare Association, representing the needs of Chinese people in Northern Ireland; Gingerbread NI, working for single parents; and Victim Support Northern Ireland, giving advice on criminal injuries and compensation. There is more information on NGOs in chapter 1F.

Assessment for learning

1. Name one group who may be marginalised by society. [1]
2. Name one law that protects people's rights in Northern Ireland. [1]
3. Describe two consequences of social inequality. [4]
4. Explain two ways that the Northern Ireland Human Rights Commission promotes human rights. [4]
5. Discuss the role of civil society in promoting social justice. [6]
6. Evaluate the role of the government in protecting people's rights. [10]

CHAPTER 1D
Democratic Institutions: Promoting Inclusion, Justice and Democracy

Chapter Summary

In this chapter you will be studying:

- **The significance and key features of the 1998 Good Friday (Belfast) Agreement.**
- **The structure and main roles of the Northern Ireland Assembly.**
- **The structure and main roles of the Northern Ireland Executive.**
- **The role and responsibilities of MLAs.**
- **The role of the Police Ombudsman's Office.**

Democratic government

In most democratic countries, there is a government of representatives elected by the people. This is known as a representative democracy. The people choose, by means of an election, someone to represent them. This person is a Member of Parliament (MP) in central government and a councillor at local level. Their job is to speak on behalf of the community who has elected them and, if necessary, fight for their rights. In a democracy, people are also given the right to vote on important issues that affect them.

Characteristics of a democracy

Different countries will have their own democratic systems of government. However, there are some features that all democracies will have:

- All adult citizens can play a part in running their country by having a **vote**. Everyone has the right to use their vote freely to choose the person they think will best represent them.
- One of the main ideas behind a democracy is that of **majority rule**. Although there are different voting systems, such as the single transferable vote used in Northern Ireland, the government in power will be the one who has received the most votes.
- In a democracy, there will be a **central government**, responsible for decisions that affect the whole country. Power will also be shared out so some decisions can be made at a **local level**.
- One of the most important functions of a democracy is to **protect the rights of everyone** in the community. These include freedom of speech and religion, the right to be protected equally under the law and the right to play a full part in the political, economic and cultural life of society.

- The government of a democracy is **elected by the people** and it should also be **accountable to the people**. This means that if someone has a complaint about a government service or organisation, then they have the right to say what is wrong and for it to be investigated fairly.

National, regional and local government

In Northern Ireland, government is organised in the following way:

1. **National government:** Decisions made by Parliament in Westminster affect people in Northern Ireland as it is part of the United Kingdom.

2. **Regional government:** The Northern Ireland Assembly has responsibility for issues that apply to the whole of Northern Ireland.
3. **Local government:** Local councils are responsible for matters concerning a smaller area, such as a town or district.

National government is responsible for matters such as defence, foreign policy and taxation. In Northern Ireland, regional government is responsible for policies concerning schools, tourism and agriculture. Local government is concerned with a particular area and looks after roads, education and housing. There are some duties that a local council has to carry out, such as refuse collections and cleaning the streets.

The Good Friday (Belfast) Agreement 1998

The Good Friday Agreement ended 30 years of conflict in Northern Ireland, known as the Troubles. The agreement was reached following multi-party negotiations and the 65-page document was signed in Belfast on 10 April 1998 (Good Friday) by the British and Irish governments. It is also referred to as **The Belfast Agreement**.

The **Northern Ireland Assembly** was elected in June 1998. The new government for Northern Ireland was formed, but did not yet have the power to rule. On 1 December 1999 at midnight, the power to rule Northern Ireland passed from Westminster to Belfast. The Northern Ireland Assembly could now govern Northern Ireland and the new **Northern Ireland Executive** met for the first time.

Activity

Draw a time line to show the key dates and events in the Good Friday Agreement, the setting up of the Northern Ireland Assembly, and any other significant events to the present day.

The key features of the Good Friday (Belfast) Agreement

- **A devolved government in Northern Ireland** – Under the agreement, Northern Ireland would have a devolved government. This means that the UK Parliament would transfer powers to the Northern Ireland Assembly, so laws and decisions on some matters would be made by Members of the Legislative Assembly (MLAs) for the people of Northern Ireland. Matters of national importance, such as defence and taxation, remain the responsibility of the UK government.
- **Cross-community power sharing** – The Assembly was originally made up of 108 MLAs but this has now been reduced to 90. The Assembly appoints Ministers to the Northern Ireland Executive and they each have responsibility for a government department. The Good Friday (Belfast) Agreement determined that the Executive Committee would be power sharing, representing both Unionists and Nationalists. This cross-community power sharing included the joint office of the First Minister and deputy First Minister, and a multi-party Executive. The First and deputy First Minister have equal powers and one can't be in office without the other.
- **The principle of consent** – When the Northern Ireland Act (1998) was passed at Westminster, it replaced the Government of Ireland Act (1920) which partitioned Ireland. The Good Friday Agreement established relations between Northern Ireland and the Republic of Ireland, and between Northern Ireland and the rest of the UK. It was agreed that Northern Ireland would remain in the UK and not become part of a united Ireland, as long as there was the consent of the majority. This is called the principle of consent.
- **The right to hold both British and Irish citizenship** – Northern Ireland is part of the UK. However, under the Good Friday Agreement, people born in Northern Ireland can choose whether to be British, Irish or have dual nationality. This means a person born in Northern Ireland is entitled to hold either a British or Irish passport, or both.
- **Safeguards for human rights and equality** – The Northern Ireland Act (1998) made it illegal to show discrimination because of race, gender, age, political beliefs, sexual orientation, having dependents, disability, religious beliefs and marital status. The new laws, particularly Section 75 (see pages 32–33), made safeguarding human rights and promoting equality of opportunity a priority. The agreement also led to the establishment of the Northern Ireland Human Rights Commission.
- **Recognition of linguistic diversity** – The Good Friday Agreement established that there should be respect, understanding and tolerance in relation to the Irish language, Ulster Scots and the languages of other ethnic minorities living in Northern Ireland. The Irish language and Ulster Scots should have cultural equality.

How has the Good Friday Agreement brought benefits to the people of Northern Ireland?

- The Good Friday Agreement was a historic breakthrough. It meant that only **democratic and peaceful** means of resolving differences could now be used.
- It gave the chance of a new start for relationships within Northern Ireland, with the Republic of Ireland, and the rest of the UK. The agreement gave the people of Northern Ireland the choice of identifying themselves as Irish, British or both.
- The Good Friday Agreement led to the passing of important new laws in the **Northern Ireland Act 1998**. Pages 32–33 look at the importance of **Section 75** in securing equality of opportunity for all people in Northern Ireland.
- The agreement is based on the ideas of human rights, equality and mutual respect for all people, and working towards a tolerant and inclusive society.
- The agreement is a way forward for all parties to commit to a power-sharing government and to show their support for the police and criminal justice systems.

However, there have been some issues with the Good Friday Agreement over the years and, on more than one occasion, power has been transferred to Westminster for periods of time.

Teamwork

Working in a group, discuss the following questions:

- How does the Good Friday Agreement bring benefits to the people of Northern Ireland?
- Why do you think this agreement has faced setbacks?
- What problems could there be with upholding this agreement in the future?

The Northern Ireland Assembly

Structure

The Northern Ireland Assembly was established as part of the Good Friday Agreement. Northern Ireland remains part of the United Kingdom, but the day-to-day running of Northern Ireland is now carried out by Northern Ireland's politicians. The governing body is the Northern Ireland Assembly, which is led by the First Minister and deputy First Minister. The Assembly has full authority to pass laws and to make decisions on the work of Northern Ireland government departments. The Assembly has several statutory committees, each one shadowing a government department at Stormont, such as education or agriculture. There are 90 elected MLAs representing 18 constituencies.

When the Northern Ireland Assembly was established, three areas of responsibility were created:

1. **Transferred matters** – Public services, such as education, health and agriculture.
2. **Reserved matters** – On-going police enquiries, Human Rights and Electoral Policy.
3. **Excepted matters** – Matters of national importance, such as defence, taxation and foreign policy.

The Assembly has full responsibility for all transferred matters. There is a minister responsible for each area and together they make up an Executive Committee, which has special powers within the Assembly. Reserved matters can be transferred to the Assembly at a later date.

Main roles

Representing constituents: MLAs represent their constituents by listening to their views and helping to solve problems in the local community. MLAs work in their constituency office when they are not in the Assembly buildings. Friday is traditionally constituency day, when MLAs hold surgeries in their offices. Local people can come along and discuss any matter that concerns them. MLAs also go to functions and visit schools and businesses, trying to keep as high a profile as possible in the local community. When MLAs return to the Assembly, their work in the local community will have given them an insight into current issues. They have a responsibility to raise any issues their constituents are concerned about, vote on new laws, speak in debates and ask ministers formal questions.

Approving legislation: The Northern Ireland Assembly has the power to make laws for Northern Ireland on transferred matters. A proposal for a new law is called a bill. Ministers, committees and individual members can propose a bill to be considered by the Assembly. The Speaker introduces a bill to the Assembly, then, after debate and careful thought, a vote is taken by members of the Assembly. If the bill is approved, then the Speaker of the Assembly will ask the Secretary of State to seek Royal Assent to enable the bill to become an act of the Northern Ireland Assembly.

Scrutinising the work of the Northern Ireland Executive: An important role of MLAs is to scrutinise the work of Ministers in the Northern Ireland Executive and the government departments that provide public services. This means they investigate what is going on and ask questions. The Assembly holds the Executive to account on behalf of the people of Northern Ireland. MLAs carry out this role through their work in the Assembly chamber and in committees.

Further thinking

The website of the Northern Ireland Assembly Education Service has a variety of activities and games to help you learn about their work. Visit http://education.niassembly.gov.uk

Assessment for learning

1. Write down one responsibility of local councils. [1]
2. Write down one responsibility of the government at Westminster. [1]
3. Describe two features of a democracy. [4]
4. Explain two responsibilities of the Northern Ireland Assembly. [4]
5. Discuss how the Good Friday Agreement promotes equality in Northern Ireland. [6]

The Northern Ireland Executive

Structure

The Executive Committee has special responsibilities and is similar to the Cabinet in Westminster. It is made up of the First Minister and deputy First Minister, and there is also a minister for each of the nine government departments. Ministers are appointed from the 90 MLAs on the Assembly and these seats are given out fairly according to how many seats each party won in the Assembly elections. The Executive Committee brings forward suggestions for new legislation in the form of bills. It also sets out a 'Programme for Government' each year, with a proposed budget.

The nine government departments, with some of their main responsibilities, are as follows:

Note: You should have knowledge and understanding of the role of any **four** departments.

- **The Executive Office** – This department's objectives include supporting ministers and the institutions of government, and building a programme for government.
- **Department of Education** – This department's main areas of responsibility are in pre-school, primary, post-primary and special education; the youth service; the promotion of community relations within and between schools; and teacher education and salaries.
- **Department for the Economy** – This department's responsibilities include economic policy development, enterprise, innovation, energy, telecoms, tourism, health and safety at work, learning and research, skills training, and promoting good employment practice.
- **Department of Finance** – This department's aims are to prioritise the use of resources available to Northern Ireland, making sure that they are used efficiently, and to modernise public services.

- **Department of Health** – This department's mission is to improve the health and social well-being of the people of Northern Ireland. Its responsibilities also include public safety, which covers policy and legislation for fire and rescue services.
- **Department of Justice** – This department has a range of devolved policing and justice functions.
- **Department for Infrastructure** – This department's main responsibilities are to develop infrastructure and services that are vital for everyone in Northern Ireland. This includes water and sewerage networks, roads and footpaths, public transport services, vehicle regulation, road safety, driver licensing, and rivers and inland waterways.
- **Department for Communities** – This department's areas of responsibility include urban regeneration, housing, social security benefits, pensions and child support, debt advice, public records, employment

service, promoting equality, and development of arts and culture.

- **Department of Agriculture, Environment and Rural Affairs** – This department is concerned with fishing, farming, recycling and pollution. It also has responsibility for the welfare of farmed animals or animals kept in boarding kennels, pet shops or zoos.

Each of these departments is headed by a minister who is a member of the Executive Committee. This minister receives help and advice from one of the statutory committees.

Further thinking

Choose four government departments and use the following website to research their work: www.nidirect.gov.uk

Main roles

Agreeing on and producing a draft budget and programme for government: Northern Ireland is currently allocated over 18 million pounds a year to spend on public services, such as health care, education and removal of waste. One of the most important roles of the Northern Ireland Executive is to produce a programme for how this money will be spent, and plan a budget. With less money available for public services, it is essential to plan the budget wisely. MLAs have the responsibility of deciding how much money will be allocated to each sector, for example, hospitals, roads and sports facilities. In Northern Ireland, the Finance Minister has overall responsibility for the budget. Assembly committees examine the draft budget and it is then debated in the Assembly chamber. Every government department and minister will have their spending checked carefully by an Assembly committee.

Making legislation: One of the roles of the Northern Ireland Assembly is to pass laws. The Northern Ireland Executive plays an important role in this process by deciding whether the proposed legislation will be accepted. MLAs and Assembly committees can propose laws, but most of them come from Executive Committee members.

Agreeing on significant or controversial issues: MLAs get to vote on decisions made by the Assembly and usually the outcome is decided by a simple majority vote. However, important decisions such as approving the budget must have cross-community support. This means that the decision must be supported by both Nationalist votes and Unionist votes. The Executive will also make a decision if an issue involves the responsibility of two or more ministers.

Teamwork

Propose a bill and make a law

- Working in a group, decide on a bill to propose to the class. You could consider the following questions:
  1. Why do we need this new rule?
  2. Who will this new rule affect?
  3. How will we enforce this new rule?
- There will then need to be class debate to decided which of the proposed bills should be introduced as a new law.
- The next stage is a class vote. If a bill is accepted, the teacher can be asked to make it law!

Members of the Legislative Assembly (MLAs)

Main roles and responsibilities

MLAs divide their time between working in Parliament buildings at Stormont and working in their constituencies. When the Assembly is in session, MLAs spend their time debating in the chamber or taking part in committee meetings.

Helping their constituents:

- MLAs are the elected representatives for their constituencies, so it is their duty to speak on behalf of the people they represent.
- MLAs represent the views of their local community in the Assembly.
- MLAs have local constituency offices that people can visit for advice or to discuss concerns.
- 'Representing constituents' on page 38 discusses this in more detail.

Making legislation: One of the important roles of an MLA is to make laws, by debating proposed bills and deciding whether or not to pass them. They also work in small groups, called committees, which scrutinise the bills in detail and play an important role in examining the work of individual government departments. They might consult experts or the views of the public to help them come to a decision. The largest parties in the Assembly appoint MLAs to act as ministers with the responsibility for a government department.

Following the Code of Conduct of the Northern Ireland Assembly: It is the responsibility of all MLAs to follow this Code of Conduct. This helps them to carry out their obligations to the Assembly, their constituents and the general public. The code aims to ensure the trust and confidence of the public in the MLAs they have voted for and to hold them to high moral standards. MLAs are expected to be honest, act with integrity, promote good relations and set a good example in the community.

As a result of the Good Friday Agreement, two new organisations were set up to protect people's rights. They are the **Northern Ireland Human Rights Commission (NIHRC)** (which was covered in Chapter 1C) and the **Police Ombudsman's Office.**

The Office of the Police Ombudsman opened in November 2000. This is a government organisation set up to investigate complaints from the general public about police officers in Northern Ireland. Before this, all complaints about the police were dealt with by the police, which some people didn't think was fair. The Police Ombudsman's Office is an independent and unbiased system for investigating complaints against the police. The Police Ombudsman's Office is fully funded by the government and administrated through the Department of Justice. It is a good example of the government taking its responsibilities seriously in protecting citizen's rights. Around 2600 complaints are made each year about police officers in Northern Ireland. These complaints include allegations that police officers have been rude or offensive, used unnecessary force or failed to do their job properly.

In addition, the Police Ombudsman's Office will also investigate the following situations, even if a complaint has not been made:

- The firing of a police firearm, except in certain circumstances such as when a firearm is used against a dangerous animal. The use of a TASER stun gun may be investigated depending on the circumstances.
- Any fatal road traffic accident involving police officers.
- Any death that might be the result of actions of a police officer.

If the Office finds that the police have acted properly, they will give an explanation to the person who has brought the complaint. If an investigation identifies failings by police, the Police Ombudsman may recommend either criminal prosecution or disciplinary action. This could lead to a prison sentence, fine, dismissal or verbal warning, depending on the seriousness of the offence.

Further thinking

Use the Internet to research how effective the work of the Police Ombudsman's Office is. Share your conclusions in a small group.

Assessment for learning

1. Write down what the letters 'MLA' stand for. [1]
2. How many MLAs are elected to the Northern Ireland Assembly? [1]
3. Describe two roles of the Northern Ireland Executive. [4]
4. Explain two ways that MLAs can represent their constituency. [4]
5. Discuss the main responsibilities of one government department. [6]
6. Evaluate the role of the Police Ombudsman's Office in safeguarding human rights. [10]

CHAPTER 1E
Democracy and Active Participation

Chapter Summary

In this chapter you will be studying:

- **The ways in which young people can participate in democratic processes, in school, the community and the wider world.**
- **The benefits of this participation for the young person and for society.**

Democracy

Democracy means 'rule by the people'. It is based on the belief that every citizen should be free and equal, and have equal access to power. It is important to remember that democracy involves everyone in society, whatever their age. It is not just the concern of people who are over 18 years of age and therefore legally entitled to vote. A sign of a strong, democratic society is one where everyone actively participates in democratic processes.

Active participation

Active citizenship is when people **actively participate** in democracy and **get involved** in society at all levels: locally, nationally and globally. Active citizens believe it's important to take notice of what is going on in society and be prepared to **take action**.

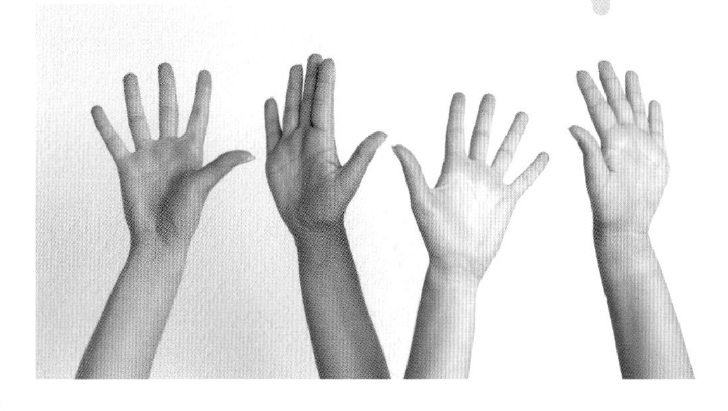

Getting involved: volunteering

Many people get involved in their community or wider society by volunteering their time and skills to help others. Volunteering can make a real difference to individuals, the local community and the environment.

Many charities and Non-Governmental Organisations (NGOs) rely on volunteer help, as they don't have the funds for all their workers to be salaried employees. Some of the groups that rely on volunteering play an important role in looking after the environment or local facilities, so the whole community can benefit from voluntary work. However, the greatest benefits from volunteering are for the volunteer. Here are some examples:

- **An opportunity to meet people and make new friends** – People of all ages and from all walks of life get involved in voluntary work, so it's a great way to get to know people from different backgrounds. However, they will probably have something in common – a commitment to the work they are doing and the belief that it is worthwhile.

- **A chance to gain some valuable work experience** – Many employers see voluntary work as being just as valuable as paid work and, in some cases, even more valuable, as it shows a high level of commitment. If someone is considering an area of work for a future career, then volunteering might help them decide if it really is for them.
- **The satisfaction of knowing they are doing something worthwhile** – Voluntary work often involves helping other people or the local community, so it can give a person the feeling of 'giving something back'. Perhaps someone has struggled with a particular issue themselves and wants to help others in a similar situation.

- **A boost to self-confidence** – Voluntary work can provide the opportunity to develop new skills or attain a personal goal. Working as part of a team, and knowing that their contribution is important can help to improve a person's self-esteem.
- **A greater involvement in the local community** – A family who has recently moved into an area might find that voluntary work can give them a sense of belonging. Helping out at a nearby charity shop, or becoming involved with a local residents' association, can help a person to feel part of their community.

Further thinking

Anyone can volunteer!

Using the Internet, research suitable voluntary work for each of the following people:

Margaret is a fit and active 72 year old. She loves to get out of the house and meet people, but since her husband passed away last year, following an illness, she has been feeling lonely. Margaret would love to do something to support her local hospice, which gave her a lot of support when her husband was ill.

What volunteering opportunities would be suitable for Margaret?

If there is one thing that makes Nathan really annoyed, it's people who treat the local environment as a rubbish dump! He lives in the country where he sees rubbish dumped in hedgerows and along the banks of a local river. Nathan is 38 and self-employed as a builder, so his working hours can be fairly flexible.

What opportunities are there for Nathan to get involved with local environmental issues and also do something practical?

Anna is 17 and has just finished her AS exams. She is hoping to go to university when she finishes school and train as a primary school teacher, as she loves working with children.

What voluntary work could Anna do during her summer holidays? She would like to have fun and also gain some valuable work experience.

Taking action: participating in democratic processes

There are many ways that people can participate in the government of their country. They can show an interest in what is going on in society by keeping up to date with current affairs or engaging in political discussion. They can also take action by participating in the following democratic processes:

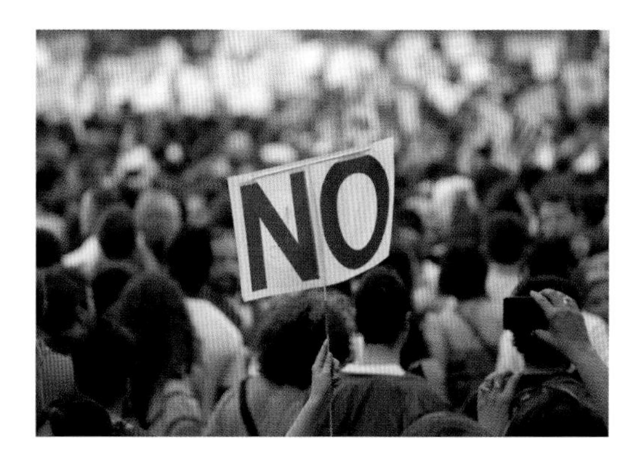

- **Voting in elections** – All adult citizens can play a part in running their country by voting for the person who best represents them in an election.
- **Writing to a local councillor or newspaper, or posting or sharing information on social media** – This can be an effective way of publicising a cause and attempting to get others to agree.
- **Petition** – Collecting signatures is a way of showing the decision-makers just how many people support a cause, and this can be very effective.
- **A march, protest or demonstration** – A peaceful march, protest or demonstration can be an effective way of raising the profile of a current issue, for example, climate change. This form of participation is also a good way of showing how many people support the cause.
- **Lobbying an MP** – This involves convincing a member of parliament that changes need to be made in a certain area.
- **Use of celebrities** – Many people are more likely to support a cause if it is promoted by a celebrity they admire.
- **Publicity stunt** – This is a planned event, aimed at getting the attention of both the general public and the media. Publicity stunts can involve celebrities, a dangerous challenge or an act of protest.
- **Join a pressure group** – This is an organised group of people who aim to influence government policy, or the laws that they pass.

Think about

Is it ever right to use violence to influence change?

Activity

- Look at the table below and consider the advantages and disadvantages of each democratic process.
- Rate each process between 1–10 according to how effective you think it is at influencing change, with '1' being the *most* effective.
- Record your conclusions in a copy of the table.

DEMOCRATIC PROCESS	ADVANTAGES	DISADVANTAGES	RATING
Lobbying an MP			
Writing to a local councillor/ newspaper; posting/sharing on social media			
March/protest/demonstration			
Petition			
Celebrities			
Publicity stunt			

Teamwork

Working in a group, discuss the following statement:

"A cause will only succeed if it has the support of the public."

Do you agree or disagree? Give reasons for your answer.

Young people and active participation

Article 12 of the **UN Convention on the Rights of the Child (UNCRC)** guarantees all children and young people the right to express their views freely in all matters affecting them. It gives them an opportunity to be heard and for their opinion to be considered, not just at home but everywhere. This means that all children and young people are entitled to play an active role in decision making, and things should change in response to their participation. Here are some of the ways that young people can actively participate in democratic processes:

In school

Most young people would agree that they should have a voice on matters that affect them, especially in school. Some schools have a school council, with elected representatives from each form class or year group. At regular meetings throughout the school year, these representatives have the opportunity to present the views and concerns of their classmates to senior teachers in the school. Being willing to stand for election as a class representative is an important way of participating in a democratic process.

Many young people see the benefit in making an active contribution to the school community. Some students choose to participate by representing their school through sports, music or drama, for example. Others might show responsibility for younger pupils by acting as mentors or taking on responsibility as a prefect. This shows the important balance between rights and responsibilities.

In the local community

Young people can show their involvement in the community through volunteering. Being involved in a youth or community group can give the opportunity to volunteer collectively and support a good cause. For example, a youth club might decide to clean up rubbish in the local area or donate toys to a hostel for homeless families. For young people who wish to actively participate in democracy, the Northern Ireland Youth Forum (NIYF) could provide the opportunity to do this. Any young person aged between 11 and 25 can join NIYF and receive regular emails about their activities. It is up to each individual to decide how much or how little they want to get involved in a current campaign.

Further thinking

Visit the website of the Northern Ireland Youth Forum (www.niyf.org) and research their active campaigns.

- What is your view on these issues?
- Would you consider getting involved with the NIYF?

Teamwork

Working in a group:

- Decide on a project for a local area. The aim of the project is to improve the area and to benefit the lives of local residents.
- In planning your project, try to include some ways to involve the whole community.
- Present your ideas to the class.

In the wider world

There are many ways for young people to take action if they feel strongly about an issue. For example, they could organise a protest or petition, hand out flyers, or use social media to raise awareness of a cause. They could lobby their MP or MLA, which involves taking their concerns to the politician representing their area and convincing them that changes need to be made. They don't have to be of voting age to do this. They could also lead by example, by only buying environmentally-friendly products or those from ethical companies, and encourage their friends and family to do the same.

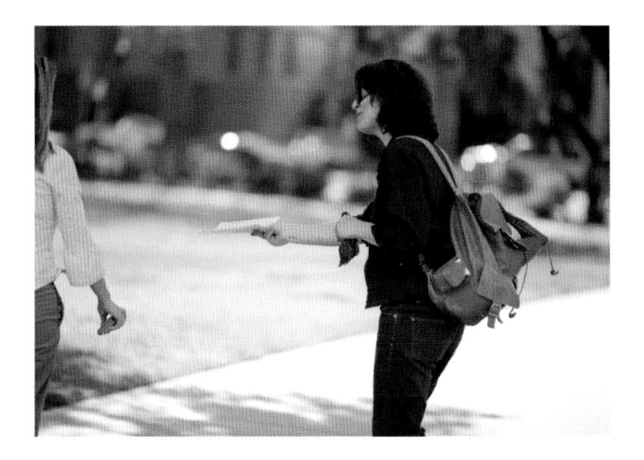

The benefits of active participation

For young people

- It gives young people a voice to speak out about the issues that affect them.
- It can improve their self-esteem and self-confidence.
- It can develop new skills, such as leadership, teamwork, problem solving and communication.
- It can help young people understand the importance of democracy, their rights and how to protect themselves.
- It allows young people to play a role in civil society and be active citizens.

For society

- It gives young people a role in decision making, which is important as they are the future of society.
- It helps to make society more democratic as everyone has a role to play.
- It helps society understand and address the needs of young people better.
- It improves relationships between younger and older members of society.
- It makes younger people feel a greater sense of belonging and investment in the community, which also improves respect towards it.

Assessment for learning

1. Write down one advantage of living in a democracy. [1]
2. Write down one way that a pupil can take an active role in their school. [1]
3. Describe two benefits that can be gained from voluntary work. [4]
4. Explain two ways people can participate in democratic processes. [4]
5. Using the information in the Source and your own knowledge, analyse why it is important for young people to be active citizens. [6]

Source

Article 12 of the United Nations Convention on the Rights of the Child (UNCRC) guarantees all children and young people the right to express their views freely in all matters affecting them. This means that all children and young people are entitled to play an active role in decision making. Every young person has a right to the opportunity to be an active and motivated citizen. Today's generation of young people is the largest in history. Over three billion people – nearly half of the world's population – are under the age of 25.[1]

Young people can show their involvement in the community through volunteering. Being involved in a youth or community group can give the opportunity to support a good cause, learn new skills and gain valuable work experience. Active citizenship can help young people to take action if they feel strongly about an issue. For example, they could organise a protest or petition, or use social media to raise awareness of a cause.

[1] Figures from Mark Cairns, 'Empowering young people to become active citizens', Winston Churchill Memorial Trust, 2016, www.wcmt.org.uk

CHAPTER 1F
The Role of NGOs

Chapter Summary

In this chapter you will be studying:

- **The role of NGOs in promoting social equality, social justice, human rights and democracy.**
- **The work of NGOs on local, national and global issues.**
- **Examples of how NGOs deal with these issues.**
- **Factors that limit the impact of NGOs' work.**

What is the role of NGOs*?

NGOs are organisations that are independent of any government and provide assistance for little or no fee. They are usually funded by donations from the public and rely heavily on volunteer help. Locally, nationally and globally NGOs promote social equality, social justice, human rights and democracy. They also tackle serious issues and areas of need that governments don't have the time or resources to address.

Here is some of the important work that NGOs carry out:

Supplying emergency relief and aid – Following a natural disaster or conflict, NGOs may send staff and volunteers to the area with food, water and medical supplies. This assistance can mean the difference between life and death in an emergency situation.

Offering practical help – This could be in the form of food and shelter for refugees, veterinary care and rehoming for an animal that has been mistreated, or advice on how to install a communal tap for a village in a developing country.

Providing long-term support – It is important that communities don't rely on NGOs, so an important aspect of their work is to form partnerships with local organisations and train people in the community with the skills to help each other.

* Some NGOs prefer to call themselves charities or voluntary organisations.

Generating income – As NGOs don't rely on cash from the government, they need to generate income. Through their work raising awareness of their cause, they hope to receive public support and donations. Apart from essential overheads, the money raised is diverted to where it's needed.

Raising awareness – Through their work, NGOs raise awareness about particular issues, provide information and keep the public informed.

Improving education – Many NGOs are dedicated to both improving education and making it a basic right for every child to attend school. Some NGOs develop resources for use in schools, which can be an important part of a Citizenship programme or used to inspire a fund-raising event. Others provide education for the people they are working with, perhaps about farming techniques.

Protesting and lobbying – For some NGOs, such as Friends of the Earth and Amnesty International, their role includes making governments aware of their campaigns and encouraging them to take action. This can be achieved in a variety of ways, such as protesting, writing letters and emails, lobbying politicians and organising petitions.

The following are just some examples of the local, national and global issues that NGOs tackle:

Natural disasters

Natural disasters are harmful natural events that cause great damage, injury or loss of life. Many are caused by extreme weather, such as drought, hurricanes, floods, tsunamis, storms and blizzards. Others are caused by geological processes, such as earthquakes and volcanoes.

Natural disasters are often devastating. They can cause injury and loss of life, and damage to property, infrastructure and essential services, such as electricity. This damage can lead to food shortages and increased health risks, as access to adequate sanitation and water supplies may be affected. Many people have to flee their homes and work for safety, and find them destroyed upon their return. Short term, NGOs can help by assisting rescue operations and providing emergency aid, including food, clean water, sanitation, medical supplies and temporary shelter. Long term, they help to rebuild homes, provide employment and prepare for future natural disasters.

The damage to property, infrastructure and essential services caused by the 2010 Haiti earthquake

Further thinking

- Use the Internet to find out what natural disasters occurred this year.
- What NGOs provided help for the areas affected?

NGO example: natural disasters

Oxfam

Oxfam started in 1942 as the Oxford Committee for Famine Relief. Today, it is an international alliance of NGOs working in around 90 countries. An important aspect of its work is helping those who need it most when natural disasters, war or famine affect their lives. Oxfam estimates that at any given time, one of their teams is responding to 25 emergencies worldwide. Oxfam takes action through:

- **Emergency response** – The priorities are clean water to drink and decent sanitation, followed by food and other essentials needed for survival, such as shelter. It is also important to make sure that the most vulnerable people, such as children, are kept safe from harm.
- **Long-term support** – Once the immediate crisis is over, Oxfam continues to support communities affected by disaster. They help with rebuilding projects so communities can come back stronger and be better prepared for disasters in the future.

Through its work, Oxfam provides the most basic human rights of clean water, a sufficient amount of nutritious food, shelter and safety from harm.

Further thinking

Visit www.oxfam.uk.org and research the following:

- How does Oxfam promote social equality, social justice, human rights and democracy? Give an example of each.
- What opportunities are there for young people to support the work of Oxfam?

Poverty

In chapter 1C, poverty was considered as one of the main consequences of social injustice and inequality. Living in absolute poverty can mean not having even the most basic of human rights, such as access to clean water, sufficient food, medical care and a safe shelter. It is thought that more than 750 million people lack adequate access to clean drinking water. Diarrhoea, caused by poor sanitation, kills approximately 2300 people a day. Preventable diseases such as diarrhoea and pneumonia cause the deaths of 2 million children each year, as their families are too poor to afford treatment. Around a quarter of the world's population live without electricity in their homes. It's estimated that 1 billion children worldwide are living in poverty and this includes children living in the UK and Ireland.

Short term, NGOs can help by providing emergency supplies of food and clean water. Long term, they work with local people to tackle poverty through agricultural projects and initiatives to install wells.

Figures from: '11 Facts about global poverty', www.dosomething.org/us/facts/11-facts-about-global-poverty

NGO example: poverty

War on Want NI

War on Want NI was founded in 1961 and for over 50 years has supported some of the poorest communities in Africa. War on Want NI has a vision of a world where everyone has access to the resources they need to achieve their full potential. Through its work, War on Want challenges the injustices that cause poverty. It supports communities in Uganda and Malawi, working in partnership with local organisations who are also fighting poverty. The aim is to break the cycle of poverty to help people achieve a sustainable livelihood. In challenging poverty, there are several other issues that War on Want NI also addresses, such as:

- Climate change
- Gender inequality
- People living with HIV and other disabilities
- Lack of access to resources

War on Want targets agricultural communities where people rely on their small farms to produce all their food and perhaps raise a little money to pay for education and medical expenses.

Further thinking

Visit www.waronwantni.org and research how the War on Want NI projects in Uganda and Malawi benefit the local people living in poverty.

Health

Social inequality means that there is often a close link between poverty and poor health, with some of the poorest people in the world having little or no access to adequate healthcare. The living conditions that result from poverty also contribute to poor health, such as inadequate shelter, poor sanitation and nutritious food.

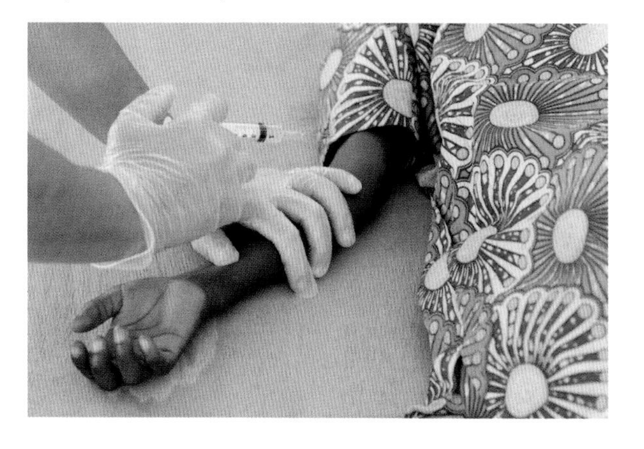

Not all health issues are caused by poverty. Illnesses such as heart disease, lung disease, diabetes, cancer and mental health problems can affect all people, worldwide.

There are many ways that NGOs can take action to improve health and the quality of life of people suffering from ill health. NGOs help to reduce many health-related problems by providing education on hygiene, diet and lifestyle. Many offer medical help for those living with ill health and provide support for sufferers and their families, for example, through hospices, respite care, alternative therapies and counselling.

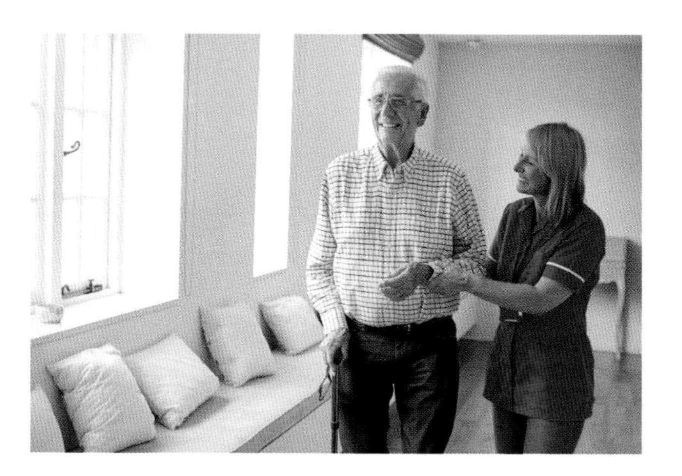

NGO example: health

Northern Ireland Chest Heart and Stroke (NICHS)

Chest Heart and Stroke has been working in Northern Ireland for over 70 years. When the work started in 1946, the initial focus was to raise awareness about the lung disease tuberculosis (TB). As the threat of TB diminished, the organisation made chest, heart and stroke illnesses its main priority. In 1976, the name was changed to The Northern Ireland Chest Heart and Stroke Association.

In Northern Ireland today, it is estimated that over 335,000 people are living with a chest, heart and stroke condition. NICHS takes action through:

- **Supporting families and individuals** – NICHS offer practical and emotional support to people who are living with a chest, heart or stroke condition, and also to their families. They provide opportunities for people to meet with others in a similar situation and share experiences.
- **Providing health education** – NICHS run programmes in schools, workplaces and within the local community.
- **Funding research** – NICHS aim to prevent chest, heart and stroke illnesses in Northern Ireland. Some of the funds they raise go towards research into the prevention, diagnosis and treatment of these conditions.

Further thinking

Visit www.nichs.org.uk and research the following:

- Why are chest-, heart- and stroke-related illnesses of particular concern in Northern Ireland?
- Find examples of NICHS's current awareness-raising campaigns.
- Evaluate the effectiveness of these campaigns.

Welfare and security

The term **welfare** refers to how the state or government looks after the health and well-being of its citizens. **Social security** is the government system of providing money for people with inadequate or no income. Article 22 of the UDHR seeks to protect this right: "Everyone has the right to social security".

Social security also refers to strategies that are designed to protect some of the most vulnerable people in society, such as children, the elderly, the sick, refugees and those who are unemployed. This includes assistance with food and shelter, and strategies to promote the overall health and well-being of the whole population.

NGOs can help by offering impartial advice on a range of issues, such as benefits, housing problems and legal issues. NGOs provide advice through various formats, such as online information, telephone advice, face-to-face interviews, leaflets and posters.

Teamwork

Working in a group, discuss the following statement:

"The social security system in Northern Ireland is unfit for purpose. That's why NGOs have to step in."

- Do you agree or disagree?
- What reasons can you give to support your view?

NGO example: welfare and security

Advice NI

Advice NI is an independent advice network, with advisers spread across Northern Ireland. It aims to give good quality, effective, independent advice to people facing problems, so they are equipped to make the best decisions. The advice covers a range of welfare and social security issues, such as tax and benefits, debt, consumer rights, housing and issues concerning older people. The advice is confidential and offered over the phone, online or through a face-to face meeting.

Advice NI is a membership organisation and local groups working in the community can become members. Advice NI runs courses and training sessions, so those providing advice can be kept up to date with welfare reform, develop their knowledge on specific subjects or become better equipped to help a particular group in the community.

Advice NI aims to:

- help people overcome their problems through advice and support.
- work with organisations in the local community.
- bring benefit to society through their work. Often, the more vulnerable people in society, such as those who are elderly, disabled or unemployed, need advice but are unable to afford professional help. Advice NI is a good example of an NGO working to promote social justice and equality.

Further thinking

- Visit www.adviceni.net and research three of Advice NI's current concerns.
- Evaluate the effectiveness of Advice NI at helping to improve welfare and security for local people.

Animal rights

Animal rights is the concept that every animal has the equal right to life, free from pain, suffering, exploitation and neglect. NGOs can support animal rights by working to protect animals from pain and exploitation; relieve animal suffering; promote awareness of their rights; and publicise incidents of cruelty and neglect.

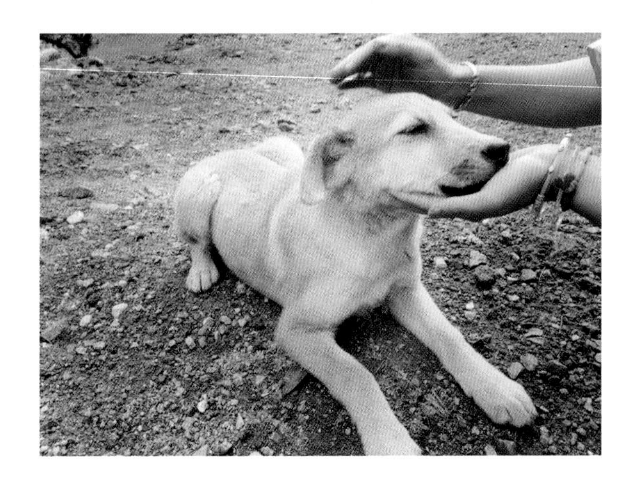

Teamwork

Many people believe in animal rights but not everyone agrees on what these rights include.

Working in a group, discuss:

- Do you agree or disagree with the following actions?
- Do any of them violate animal rights?
- Can animal rights change depending on the circumstances?

• Hunting animals • Dog fighting
• Using animals for medical research
• Wearing a fur coat • Buying leather products
• Eating meat • Consuming dairy products
• Disciplining an animal using physical force
• Breeding endangered species in captivity

NGO example: animal rights

Ulster Society for the Prevention of Cruelty to Animals (USPCA)

The USPCA has been working to protect the rights of animals in Northern Ireland for over 175 years. The original aim was to prevent cruelty to animals and relieve suffering. One of the society's first priorities was to challenge the abuse of working horses, a common occurrence in the Victorian era. Today, the work of the USPCA covers the welfare of all animals, including pets, farm animals and wildlife.

The USPCA acts to prevent animal cruelty in the following ways:

- **Providing information** on how to report animal cruelty.
- **Campaigning** to prevent animal cruelty and putting pressure on the government to make changes to the law to protect animal rights.
- **Operating an animal hospital** dedicated to the relief of animal suffering and offering affordable veterinary care for pet owners on a reduced income.

Further thinking

- Visit www.uspca.co.uk and research some of the USPCA's current campaigns to protect animal's rights and prevent cruelty.
- Produce a leaflet to publicise its work.

The environment

Humans are damaging the environment. Their activity has many negative effects, including pollution, loss of biodiversity, deforestation, depletion of natural resources and global warming. Urgent environmental issues include the need for responsible waste disposal, a reduction in both waste and pollution, and investment in sustainable forms of energy. NGOs work to protect the environment. They raise awareness of the impact of human activity and offer advice on how to limit it. They also promote sustainability, conservation and renewable energy.

NGO example: the environment

Friends of the Earth (FoE)

Friends of the Earth is an international network of environmental organisations across the world. It is also active in tackling environmental issues at national and local level. In the UK, an important part of FoE's work is organising campaigns to persuade the Westminster government to change legislation. For example, a campaign by Friends of the Earth called 'Big Ask' led to the Climate Change Act of 2006. This law commits the UK government to cutting CO_2 emissions by 3% each year.

FoE has local groups in England, Wales and Northern Ireland. These groups are run by thousands of volunteers from many different backgrounds. However, they all believe that the following causes are important:

- Protecting homes and local environments.
- Promoting safe food and water.
- Supporting alternative energy solutions.

FoE's campaigns are an example of how NGOs can act within a democratic society, putting pressure on the government to bring about changes that will benefit everyone.

Further thinking

- Visit www.friendsoftheearth.uk and research some of Friends of the Earth's current campaigns at national level.
- Try and find out if there are any campaigns in your local area.

War and conflict

War can be defined as an organised conflict, usually involving intense violence and carried out by one state against another. However, there are also conflicts that occur within nations, which can be devastating in terms of loss of life and structural damage. The causes of any war or conflict are complicated, but are often to attack or invade an area or gain possession of a natural resource. Sometimes a war may be declared to resist such an attack by another group or to protect an ally.

The effects of war are damaging in a number of ways. Most obviously, there is the cost in terms of human life, which often includes children and innocent civilians as well as armed combatants. A war can also leave an area devastated in terms of damage to homes, schools, hospitals and essential services, such as clean water supply, electricity and infrastructure. The rebuilding following a war can take many years. Other concerns include the long-lasting psychological damage to survivors of the war and the damage to the environment.

In situations of war and conflict, NGOs can take immediate action to keep people safe, for example, by evacuating them from an area of danger. Long-term measures are equally important, to help rebuild devastated communities and help victims of war return home or be comfortably resettled elsewhere.

NGO example: war and conflict

British Red Cross

The British Red Cross is a national society, which is part of the International Red Cross and Red Crescent Movement, an independent humanitarian organisation. Most countries around the world have a national Red Cross or Red Crescent society. Each society has a responsibility to help vulnerable people within its own borders, and to work in conjunction with the movement to protect and support those in crisis worldwide.

Protecting people in conflict is an important area of their work. They help victims of armed conflict and internal disturbances, including prisoners-of-war. In conflicts, the Red Cross makes sure International Humanitarian Law (IHL) is observed. IHL is a set of rules that seeks to protect people who are not/ no longer, participating in armed conflict, such as civilians and wounded, sick or shipwrecked members of the armed forces. It also restricts the means and methods of warfare.

The British Red Cross shows how NGOs can protect human rights and promotes justice through their work.

Further thinking

- Visit www.redcross.org.uk and research the seven fundamental principles of the Red Cross.
- In groups, discuss how these principles help the Red Cross to work effectively whenever a humanitarian crisis occurs.

Human rights abuse

Human rights are the "The basic rights and freedoms that belong to every person in the world".[1] They include the right to life, equality, a fair trial, freedom from slavery and torture, and freedom of thought and expression. When these rights are ignored or deliberately taken away, this is considered to be an abuse or violation of human rights. The Universal Declaration of Human Rights (see page 21) is an attempt to set an agreed standard that all governments should respect. Some of the most serious human rights abuses include war crimes and crimes against humanity, such as genocide, torture, slavery, rape, enforced sterilisation or medical experimentation, and deliberate starvation. Sometimes these violations of human rights are implemented by governments as part of their policies, so limiting the power of the state is an important part of international law.

NGOs working to prevent human rights abuses can offer practical support to victims and their families. They also help through campaigns to change government policies and raise public awareness when abuses take place.

NGO example: human rights abuse

Amnesty International

Amnesty International is a campaigning organisation made up of ordinary people from across the world. They all have one thing in common – a desire to stand up for human rights and protect people who are denied justice, fairness, freedom and truth.

Amnesty International is a global movement, with an estimated 7 million members. It is independent of any government, political party or religion. It was awarded the Nobel Peace Prize in 1977 for its campaign to stop torture around the world.

The aim of Amnesty International is to prevent and end abuses of human rights, by promoting the values contained in the Universal Declaration of Human Rights.

Amnesty International acts to encourage:

- people to accept that human rights must be protected.
- governments to enforce international standards of human rights.
- organisations, businesses, other groups and individuals to support and respect human rights.

Further thinking

- Visit www.amnesty.org.uk and research some of Amnesty International's current campaigns against human rights abuses.
- Are there any examples that are relevant to Northern Ireland?

Homelessness

Homelessness doesn't necessarily mean that a person is sleeping rough or living on the streets. Anyone who is staying at a friend's or relative's, or living in temporary, overcrowded or unsuitable accommodation may still be homeless. There are many reasons why a person may experience homelessness, including poverty, unemployment, unaffordable housing and relationship breakdown. Difficulties at home might lead to a young person leaving and with no family support, they may be in a vulnerable position.

People who are homeless have a number of difficulties to face. Of primary importance is the need to stay safe and healthy. Homelessness puts people at greater risk of violence, addiction, and poor physical and mental health. Homelessness can also make maintaining relationships and employment more difficult.

[1] Source: Equality and Human Rights Commission, www.equalityhumanrights.com/

NGOs tackling homelessness can help by providing short-term emergency accommodation. Long term, they can help by supporting a homeless person or family to move on to more permanent accommodation. Campaigning on the issues that can lead to homelessness is also an important part of their work.

NGO example: homelessness

Simon Community NI

People who are homeless are denied some of the most basic human rights. Simon Community NI works to promote social justice by supporting people who are experiencing, or at risk of, homelessness. The Simon Community is a UK-wide organisation, with the Belfast branch established in 1971. Simon Community NI helps over 3000 people each year, across 22 projects throughout Northern Ireland. It is working towards a society where homelessness is ended, and everyone has a home. Simon Community NI has the following strategies to help towards this goal:

- **Preventing homelessness** – It does this through providing advice and support to people who are at risk, and by campaigning to keep homelessness a priority.
- **Providing support** – It provides people who become homeless with safe and comfortable emergency accommodation.
- **Offering solutions to end homelessness** – It provides assistance for people, at the right time, to help them keep their home. It also provides 'move-on' and permanent accommodation for people who are homeless.

Further thinking

- Visit www.simoncommunity.org to find out more about homelessness in Northern Ireland.
- Produce a short presentation to highlight:
  - the main issues with homelessness.
  - how Simon Community NI is making a difference.

Factors that limit the impact of NGO's work

- **Limited funds** – NGOs are usually funded by donations from the public, private donors, larger charities, and government grants. NGOs therefore rely heavily on their supporters and their funding is limited by what their donors can provide. This can vary from year to year, which can make funds uncertain.
- **Limited resources** – Resources need paid for, so limited funds leads to limited resources. For example, often NGOs can provide only a small amount of aid compared to large aid agencies and the government.
- **Limited staff** – Many NGOs can afford only to have a small staff of salaried workers and rely heavily on volunteer help. While volunteers may offer a huge amount of expertise, enthusiasm and commitment, sometimes their long-term contribution is uncertain.
- **Working in difficult situations** – An essential part of the work of many NGOs is to provide an emergency response following a crisis. This may mean that aid needs to be taken into areas of conflict or a natural disaster. Violence or damage to infrastructure might make it difficult to quickly reach those who are most in need of help.

- **Limited long-term support** – Following a natural disaster, famine or crisis following conflict, emergency aid is often needed. However, in the longer term, it is important that the approach is one of empowering people to help themselves, rather than relying on aid. If NGOs are not able to offer adequate long-term support, this can impact the overall effectiveness of their work. In the event of a further crisis or disaster, individuals and communities need to be able to cope, rather than being entirely dependent on aid.

Assessment for learning

1. Name one NGO that campaigns to protect the environment. [1]
2. Name one NGO working to fight poverty. [1]
3. Describe two ways NGOs can raise public awareness. [4]
4. Explain two ways NGOs protect people's rights. [4]
5. Discuss some of the limitations on the work of NGOs. [6]
6. Evaluate the effectiveness of NGOs in tackling homelessness. [10]

Teamwork

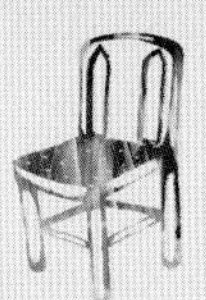

In The Hot Seat

- Imagine you are a fundraiser for an NGO and the rest of your class are wealthy business people who want to support a good cause.
- What would you say to convince them to support your NGO?
- They might put you 'in the hot seat' and ask you some tricky questions. You need to be sure of your facts!

Teamwork

- Working in a group, organise an 'Action Week' in school where you focus on the work of one of the NGOs you have studied.
- Discuss which activities you think would be most effective. The spider diagram below gives some suggestions.

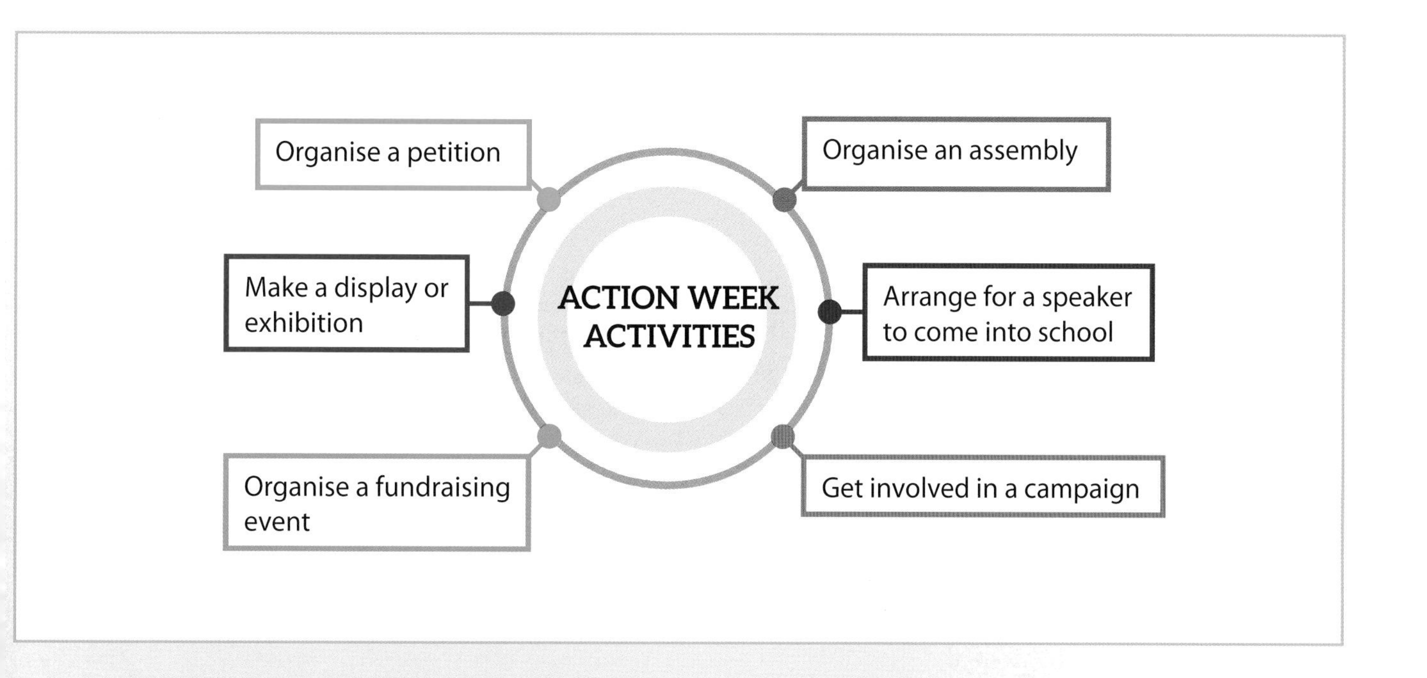

CHAPTER 2A
Personal Health and Well-Being

Chapter Summary

In this chapter you will be studying:

- **The impact of diet, exercise and attitudes to health and well-being.**
- **The causes and consequences of drinking alcohol, smoking and using drugs.**
- **The impact of lifestyle factors on physical and mental health.**
- **Dealing with anxiety, stress and depression.**
- **Support for young people with addictions and mental health issues.**

Health

What does it mean to be healthy?

There is more to being healthy than simply not feeling ill. A healthy person is at the peak of condition, will be around the right weight for their height, take regular exercise and have a balanced diet. Being healthy involves the whole person. It is a combination of feeling good physically, emotionally and socially. These three elements are often referred to as the 'Health Triangle'.

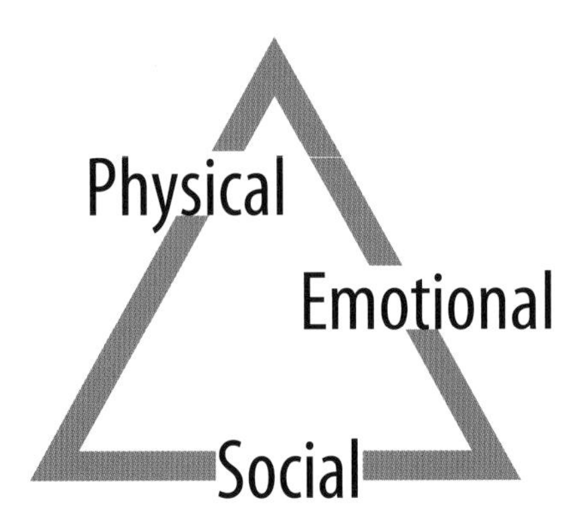

Different types of health

Physical health: Think of the body as a complex machine, where all the parts are operating correctly and efficiently, receiving the right type and amount of fuel. For people in physical health, everything is in good working order. However, we are more than just machines – other factors go towards a healthy human.

Social health: People are generally sociable – they need meaningful interaction with other humans for general well-being.

Relating socially with others is thought to release chemicals into the brain that can affect personality and general well-being. So having good relationships can give people more positive attitudes to life.

Social health is also concerned with the environment a person lives in. Inadequate housing, over-crowded living conditions, low income, work-related stress and poor education can all have a negative impact on health.

Emotional health: Good emotional health is a state of mental well-being that allows a person to lead a full life, confident that they can cope with life's stresses and challenges. People with positive emotional health are also good at helping others. Poor emotional health is when a person feels low and finds it hard to cope; they may also feel lonely and isolated.

Factors affecting health

People are not automatically in good physical, social or emotional health. There are many factors that influence health:

- Physical health can be affected by injury, illness, diet, exercise, rest, genetic make-up and the environment in which people live.
- Social health can be affected by relationships, living conditions, work, income and education.
- Emotional health can be affected by relationships, stress, unemployment, bereavement and mental illness.

There is a lot of positive action people can take to try and improve their well-being:

- Eat a balanced, healthy diet.
- Take regular exercise.
- Get enough rest and sleep.
- Avoid drinking alcohol, smoking and using drugs.
- Maintain good personal hygiene.
- Develop and maintain positive relationships.
- Talk to someone about your problems rather than bottling them up.
- Maintain a healthy work-life balance.
- Take some time for yourself.
- Be kind to yourself and try not to be too self-critical.
- Try to be positive.
- Try new things, such as new hobbies or skills.

Activity

Design a poster to help promote a healthy school environment. Remember to refer to physical, social and emotional health.

Teamwork

Working in a group:

1. Discuss how each of the following may have a negative effect on a person's emotional health:
   - Loss of friendship
   - Bereavement
   - Loss of job
   - Moving school or house
   - Difficulties with parents or carers
2. Here are some factors that could have a positive effect on a person's emotional health:
   - Forming a new friendship
   - Developing a new skill

   What others can you think of?

Assessment for learning

1. Write down what is meant by the term 'Health Triangle'. [1]
2. Name one way a person can improve their physical health. [1]
3. Describe one social benefit from following an exercise programme. [2]
4. Explain two strategies to help improve emotional health. [4]
5. Discuss some of the factors influencing a person's overall health. [6]

Diet

A balanced diet

The food we eat can be divided into five main groups:

- Proteins, such as meat, fish, eggs and beans.
- Fruit and vegetables.
- Carbohydrates, such as rice, pasta and bread.
- Dairy products and alternatives.
- Foods containing fat and sugar.

In the UK, many people eat a diet containing too much fat, salt and sugar, but not enough wholegrains, fresh fruit and vegetables. A healthy diet is a balanced diet – there needs to be the right proportion of foods from each group. A sensible diet will include plenty of carbohydrates, fruit and vegetables, enough protein, dairy products or alternatives, but will go easy on fatty and sugary items. Eating a variety of foods in the right proportion means that our bodies get all the nutrients needed for good health.

Activity

Plan a menu for a teenager for the next three days. Make sure you include all the food groups and limit the amounts of fatty and sugary foods.

Special diets

Some people have to follow a special diet and eliminate or restrict certain foods, perhaps because of a health condition. Others choose not to eat particular types of food because of their beliefs. Two examples of this are vegetarians and vegans.

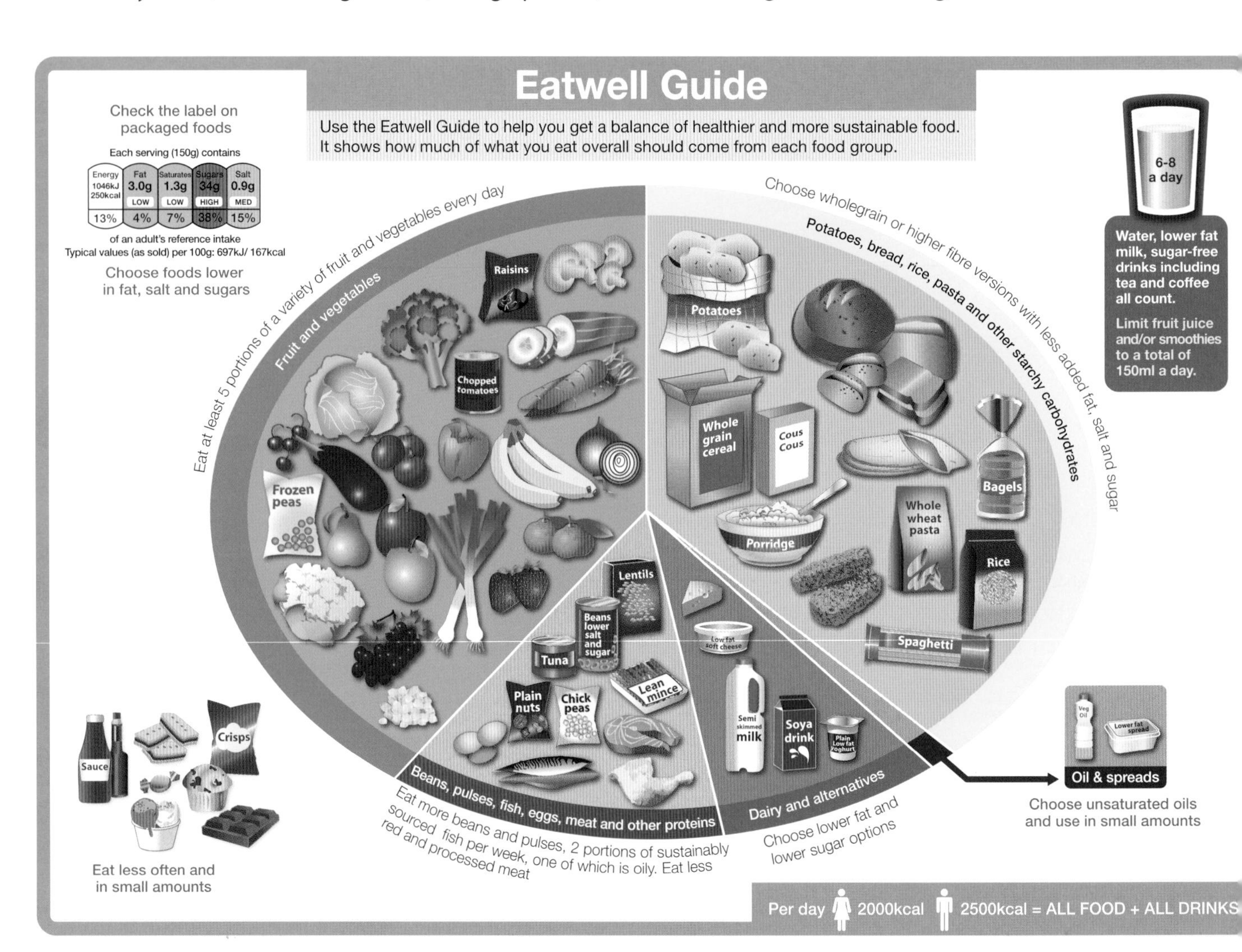

Source: Public Health England in association with the Welsh Government, Food Standards Scotland and the Food Standards Agency in Northern Ireland. © Crown Copyright 2016

Vegetarians avoid all products that come from killing an animal. This means they will not eat any meat, poultry or fish. Vegetarians can eat eggs and dairy products, such as milk, yoghurt and cheese.

Vegans avoid all animal products. This means no meat of any kind, but also no eggs, honey or dairy products. Vegans will also avoid buying products made from leather (such as shoes, handbags and belts), choosing synthetic alternatives instead.

Most supermarkets stock **organic foods**. Organic food is farmed naturally without the use of potentially harmful chemicals, growth hormones or genetic modification. Some people try to base their diet entirely on organic produce as they are concerned about the use of artificial pesticides and fertilisers.

Fast food, convenience food and junk food

Achieving the right balance and eating a healthy diet can be difficult and often the pressures of modern living don't make it easy. After a busy day it can be tempting to go to the local takeaway **(fast food)** or grab a microwave meal from the supermarket shelf **(convenience food)**.

Eating these kinds of foods occasionally isn't going to cause health problems. Some convenience foods are additive-free and available in healthier options. However, many fast foods and convenience foods contain high levels of fat, sugar and salt, with very little fibre, vitamins or minerals. Many nutritionists would consider them to be '**junk food**' as they have very little nutritional value. Snacks, such as crisps and sweets, would also be considered junk food.

Processed food includes items that are frozen, tinned or dried. Processed food can be eaten as part of a healthy diet, but sometimes they contain high levels of sugar, fat and salt to preserve them and extend their shelf life. This can also make them higher in calories than fresh food.

Teamwork

Working in a group, discuss the following statement.

"The fast food industry is booming – there's always a new chip shop or pizza delivery service starting up. It's what people want to eat, so it can't be all bad, can it?"

- Do you agree? How would you respond to this statement?
- Do you think that adverts for junk food ought to be banned? Explain your answer.

Teamwork

Keep a food diary for a week. In a small group, compare your results.

- Identify the five food groups.
- Identify the healthy and unhealthy parts of each person's diet.
- For any unhealthy parts, suggest healthy alternatives.

The impact of diet on health and well-being

ADVANTAGES OF A HEALTHY DIET	DISADVANTAGES OF AN UNHEALTHY DIET
Good health, ensuring your body gets the nutrients it needs to keep well and fight disease.	Poor health, as an unhealthy diet doesn't provide the body with all the nutrients it needs to keep well and fight disease.
Avoiding health problems, such as high cholesterol, heart disease, diabetes and liver damage.	Increasing the risk of health problems, including: • High cholesterol – Too much saturated fat in the diet can increase cholesterol levels in the blood. This can cause the arteries to block, increasing the risk of heart disease, heart attacks and strokes. • Diabetes – Too much sugar in the diet can damage the pancreas, which is essential for controlling blood sugar levels. Diabetes causes a person's blood sugar level to become dangerously high. • Liver damage – Too much salt in the diet can damage the liver. Many convenience foods and snacks have a high salt content.
Being a healthy weight and avoiding problems associated with obesity.	Gaining weight. Regular overeating can lead to weight gain and obesity, increasing the risks of health problems, reduced mobility and low self-esteem.
Feeling fit and full of energy.	Feeling unfit and lacking energy.
Achieving good levels of concentration and mental alertness.	Struggling to concentrate and stay alert.
Getting the correct nutrients may lead to clear skin, strong nails, and healthy teeth.	Lacking the right nutrients can lead to poor skin and brittle nails. Too much sugar in the diet can damage the teeth and cause decay.
Improved emotional health, as people who are getting the right nutrition feel fit, healthy and good about themselves. Having a positive attitude can also boost social health and provide opportunities for activities with others, such as playing sport or going to the gym.	Poorer emotional health, as people who are not getting the right nutrition can feel unfit, gain weight and suffer illness more frequently. This can lead to anxiety, poor body image and self-esteem, and have a negative impact on social health.

Obesity

Obesity is a medical condition, where a person has become very overweight and this is having a negative effect on their health.

There are a number of factors that can lead to obesity but the most common are a lack of exercise and eating more calories than the body needs. There are also some medical conditions that can cause weight gain (e.g. Cushing's syndrome and an underactive thyroid gland).

Obesity is a serious issue, regarded by some health professionals as a major concern for the twenty-first century. Many people live a less active lifestyle than in the past and diets are now more likely to include high calorie foods.

Obesity is associated with the following risks:

- **Health problems** – It can increase the chances of developing conditions such as high blood pressure, heart disease, diabetes and some types of cancer.
- **Reduced mobility** – It can make it more difficult to move around comfortably.
- **Low self-esteem** – Ill health, reduced mobility and poor body image can all affect self-confidence and self-esteem. This can lead to poor emotional health.

How to avoid obesity:

- Eat a healthy, balanced diet.
- Eat less fast food, convenience food and junk food.
- Eat appropriate food portions, rather than eating more calories than the body needs.
- Be active, as exercise burns calories.

Further thinking

Use the Internet to research obesity.

- Find some obesity facts and figures for Northern Ireland.
- To what extent is obesity a major cause for concern in our society?
- What, if anything, do you think needs to be done to address the problem?

Assessment for learning

1. Write down one way that obesity can affect physical health. [1]
2. Write down what a vegan diet is. [1]
3. Explain two benefits of eating a balanced diet. [4]
4. Explain two disadvantages of eating fast food. [4]
5. Evaluate the impact of diet on health and well-being. [10]

Exercise

Why are there concerns about exercise?

Many people live a less active lifestyle than in the past. It isn't that people are lazy; in fact one of the reasons why people don't exercise enough is that they are too busy with other activities, such as school work, demanding jobs and hectic lifestyles.

Many modern occupations involve very little physical effort and people spend long periods of time sitting at an office desk. More people travel by car or public transport than in the past, rather than active alternatives such as walking or cycling. At home, the use of labour-saving machines makes housework less of a physical chore than it was for previous generations. However, this too reduces physical activity.

Screen time

Changing trends in lifestyle are having a huge impact on young people. The most popular leisure activities involve doing something in front of a screen and very little exercise. There needs to be a balance between screen time and physical activity.

Teamwork

Survey the sports fans in your class.

- How much time do they spend watching sport on a TV or the Internet, or playing sport-themed computer games?
- How does this compare to the time spent actually playing sport?

How much exercise do you need?

School age children will have PE and Games on their timetables. However, this is not enough physical activity for good health. Young people need around one hour of exercise each day. This does not need to be taken all at once; in fact it is better in sessions of around 10–15 minutes.

Active play and sport are great ways to get exercise, so it need not be boring. Going to a fitness or martial arts class with a couple of friends can be an opportunity to socialise as well as get some exercise. Joining a team or taking up swimming or running might appeal to a competitive person. Regular exercise is essential for a healthy lifestyle.

Activity

How do you exercise?

- Keep a diary for a week and include all exercise that you do. For example, walking to school, PE classes, sports clubs, team training, etc.
- How much time do you spend on physical activity each day?
- How does this compare with others in your class?
- Do you think you get enough exercise?

Physical fitness

An effective exercise session is one that will involve aerobic or cardiovascular exercise, combined with bending and stretching. It is important to get out of breath and get the heart pumping (but don't overdo it!), and to build up suppleness in muscles and joints.

There are three main elements to physical fitness:

1. **Stamina:** This means having a slow, powerful heartbeat and the ability to keep going for a long time without gasping for breath.

2. **Strength:** This comes from having well-toned muscles through regular exercise.

3. **Suppleness:** This means having flexibility in key areas of the body, such as neck, spine and joints.

The impact of exercise on health and well-being

THE POSITIVES the benefits of regular exercise	THE NEGATIVES what can happen if you don't
In the short term, regular exercise can: • help maintain a healthy weight. • improve health, as exercise stimulates the body's own repair and defence mechanism. • improve brain function and mental awareness. • strengthen bones and muscles, helping the body withstand injury. • improve balance, strength and mobility. • provide more social opportunities. • provide a sense of achievement. • improve body confidence and self-esteem.	In the short term, a lack of regular exercise can: • cause weight gain. • lead to poor health. • contribute to sleep problems. • increase breathlessness. • contribute to decreased energy levels. • increase the risk of injury. • reduce balance, strength and mobility.
In the long term, regular exercise can: • maintain mobility and independence with age. • help muscles, bones and joints stay healthier for longer. • reduce the risk of some serious health problems.	In the long term, a lack of regular exercise can: • reduce mobility and independence with age. • lead to stiff joints with age. • increase the risk of some serious health problems, including coronary heart disease, strokes, diabetes, osteoporosis, high blood pressure and high cholesterol.
Regular exercise can have a positive impact on social and emotional health by: • reducing stress, as exercise releases chemicals called endorphins into the bloodstream and these create feelings of well-being. • improving sleep. • increasing energy levels.	A lack of regular exercise can have a negative impact on social and emotional health by: • contributing to stress. • reducing some social opportunities. • lowering body confidence and self-esteem.

The impact of attitudes to health and well-being

Living a healthier lifestyle does not have to be seen as boring, a punishment or something to put off until tomorrow, next week, or sometime in the future. Most people are aware of the importance of a balanced diet and regular exercise, but often find this difficult to maintain on a long-term, regular basis. Sometimes there is the temptation to make excuses, try a short-term solution, such as 'crash diet', or expect to see dramatic results in a short space of time.

These negative attitudes rarely lead to a long-term improvement in health and well-being.

When children and young people are encouraged to have a positive attitude towards a healthy lifestyle, this can lead to good habits that last a lifetime. Eating a healthy, balanced diet and getting the right amount of exercise can become a natural part of life. Parents and carers can encourage a healthy attitude by:

- Being a good role model for a healthy lifestyle.
- Not using food (especially sweets) as a reward or a way of showing praise.
- Providing healthy meals and snacks.
- Encouraging outside playtime and sporting activities.
- Limiting screen time, as children can be more likely to 'graze' on unhealthy snacks when in front of a screen, as well as getting less physical activity.

Assessment for learning

1. Name the three main elements to physical fitness. [1]
2. Write down one long-term benefit of regular exercise. [1]
3. Describe one disadvantage of not getting enough exercise. [2]
4. Explain two ways that exercise can improve mental well-being. [4]
5. Discuss the ways that a young person could develop a positive attitude towards health. [6]

Lifestyle choices: using drugs, drinking alcohol and smoking

The use of addictive substances is a lifestyle choice that can have a significant impact on health and well-being. Even substances that are legal and socially acceptable can have serious consequences if misused.

Using drugs

What is a drug?

The term 'drug' can be used to refer to any chemical that affects how your body works, how you behave or how you feel.

Drugs act on the central nervous system when taken into the body by being swallowed, injected or inhaled. These chemicals then interfere with the functioning of the brain.

Neurotransmitters enable the brain to send and receive messages throughout the body; however, drugs can block or enhance the effect of a neurotransmitter. This means that drugs can alter a person's mood and state of mind; affect vision, coordination and speech; create hallucinations or even cause unconsciousness and death.

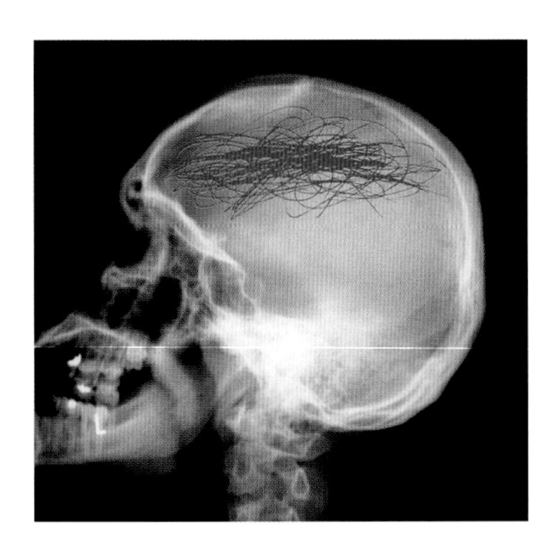

How are drugs classified?

Drugs can be classified according to how they affect the mind and body. There are four main groups:

1. **Stimulants** – These drugs cause the body to be stimulated, or speed up. A person using a stimulant drug may appear to be very lively, talkative and

energetic, but this can also turn to agitation and aggression. Ecstasy and cocaine are stimulants.

2. **Depressants** – These drugs depress the nervous system and cause feelings of sleepiness and relaxation. A person using depressants may have slurred speech and uncoordinated movements, or may even slip into unconsciousness. Cannabis and alcohol are depressants.

3. **Hallucinogens** – These drugs create hallucinations where the user will 'trip', seeing odd shapes and colours or perhaps hear strange sounds. Trips can be either pleasant or terrifying; there is no guarantee how a hallucinogen will affect the body. However, if a person is feeling tense or unhappy before taking a hallucinogenic drug, the result will probably be unpleasant as they tend to magnify whatever mood they are in. LSD is a hallucinogen; ecstasy and cannabis also have hallucinogenic effects.
4. **Opiates –** These drugs can have a medical use in controlling severe pain. When abused they have the effect of blocking out feelings and making the user appear cut off from the world. Heroin is an opiate.

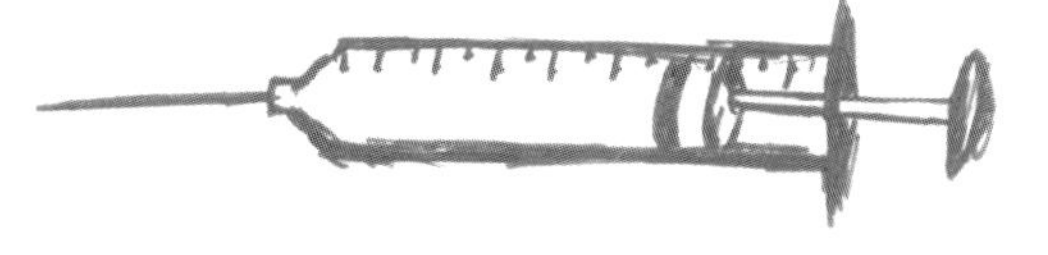

Legal drugs

Not all drugs are illegal. The following drugs are legal but can still have negative impacts on health if misused.

Caffeine – This is a chemical found in tea, coffee, cola and other soft drinks, often sold as 'energy drinks'. Caffeine is a stimulant that affects the central nervous system. It is often used to improve mental alertness.

Alcohol – In Industry, alcohol is a chemical compound. It is found in a range of drinks of varying strengths, colours and tastes. Although alcohol is legal, it is a dangerous and addictive drug if misused.

Nicotine – This is a stimulant found in many types of plant, including the tobacco plant. When nicotine is inhaled through smoking it has an immediate effect on the brain, causing changes in mood and concentration levels. It is highly addictive.

Prescription drugs – These are legal drugs, prescribed by a doctor. Misuse of prescription drugs means taking them in a way other than the doctor intended. This can include taking someone else's medication, exceeding the dose or using it for recreational purposes (to 'get high').

Info box

The law and drugs

Illegal drugs can also be classified according to how dangerous they are, as this affects the legal penalties for having them in your possession or supplying them to others.

There are three categories:*

CLASS A: These are considered to be the most harmful.

Examples: Ecstasy, LSD, heroin, cocaine, crack cocaine.

Penalty for possession: Up to 7 years in prison, an unlimited fine or both.

Penalty for dealing: Up to life imprisonment, an unlimited fine or both.

CLASS B: These are considered not as dangerous, unless they are injected (if this is the case, then they receive the Class A penalties).

Examples: Amphetamines, pholcodine.

Penalty for possession: Up to 5 years in prison, an unlimited fine or both.

Penalty for dealing: Up to 14 years in prison, an unlimited fine or both.

CLASS C: These are considered to be less harmful than other illegal drugs.

Examples: Cannabis, tranquilisers.

Penalties for possession: Up to 2 years in prison, an unlimited fine or both.

Penalties for dealing: Up to 14 years in prison, an unlimited fine or both.

* Sometimes the laws relating to drug classification are updated. The laws listed here are current at the date of printing in 2019.

Causes of drug use

Most people know that misusing drugs is bad for their health, yet some people decide to take them anyway. Here are some of the reasons why:

- **Rebellion** – People are more likely to take risks when they are younger. Even though they have been told that drugs are bad for them, they take them anyway.
- **Pleasure** – The initial effects of taking certain drugs can be exhilarating and exciting. The problem is that these feelings and sensations don't last.
- **Curiosity** – Most young people are naturally curious and want to try new things. If some of their friends are taking drugs, they might be tempted to try them too.
- **Peer pressure** – Their friends might persuade them to try drugs.

- **Stress** – Some people find it hard to cope with the pressures of work, school or relationships and turn to drugs to try and escape.
- **Lifestyle** – Drug-taking is more common in certain environments, such as in night clubs and music venues.
- **Risk-taking behaviour** – Taking drugs can make people reckless and more likely to take risks, harm themselves or others, or commit a crime. It also makes people less likely to consider their personal safety.
- **Addiction** – Some people become addicted to drugs and are compelled to keep taking them even thought they know it's bad for their health.
- **Changes in behaviour** – If a person becomes addicted to drugs their behaviour may change. For example, a conscientious student may start to ignore schoolwork, fail exams or drop out of clubs and sporting activities. Someone with a friendly, easy-going personality may become more secretive or aggressive.

Consequences of taking drugs

- **Health problems** – There are many health problems linked to taking drugs. Cannabis has been linked to schizophrenia and is even more damaging to the lungs than smoking cigarettes. Cocaine and amphetamines have been linked to heart problems. Ecstasy can cause liver failure and panic attacks. Although prescription drugs can be beneficial when prescribed by a doctor, taking a drug prescribed for someone else, or taking it in larger quantities than instructed by a doctor, can have unwelcome side-effects and can be very dangerous.
- **Damage to relationships** – Addiction to drugs often impacts personal relationships. The user's priorities may change, as their energy is directed towards their addiction and away from their relationships.
- **Financial difficulties** – Drugs are expensive and it can cost a lot of money to sustain an addiction. Some drug users find it difficult to hold down a job. Some addicts will do anything to fund their habit, such as stealing from family or friends or selling drugs.
- **Trouble with the authorities** – A student may be suspended from school or in trouble with the police if suspected of possessing or distributing drugs.

Addiction

Drugs are addictive. This means the body quickly becomes used to them, so more and more have to be taken to achieve the same effect.

When a person is addicted, it means they have a compulsion to keep taking or using something even though they know it's bad for their health. Addiction can be either physical or psychological.

- **Physical addiction** is when a person's body becomes dependent on a drug in order to function properly. After a certain number of doses of the drug, their body will actually need to have the drug, or else they will suffer from withdrawal symptoms such as sweating, dizziness, stomach cramps, alternating feelings of hot and cold, vomiting and diarrhoea. Heroin causes physical addiction.
- **Psychological addiction** is when a person's mind becomes dependent on a drug. Cannabis, solvents and ecstasy are all drugs that cause this kind of dependence. If a person takes them for a while, and then stops, their body would continue to function normally. However, they would crave the good feelings that the drug artificially and temporarily creates.

Think about

Why do you think young people use drugs? Make a list of reasons.

Drinking alcohol

Info box

The law and alcohol

In the UK and Ireland, it is against the law for a young person under the age of 18 to:

- buy alcoholic drinks in a shop or bar.
- ask someone else to buy it for them (even if this person is over 18).
- pretend to be 18 and drink alcohol in a public place.

Police can confiscate alcoholic drinks from a person under the age of 18, even if they say they are not drinking it but looking after it for someone else.

Causes of drinking

Most young people know that drinking alcohol before they are 18 years old is bad for their health. However, many still experiment with alcohol anyway. Here are some of the reasons why:

- **Curiosity** – If their friends are talking about and drinking alcohol it may tempt them to try it too.
- **Peer pressure** – Their friends might persuade them to drink alcohol.
- **Fitting in** – Drinking alcohol makes some people feel more at ease and sociable with others.
- **Excitement** – Drinking alcohol gives some people a buzz and can make them feel good. However, it can also make them feel nauseous.
- **Promotion and availability** – Alcohol is advertised on TV, online and can be purchased from supermarkets, off-licences and bars. Although it is illegal to sell alcohol to anyone under 18, it's still possible for young people to get hold of it by using fake IDs or asking older people to buy alcohol for them.

Binge drinking

Binge drinking is when people go out with the intention of getting as drunk as they can as fast as they can. With young people, it usually takes place in the company of others, where there is considerable peer pressure to drink large quantities – perhaps it may even be part of a game to down a drink in one go.

The increase in a binge-drinking attitude to alcohol, particularly among young people, is a cause for concern.

Consequences of drinking

- **Side effects** – Drinking alcohol has many negative side effects including slurred speech, loss of coordination, drowsiness, nausea, vomiting, headaches, memory lapses and even unconsciousness.
- **Heath problems** – There are many health problems associated with drinking alcohol, including alcohol poisoning, liver damage, malnutrition,

high blood pressure, coronary heart disease, strokes, oral cancer and mental health problems such as depression. If a person's body is still growing and developing, then their bodies are even more likely to be damaged from alcohol.

- **Risk-taking behaviour** – Like using drugs, drinking alcohol can make people reckless, as it lowers inhibitions. It can make people less likely to consider their personal safety, such as how to get home.
- **Drink driving** – A person who drives after drinking alcohol is particularly likely to harm themselves and others.
- **Aggression** – Drinking alcohol can make a person aggressive and more likely to get into a fight or commit a crime. This can be particularly dangerous if anyone involved is carrying a weapon.

- **Regret** – Alcohol and some other drugs can cause a person to lose their inhibitions, doing things they wouldn't normally do. Drinking alcohol affects a person's judgement and this could lead to them doing something stupid or embarrassing that they regret the next day.
- **Addiction** – Young people who start drinking in their early teens are more likely to develop a problem with alcohol in later life.

Choosing NOT to drink alcohol

Under-age drinking has become a very serious issue. However, many young people choose not to drink at all. This could be for religious reasons; because they are aware of some of the dangers associated with drinking alcohol early in life; or simply because they don't like it! Making a positive decision not to drink alcohol is sometimes known as **abstinence**.

Teamwork

Working in a group, discuss the following controversial issues:

Supermarkets often have 'special offers' on alcoholic drinks and some bars and clubs have a 'happy hour' when drinks are cheap. Are these wrong because they encourage people to drink too much?

Should people be treated on the NHS if their condition is the result of alcoholism or drug abuse?

Some people argue that alcohol is more harmful than cannabis, so why is cannabis illegal and alcohol not?

Smoking tobacco

Info box

The law and smoking

You must be over 18 to buy cigarettes or other tobacco products in the UK and Ireland.

If a young person under the age of 16 is smoking in public, the police have the right to confiscate the cigarettes.

Smoking is banned in the UK and Ireland in any enclosed workplaces, public building or on public transport.

Causes of smoking

Most young people know that smoking tobacco is bad for their health. However, many take up smoking anyway. Here are some of the reasons why:

- **Rebellion** – People are more likely to take risks when they are younger. Even though they have been told that smoking is bad for them, they might try it anyway.
- **Curiosity** – If their friends are talking about and smoking tobacco, it may tempt people to try it too.
- **Peer pressure** – Their friends might persuade them to try smoking.
- **Weight control** – Smoking can cause appetite loss, which some young people think is worth the adverse health effects.

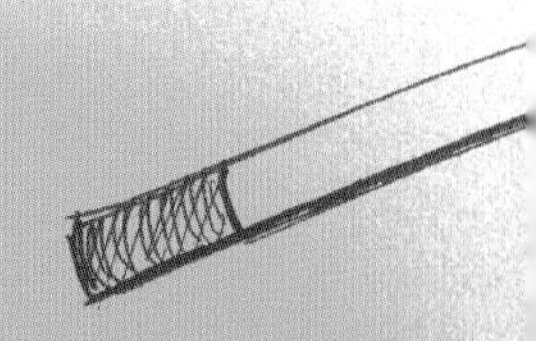

Consequences of smoking

- **Health problems** – There are many health problems associated with smoking tobacco, including high blood pressure, coronary heart disease and strokes; oral, throat and lung cancers; and respiratory problems such as chronic bronchitis and emphysema.
- **Addiction** – Nicotine, the drug contained in tobacco, is highly addictive.
- **Appearance** – Smoking can discolour teeth and fingernails, as the tar in tobacco stains them yellow. The chemicals in cigarettes can also cause premature ageing of the skin.
- **Harm to others** – Passive smoking can cause harm to other people. Smoking during pregnancy can harm the baby, causing premature birth and low birth weight.

Activity

Design a poster or leaflet on the disadvantages of smoking. You are aiming to target children/young teenagers with your message.

Vaping

Vaping, or the use of e-cigarettes, is becoming more popular. E-cigarettes are not risk free but, based on current evidence, they carry less risk to health than ordinary cigarettes. Public Health figures suggest that using an e-cigarette is around 95% safer than smoking. However, as well as nicotine, e-cigarette liquid and vapour can contain potentially harmful chemicals. It is also worth remembering that e-cigarettes can still lead to nicotine addiction.

Assessment for learning

1. Name one way prescription drugs can be abused. [1]
2. Write down one health risk associated with drinking alcohol. [1]
3. Describe one consequence of physical addiction. [2]
4. Explain two physical consequences of a young person smoking cigarettes. [4]
5. Discuss the impact of drinking alcohol on the lives of young people. [6]
6. Evaluate the impact of peer pressure on young people abusing drugs. [10]

Further thinking

Use the Internet to find out more about the help available for people affected by addiction to drugs, alcohol or smoking tobacco. Look at both professional organisations and voluntary groups.

Lifestyle factors

This topic examines the causes and consequences of certain lifestyle factors on a person's physical and mental health. In some cases, a lifestyle factor may be caused by a problem with physical or mental well-being. For example, a person suffering from depression may neglect their self-care and appearance. Sometimes these lifestyle factors can lead to stress, anxiety and feelings of low self-esteem.

Poor hygiene

Personal hygiene is important for feeling clean and comfortable, and also for making your company more pleasant for other people – not many people like to be beside someone with strong body odour or bad breath.

Good personal hygiene involves looking after yourself in the following ways:

- Keeping your body clean, through washing, bathing or showering at least once a day.
- Using an antiperspirant deodorant.

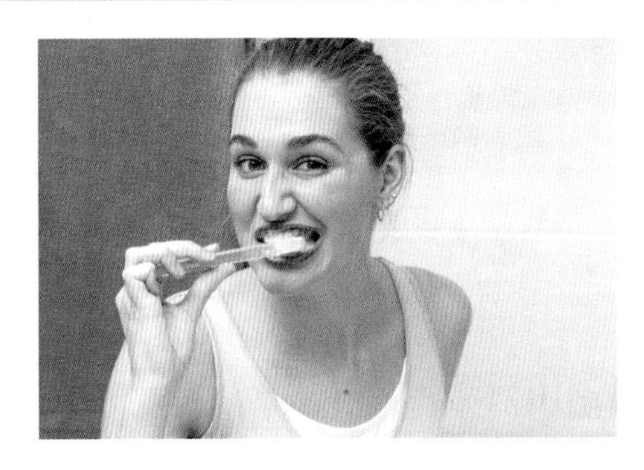

- Washing your hands after going to the toilet and before handling food.
- Cleaning your teeth at least twice a day.
- Washing and brushing your hair regularly.
- Wearing clean clothes, with underwear changed on a daily basis.

Not maintaining good personal hygiene can have a negative impact on a person's health and well-being:

- Without daily bathing, a build up of bacteria on the skin can cause skin complaints and body odour.
- Neglected teeth can lead to bad breath, gum disease and tooth loss.
- Greasy hair in close contact with the face can encourage spots.
- Unwashed hands increases the likelihood of getting a cold or stomach upset.
- Poor personal hygiene can also affect a person's mental health, as it can lead to insecurities and low self-esteem. If someone does not feel good about themselves, they may be even more likely to neglect their appearance and personal hygiene.
- If a person is unpleasant to be around, then their social well-being will also deteriorate.

Think about

What would you do?

You notice that a friend has recently developed a problem with body odour and is wearing dirty clothes. Other people have noticed and have started to make remarks.

- What would you say to your friend to try and help them?
- Why might there be a need for some tact and sensitivity?

Work-life balance

Work-life balance involves dividing your time between work and personal life in a way that works for you. It doesn't necessarily mean an equal balance of hours, as some people are comfortable working longer hours than others. For some, it might be difficult at times to distinguish between work and personal life, especially if someone is a full-time parent or carer, or works from home.

An unhealthy work-life balance usually occurs when someone feels their work is too demanding on their time, leaving limited opportunities for leisure. As a result, someone may suffer from stress or exhaustion due to overwork, leading to problems with both physical and mental health.

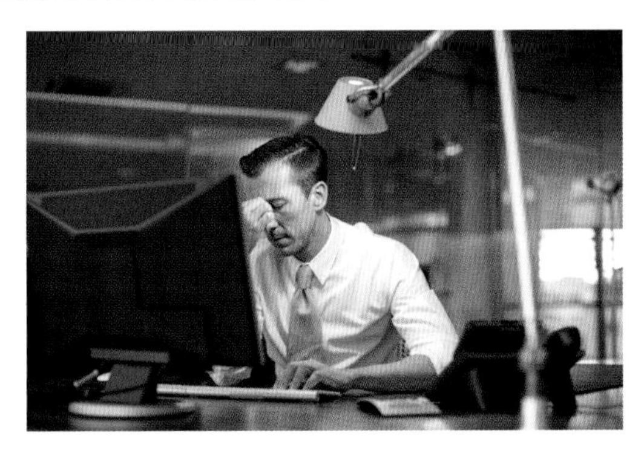

People suffering from stress from an unhealthy work-life balance can:

- become short-tempered.
- feel anxious.
- find it difficult to concentrate and make mistakes in work or study.
- feel exhausted but be unable to sleep well because they are worried about work.
- suffer from frequent colds or infections as the body is unable to cope with the demands placed on it. This can lead to even more stress if time has to be taken off work or school and there is the worry about falling behind.

Whether you are an adult at work or a pupil at school, it is often necessary to work hard. However, it's also important to try and achieve a healthy balance between work and leisure. A healthy work-life balance will mean:

- **you are less likely to suffer from job burnout** – This is a special type of job stress, where a person is in a state of physical and mental exhaustion at work, combined with doubts about their competence and the value of their work.
- **you can be more successful** – Forgetting about work for a while and spending time with friends or family can help with relationships. You can then return to work feeling refreshed and work more efficiently.
- **your health is better** – Taking the time to eat well, exercise and enjoy leisure activities means you are less likely to become run down and prone to illnesses.

Income

Living on a low income can have an impact on **physical health**, particularly if there isn't enough money for nutritious food or a warm home. Living on a low income is often associated with poor diet, poor-quality housing and poor hygiene, leading to illness, malnourishment, obesity, diabetes, respiratory illnesses and addiction. In our society, the people who are most likely to live on a low income include:

- those on a very low wage.
- elderly people.
- one parent families.
- unemployed people.
- sick or disabled people.

Coping with a low income can also have an impact on a person's **mental health**. Living on a low income is often linked to low self-esteem, anxiety, stress and depression. Children and young people may feel different to their classmates if they don't have the same possessions or feel embarrassed about inviting friends to their home, which can lead to low self-esteem. For parents struggling to raise a family on a low income, the constant pressure of paying the bills can lead to stress, depression and anxiety. A person who has been made unemployed, or who is unable to find work, may suffer from feelings of helplessness and low self-esteem.

Assessment for learning

1. Write down what is meant by the term 'job burnout. [1]
2. Name one group of people who may have to live on a low income. [1]
3. Describe two consequences of an unhealthy work-life balance. [4]
4. Explain two ways of coping with anxiety. [4]
5. Discuss how poor hygiene can have an impact on self-confidence and self-esteem. [6]
6. Discuss the impact of low income on all members of the family. [6]

Developing a healthy mind

This section looks at the causes and consequences of anxiety, stress and depression. Having good mental health is very important, as it can help you to have good relationships, cope with challenges and reach your potential. Feeling upset, angry or tense are emotions that everyone feels from time to time. However, if these feelings continue for long periods and have an effect on everyday activities, they may be part of a mental health problem. An important step in developing a healthy mind is to recognise the signs that something isn't right, then take action to cope with the problem. This may be as simple as sharing how you feel with someone you trust.

Causes of anxiety, stress and depression

Anxiety, stress and depression are often closely linked together, for example, being under stress can lead to depression, which in turn can cause anxiety, leading to even more stress for the sufferer. They are often associated with negative life experiences, such as:

- unhappiness at work or school.
- exams.
- emotional trauma, such as bereavement.
- ill health (either yourself or someone close to you).
- changes (in home, school or work-life).
- relationship problems, with family, friends or partners.
- unemployment.
- financial worries.

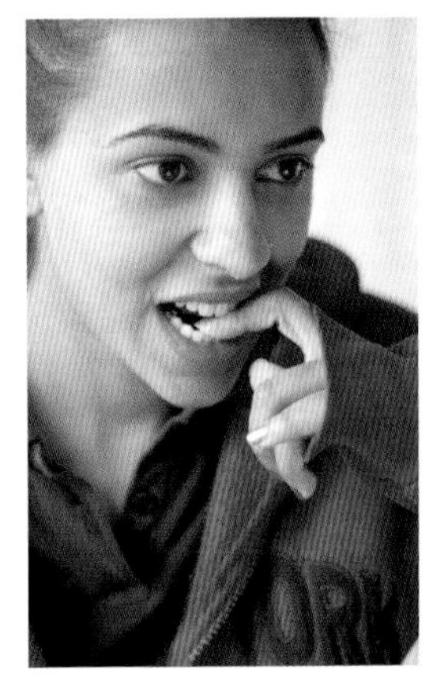

Anxiety

What is anxiety?

Anxiety is the body's way of coping with difficult situations, such as doing an exam or having to speak out loud in front of others. Feeling slightly anxious can help to improve performance but it can become a problem if anxiety gets in the way of daily life.

Consequences of anxiety

- Anxiety can cause a person to worry about things they can't change, such as negative experiences in the past, an event that might happen in the future or something they have created in their mind.
- Anxiety can make a person so worried that they are unable to sleep, enjoy leisure activities or time with friends and family.
- The physical symptoms of anxiety can include breathing faster, 'butterflies' in the stomach, and nausea. Sometimes these feelings can be so severe that a person is physically unwell or unable to complete a task.
- Extreme anxiety can lead to a panic attack, where someone might feel like they can't breathe or are having a heart attack. A panic attack may only last for a few minutes, but it can be a terrifying experience.

Coping with anxiety

For a person trying to overcome anxiety, an important consideration is what situations trigger this feeling. Avoiding such situations (where possible) is a good short-term solution. However, learning ways to cope with anxiety is usually more effective in the long term. These are known as self-help techniques and include:

- **Looking after yourself** – Managing anxiety starts with taking care of your mind and body. This involves eating well, getting enough sleep, keeping fit, and avoiding drugs and alcohol as they will only make things worse in the long term.
- **Spending time on relaxation** – Breathing exercises, listening to music or mindfulness activities can lower anxiety and help towards getting a better night's sleep.
- **Doing something practical** – Listening to music, going for a walk, attending a club or an exercise class, or having a massage are just some practical ways to relieve tension and forget about things, even if it's only temporary. Regular physical activity, such as going for cycle or playing sport, can also aid relaxation and sleep.
- **Having the right mental attitude** – Be positive that you can learn to cope with anxiety and prevent it from interfering with your daily life. There are many apps and websites offering advice and techniques that may be useful.
- **Talking to someone –** Sharing how you feel with a person you trust can provide reassurance.

Mindfulness

Mindfulness is about being aware of your own feelings and also what is going on in the world around you in the present moment. Being mindful can help people to get more enjoyment out of life and understand themselves better, both of which have a positive impact on mental well-being.

Info box

Smiling Mind is an Australian not-for-profit organisation that works to provide children and adults with mindfulness techniques, such as meditation and breathing. An increasing number of schools and businesses worldwide are using their programmes. There is more information on their website and an app giving 10 minutes of mindfulness techniques: www.smilingmind.com.au

Stress

What is stress?

Feeling under pressure is part of everyday life and people often say they feel stressed when they have too much to do or other people are making demands on them. To a certain extent, stress can be positive and these feelings can help deadlines to be met and tasks to be completed. However, if stress causes a person to feel totally overwhelmed and unable to cope, this is a cause for concern.

Consequences of stress

- Stress is not an illness, but it can cause illnesses, some of which are potentially serious, such as high blood pressure.
- The physical symptoms of stress can include headaches, an upset stomach, skin conditions and asthma.
- Stress can lead to poor relationships at home, school or work.
- As a result of the factors above, a person may have feelings of low self-confidence and self-esteem, which can contribute to unhealthy mental well-being.

Coping with stress

The techniques for coping with anxiety can also be effective in managing stress, as they are closely linked. Some people find it helpful to try and work out what causes them to experience high levels of stress. Keeping a diary for a couple of weeks and noting what triggers stress can help someone predict and prepare for difficult situations.

Teamwork

Working in a group, discuss the following:

1. In what ways can the following situations cause stress?
   - Trying to do well in exams.
   - Wanting to meet the expectations of family.
   - Coping with a difficult situation at home.
   - Trying to look good.
   - Fitting in with others and making friends.
2. What advice would you give on how to cope?
3. What other situations can cause a young person to feel stress?

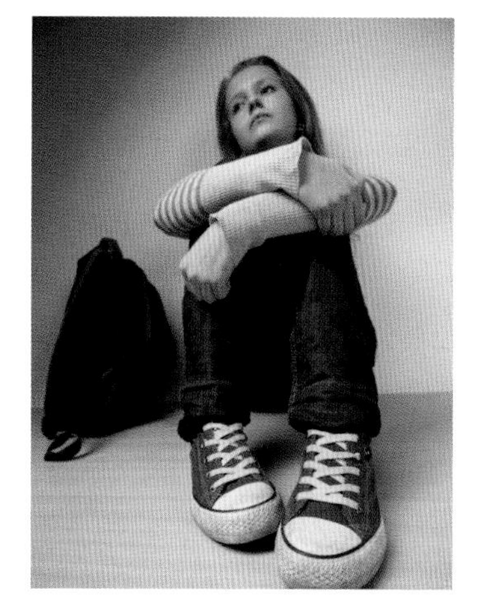

Depression

What is depression?

It is normal to be sad or upset from time to time, even if there is no obvious reason for these feelings. Especially during adolescence, mood swings are very common. Depression is more than just feeling down on occasions. The warning signs of depression can be when the feelings last for longer than a couple of weeks and start to have an impact on daily life.

Consequences of depression

- Depression can cause a person to feel sad, upset or worried for long periods of time. In some cases, these feelings can be so overwhelming that a person loses motivation and interest in daily life.

- The physical symptoms of depression can include fatigue, insomnia, loss of appetite and unexplained aches and pains.
- Depression can cause other problems, such as anxiety, panic attacks, stress and in extreme cases self-harm or suicidal thoughts.

Coping with depression

The techniques for coping with anxiety can also help people who are suffering from depression. It is particularly important for sufferers to express their thoughts and feelings and let other people know what they are experiencing. Sometimes the feelings of sadness can be helped by doing something they enjoy, perhaps an activity they used to do in the past, or trying something new. However, depression is a serious condition and in some cases it is necessary to seek expert help. The NHS recommends visiting a GP if anyone experiences symptoms of depression for most of the day, every day, for more than two weeks.

Assessment for learning

1. Write down what mindfulness is. [1]
2. Name one cause of stress. [1]
3. Describe one physical effect of depression. [2]
4. Explain two consequences of anxiety. [4]
5. Using the information in the Source and your own knowledge, analyse some of the self-help techniques for dealing with anxiety and stress. [6]

Note: In your answer to question 5 you should identify and comment on at least **two** relevant points from the source.

Source

Mental health issues affect many people in society. As a result, there is a range of help available, including health professionals, voluntary organisations and online information. Anxiety, stress and depression can be caused by negative life experiences, so some people find learning to identify and avoid certain situations can be an effective short-term solution.

Many people find that self-help techniques are a helpful way of coping with anxiety, stress and depression. They focus on looking after themselves, both physically and mentally. This includes eating a healthy diet, regular exercise and plenty of sleep. Some people find that spending time on relaxation, such as breathing exercises, yoga or mindfulness techniques helps to improve their mental well-being.

Support for young people

It is widely recognised today that mental health issues and addiction are serious problems for society and affect many people. As a result there is a range of help available, including health professionals, self help groups and voluntary organisations.

Dealing with addiction

Alcohol Change UK is a national charity working to make people aware of the dangers of drinking too much alcohol. They do this by offering information and support to individuals, as well as working with health professionals who support people with alcohol problems. The aim of Alcohol Change UK is to create a society in which alcohol does no harm. Giving advice, either to people who may be worried about their own drinking or someone else's, is an important part of their work. Alcohol Change UK run Drinkline, a free confidential telephone helpline. They offer advice to anyone, regardless of the caller's age, gender, sexuality or ethnic background.

Many people choose to use the Internet for information and support. **Talk to Frank** is a drug education website offering information on commonly abused drugs and advice about where to get help. They offer support through live chat, email, and text and phone. Frank was set up in 2003 as a joint project by the Department of Health and the Home Office of the UK government. It aims to reduce drug abuse by educating teenagers and adolescents about the potential dangers of drugs and alcohol.

Dealing with mental health issues

Being healthy involves more than just physical health. There is an increasing awareness that young people have many pressures to face in daily life and may need support with mental health issues. Getting the right help and advice when needed is important in helping young people reach their potential.

Young Minds is one of the main charities in the UK committed to improving the well-being and mental health of children and young people. They do this by offering information on their website, campaigning to raise awareness and running a telephone helpline. The NHS website gives tips and advice to boost mental health. These include self-help treatments, such as mindfulness and breathing exercises for stress.

Info box

For more information, you could visit the following websites:

Alcohol Change UK – www.alcoholchange.org.uk

Talk to Frank – www.talktofrank.com

YoungMinds – www.youngminds.org.uk

NHS – www.nhs.uk/conditions/stress-anxiety-depression/

Info box

WHO World Mental Health Day

The World Health Organisation (WHO) have established a World Mental Health Day, which is on 10th October every year. The aim of the day is to raise awareness of mental health issues and encourage efforts to support better mental health. In 2018 the theme of the day was 'Young people and mental health in a changing world'. The goal was to help raise mental health awareness, to ensure that young people dealing with problems concerning mental health can live better lives with dignity.

Further thinking

Use the Internet to research the WHO World Mental Health Day theme for this year. Perhaps your class could organise an activity or campaign to raise awareness for World Mental Health Day.

The **Public Health Agency** for Northern Ireland is an organisation run by the government. They aim to raise public awareness through their posters and publications. These cover a wide range of health-related topics, such as drugs, alcohol, nutrition and mental health. They are designed to have maximum impact in schools, workplaces and public areas outdoors. You may have noticed some of their posters on bus shelters or billboards.

How schools could help

Schools can play a vital role in helping and encouraging students to have a healthy lifestyle and achieve optimum physical, social and emotional well-being. Schools can do this through:

- **The school curriculum** – This can be developed to support a healthy lifestyle, with a variety of subjects contributing to lessons on diet, nutrition, exercise and lifestyle choices. It is also important for students to have sports, PE and games on their timetables, to encourage physical activity and teamwork.

- **Pastoral care** – Specially trained teachers, working alongside counsellors, should be equipped to help and advise students about emotional issues.

- **School counsellors** – Schools could have a counsellor to support the work of the pastoral care teachers. Counselling can be an effective way of helping young people cope with issues that cause upset. It involves the process of talking and listening in a safe place. Young people can find it helpful to talk to someone in school who is not a teacher.
- **A healthy eating policy** – Vending machines could replace fizzy drinks, crisps or sweets with water, fresh juice or healthy snacks. Drinking water could be freely available. The school canteen could provide a choice of nutritious, fresh food.
- **Promoting cycling or walking to school** – Bicycle sheds and changing facilities could be provided by the school, along with luminous armbands to ensure students' safety when cycling or walking to school.
- **An effective anti-bullying policy** – It is important for students to feel safe and unthreatened in their school environment. Being bullied at school could have a detrimental effect on a person's emotional health.

Teamwork

Working in a group:

- Make a list of the ways in which your school encourages students to make healthy choices.
- Suggest ways in which your school could do more to encourage good health.
- Create a school policy to help promote a healthier lifestyle for pupils.

Activity

- Choose one of the aspects of living a healthy lifestyle covered in this chapter.
- Produce a PowerPoint presentation that could be shown to the rest of your class.

Assessment for learning

1. Write down one source of support for a person with an addiction problem. [1]
2. Write down one source of support for a person with mental health issues. [1]
3. Explain two ways that a voluntary organisation can support a young person with a mental health issue. [4]
4. Discuss how a young person could use the Internet to obtain support and advice with a personal issue. [6]

CHAPTER 2B
Emotions and Reactions to Life Experiences

Chapter Summary

In this chapter you will be studying:

- **Developing a positive concept of self.**
- **Managing emotions and reactions to life experiences.**
- **The impact of change on a young person's development.**
- **Managing change in positive ways.**

Developing a positive concept of self

You are unique. Everyone has their own particular talents and abilities, as well as weaknesses. Life would be very boring if everyone was exactly the same.

Each person has a mental picture of themselves, or self-image, with a mix of both positive and negative ideas. This is their concept of self.

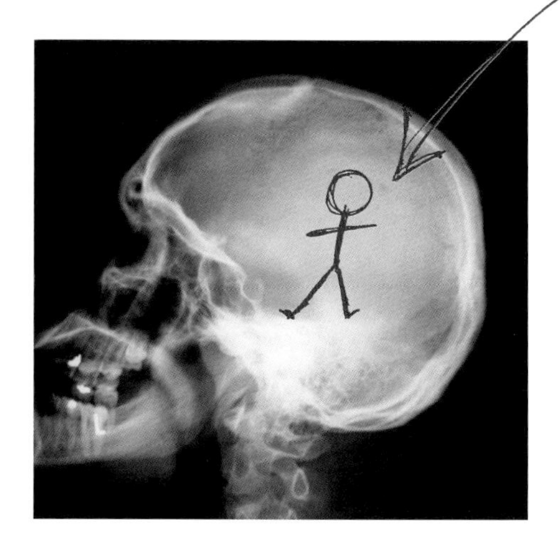

What factors can have an influence?

There are a number of factors that can have an influence on a person's concept of self, such as:

Friends: Having a circle of friends who enjoy your company and will support you can have a very positive effect on your concept of self. On the other hand, poor relationships can lead to feelings of low self-worth. Your self-esteem can also be lowered by comparing yourself to others or worrying too much about what others think of you.

Family: Most families do their best to support and encourage each other. Knowing that you are valued by your family can give you a positive concept of self. Family also help each other improve, by offering constructive criticism and teaching good behaviour. However, criticism should never make anyone feel useless or unloved, as this will have a negative impact on self-esteem.

Success: Feeling successful in just one aspect of life that can help improve your concept of self. This could be academic success, achieving in music, drama or sport – there are many possibilities! However, you can't be successful at everything or even successful at the things you're good at all of the time. Try not to let this get you down.

Body image: Someone who is generally content with their appearance is more likely to have a positive concept of self. However, very few people are totally happy with their looks and most people would change something about their appearance if given the chance. It is important to focus on the things you like about yourself, rather than the things you are unhappy with.

Sexual relationships: Sexual relationships can have a huge effect on people's concept of self. Healthy dating relationships should make both people feel loved, respected and happy. While unhealthy relationships could make people feel insecure, pressurised or unhappy. If a relationship has a negative effect on your concept of self, it might be time for the relationship to end.

Self-esteem

Self-esteem refers to your personal feelings about yourself. If you are generally happy with who you are as a person, you could be described as having high self-esteem. If you are self-critical, hard on yourself or find it difficult to accept praise for doing something well, you could be described as having low self-esteem.

Think about

- Take a few minutes to rate your own self-esteem out of ten.
- Does this change from day to day?
- Why do you think this is?

Teamwork

1. Outline a situation that could lead to a young person having a negative concept of self. What advice could you give to this person to try to help them feel positive about themselves?
2. What difficulties might be experienced in relationships with others? How might these difficulties affect a person's concept of self?
3. Explain how parents can help their teenage children to have higher self-esteem.

Assessment for learning

1. Write down one benefit of having a close circle of friends. [1]
2. Write down one consequence of low self-esteem. [1]
3. Describe two ways good family relationships can benefit a young person. [4]
4. Discuss how sexual relationships can affect a person's concept of self. [6]

How to develop a positive concept of self

We often have very little control over the way other people treat us. However, we can have a very significant influence on our own concept of self. Here are some suggestions:

Positive thinking: It is important to keep a sense of perspective. In most situations there will be good points and bad, but it is important to focus more on the positives than the negatives. Positive thinking involves thinking well of yourself, not being too critical or putting yourself down. It also means dealing with other people in a positive way.

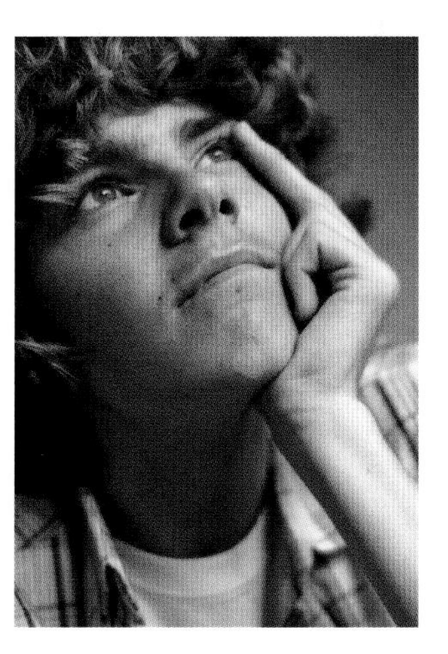

Believe in yourself: If you really believe that you can achieve something, and you are prepared to make an effort, then you will probably enjoy some success. If you approach things negatively and are unwilling to try, you are more likely to fail, which often leads to more negative feelings.

Be realistic: It is great to aim high and set yourself a challenge, but make sure you are not expecting too much of yourself. Try not to compare yourself to others who may find a particular task easier than you.

Managing emotions and reactions to life experiences

Emotions are the feelings we have. They can be caused by different situations, other people and our own thoughts. Emotions are part of human nature and can be both positive and negative. Negative emotions, such as frustration, sadness and loneliness, can be difficult to cope with, so it's important to know how to manage your feelings and how you react to different situations.

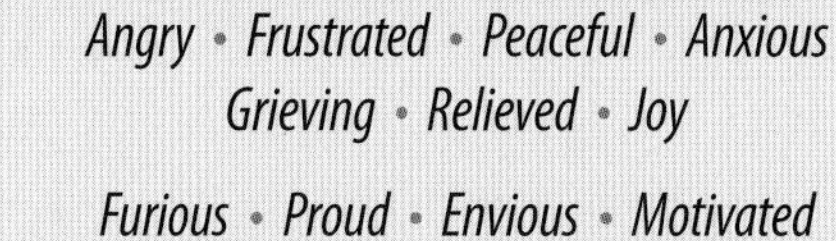

Teamwork

Angry • Frustrated • Peaceful • Anxious
Grieving • Relieved • Joy

Furious • Proud • Envious • Motivated
Worried • Miserable • Embarrassed

Ashamed • Happy • Resentful • Hopeful
Sad • Depressed • Irritated • Determined

Bored • Hurt • Satisfied • Confused
Insecure • Self-conscious • Lonely
Tense • Content

Lost • Terrified • Excited • Nervous
Worthless • Inadequate • Scared
Shocked • Jealous

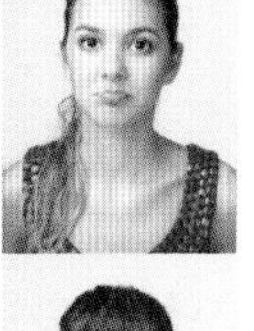

Working in a group, discuss the following:

- Which of the emotions above are positive and which are negative?
- Which emotions can be either positive or negative depending on the situation?
- Choose the five emotions that you think could have the most negative impact on a young person.
- Think of ways to cope with these emotions positively.

Positive coping

'Coping' is the way the body deals with something difficult, stressful or challenging. It is any behaviour that can help to manage emotions. For some people, this might involve directing anger, aggression or violence against other people, themselves or perhaps everyday objects. Some people turn to drugs and alcohol, or develop an unhealthy relationship with food as a means of coping. These reactions may give some short-term feelings of release but are more harmful in the long term.

Alternatively, positive coping skills can provide an outlet for stress that isn't negative or destructive and doesn't hurt other people's feelings. These skills can be learnt at a young age and developed throughout a person's life. An important part of the process is learning what works best for you in a variety of difficult situations. Positive coping skills can help to maintain long-term well-being.

Positive coping skills

- **Look after yourself** – Get plenty of sleep, take some exercise and eat a healthy, balanced diet.
- **Learn some relaxation and breathing exercises** – They are simple to learn and easy to use.
- **Role play** – Practice how you will cope in situations that cause stress.
- **Listen to music** – It can be a great way to relieve stress.

- **Practice taking control of your impulses** – Before you lose your temper, try writing down or drawing how you feel.
- **Be aware of triggers** – These are the people, places or situations that may cause negative emotions.
- **Develop a positive attitude** – This can take practice, but will lead to better health and less stress.
- **Learn to say 'no'** – Having too many commitments can be a major source of stress.
- **Work on your organisational skills** – This will help you meet deadlines and cope with daily tasks.
- **Get some help** – Don't try to manage on your own. Know when it might be best to seek support, either from someone you know or a professional.

Building resilience

Do you see obstacles as challenges to be overcome? When things go wrong, do you look on this as a potential learning experience? If so, you might be described as resilient. Resilience is the ability to recover from setbacks, adapt to change and keep going in difficult situations.

A person who is resilient can cope with life's challenges and often has an optimistic attitude. Resilience is an important quality and can be learnt through practicing positive coping skills. It can be especially useful for teenagers who find their adolescent years stressful and difficult to cope with. During this stage in life, there are also a significant number of changes to face. These can include moving or leaving school, changing friendship group, managing study and exams, and possibly leaving home for the first time.

The impact of change

There are various events at different stages in life that can bring significant changes. These can present challenges, but also new and exciting opportunities.

Starting a new school

Whether starting school for the first time, moving to secondary level education or sixth form, or changing schools because you moved house, this is a sign of moving on and growing up. The change will bring new opportunities for studying different subjects and taking part in new activities.

However, a young person may be worried about making friends, adjusting to a different routine, possibly a much larger school or coping with new subjects.

Going to college or university

Going to college or university might mean going somewhere new or moving away from home for the first time. It is also the opportunity for a student to study something they are really interested in and take important steps towards their future career.

However, for some young people, the thought of leaving home could be very stressful. They may be anxious about where they are going to live and whether they will miss their family. Other worries might include coping with the work and fitting in with a new social group.

Starting a new job

Starting a new job can be very exciting, perhaps bringing opportunities for promotion, better pay and working conditions. Some people may be making a career change as they were dissatisfied with their previous employment. For others, it might be a chance to start their first job or get out of unemployment.

However, starting a new job can also be very stressful, especially if someone is moving to an unfamiliar workplace with different expectations. There will be new relationships to form with colleagues and possibly a more demanding role, if the move is the result of a promotion.

Moving in with a partner, getting married or entering into a civil partnership

When a couple decide to live together, get married or enter into a civil partnership, this is the sign of a serious commitment to the person they love. They may plan to start a family together and look forward to a long and happy relationship. These changes in a person's life can be very positive and bring feelings of happiness and contentment.

However, there may also be nervousness about settling in with another person, with possible tension and arguments as they get used to each other's routines. This may be the first time someone has moved out of the family home, which may bring added stress as the couple adjust to living together.

Becoming unemployed

Unemployment might bring the chance to try something new, or retrain for something different. A person may have felt unhappy at work for some time and unemployment could be seen as an opportunity and a challenge to do something better.

However, losing a job can be one of life's most stressful situations. Unemployment can bring serious money worries, with anxiety about paying the bills and maintaining a decent standard of living. Job loss and unemployment brings a lot of changes at once, which can lead to feelings of rejection and possible low self-esteem.

Managing change in positive ways

It is important to find a way to cope with the stress and tension that can arise from challenging life experiences. There are many positive ways to cope:

- **Talk to a friend** – It is important to feel that you are not alone, that there is someone who is on your side. A friend may have some useful advice.
- **Set achievable targets** – You might find it helpful to write down your targets for the coming week, to prioritise what is most urgent and remind yourself of what you are trying to achieve. This may be an effective strategy to try and cope with a new situation, such as starting a new school or going to university.
- **Do something practical** – Listening to music, going for a walk, playing sport or having a massage are just some ways to relieve tension and forget about things, even if it's only temporary.

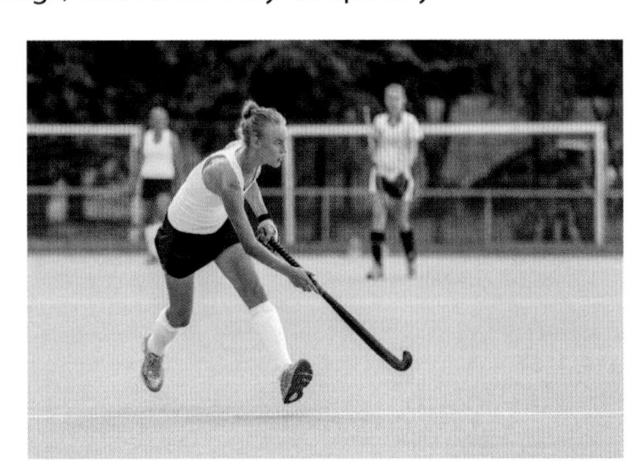

- **Find some personal space** – Finding time for yourself can be an effective way of coping with a lifestyle change, such as moving in with a partner or getting married. This might involve taking up a new activity or simply relaxing in the way that suits you best.

- **Try to find out about the new situation** – Unknown situations can cause stress, so finding out as much information as possible about the new job, school or area where you will be living can help to make change more manageable.
- **Remember that change is a part of life** – Try to turn any anxiety you may be feeling into excitement. Think positively about new opportunities for the future and try to be resilient to change. These are important skills to develop for the rest of your life.

Think about

What do you do to cope with pressure?

Assessment for learning

1. Write down one way to cope with challenging life experiences. [1]
2. Write down one benefit of starting a new job. [1]
3. Explain two ways that becoming unemployed can cause anxiety. [4]
4. Describe one strategy to cope with pressure. [2]
5. Evaluate the impact of unemployment on all members of the family. [10]

CHAPTER 2C
Relationships and Sexuality

Chapter Summary

In this chapter you will be studying:

- **The positive factors that contribute to healthy relationships.**
- **The different types of sexual orientation and gender identity.**
- **The physical and emotional effects of unhealthy relationships.**
- **Support for people in unhealthy relationships.**

Healthy relationships

What is a healthy relationship?

You have many different relationships with lots of different people, including your family, friends and boyfriends or girlfriends. A healthy relationship is one that makes you feel good about yourself. It should make you feel at ease, safe, valued and respected. An unhealthy relationship is one that makes you feel scared, anxious, insecure or angry.

A healthy relationship involves an equal balance of give and take; one person should not feel that they are making all the effort, nor should one person be dominated by the other. A healthy relationship should also be enjoyable. It should be fun being with that person, doing activities that you both enjoy.

Positive factors in a healthy relationship

Relationships with others can be the best part of people's lives, but they can also be the most challenging. Building and maintaining healthy relationships takes time, energy and effort. A person has the power to create healthy relationships around them but they don't happen by accident.

No two relationships are the same, but a healthy relationship is likely to include some or all of the following qualities:

Mutual respect: People in a healthy relationship should respect and value each other for who they are.

Communication: People should be able to talk – and listen – to each other.

Trust: People should be able to trust each other, rely on each other for support and know that secrets will not be shared.

Sharing: The degree of sharing depends on the relationship. This can mean sharing thoughts and feelings, a few hours of time or an entire life with someone.

Honesty: While it is necessary to respect other people's feelings, honesty is also important. This means not telling lies. However, some situations require tact and sensitivity.

Tolerance: This means respecting the fact that everyone is different. A healthy relationship should be able to cope with other people's weaknesses and annoying habits.

Commitment: Building healthy relationships takes time and effort. The people involved need to be willing to work at a relationship and to try and overcome any difficulties that may arise.

Compromise: Disagreements are part of most relationships. A healthy relationship involves working through these disagreements to reach a decision that suits everyone.

Taking responsibility: Relationship difficulties are rarely the fault of one person. Both people need to take responsibility for their actions, admit when they are wrong and apologise for any unkind behaviour, even if it is unintentional.

Forgiveness: No one is perfect; people upset and disappoint each other often without meaning to. This is why forgiveness is important in a healthy relationship.

Teamwork

Look at the following situations. Discuss which positive factor is missing from each relationship.

"It's really unfair! I'm not allowed to go on the ski trip. Mum says we can't afford it and she has the rest of the family to think about. She's being really mean!"

"My gran has got to come and stay with us for a whole month when she gets out of hospital. I've got to give up my bedroom and share with my younger brother, who's a real nerd. I won't be able to play my guitar or have my mates round."

"You'll never guess what's happened to Sophie! Of course, I was told in confidence as I'm her best friend, but just wait until you hear this…"

"I'm asking Cathy to go with me to the party … okay, I'm still dating Beth, but she's away for the weekend. It's all right, she won't find out."

"Dad can't seem to realise that I'm nearly seventeen! He says he's 'worried about me' going to Mark's party. There's no point talking to him, he never listens. I don't care, I'm going anyway. I'll tell him I'm babysitting."

Family relationships

Healthy family relationships can help to create strong, healthy individuals. The family home is where most people learn how to relate to other people and cope with life in the outside world. We can choose our friends but we can't choose our family, so sometimes more effort is needed to build good relationships.

Types of family

Families come in all shapes and sizes and there is no such thing as a typical family. Some of the different types are listed below:

Single-parent family – A parent raising children without a partner, perhaps due to separation, bereavement, sperm donation, adoption and/or having never lived with the other parent.

Extended family – Parent(s) and children, plus other relatives, such as grandparents, living in the family home.

Foster family – Family care for a child whose own parent(s) is facing a crisis; a foster family will provide temporary care.

Adoptive family – Permanent care for a child where this can't be provided by the birth parent(s); adoptive parent(s) have full legal responsibility for the child.

Blended family or step-family – A family where one or both parents have children from a previous relationship, but they have combined to form a new family.

Healthy family relationships

Good communication is very important in a family relationship. Taking the time to talk – and listen – to others in the family can help to ensure that family relationships stay strong and happy.

It is also important to learn how to handle conflict, by trying to **avoid arguments** and aiming for a compromise instead. Reaching a compromise is all about negotiation. This means calmly explaining a point of view and listening to what the other person has to say; the next stage is to work out a way forward that is acceptable to everyone involved.

When children are very young they rely on their parents and carers to do everything for them, which includes making decisions on their behalf. Parents and carers need to provide protection for children to keep them safe from harm. They should also teach their children responsibility, moral values and good behaviour. As children grow older, they need **greater independence**. This means being willing to help out with the day-to-day responsibilities to be done in the home, but also having a role to play in decision making.

Healthy family relationships involve people **caring for each other**. They try to be positive even if someone has made a mistake. In a healthy family relationship, family members offer encouragement to each other and try to promote one another's self-esteem.

Forgiveness is also very important in family life. If someone in the family will not forgive, this can create an unhappy and unequal relationship, with one person made to feel like they owe the other for making a mistake.

Teamwork

Role play

Johnny is 16 years old and he really wants a part-time job and his own transport. He has been given the offer of work at a local takeaway food shop, which will involve working on Thursday, Friday and Saturday evenings. He will have to work very late on a Friday (until 2 am) but this means he will be able save up for a moped. Johnny's parents have the following concerns:

- *His school work might suffer.*
- *He will be out later than he is normally allowed to be on a Friday.*
- *They are worried about his safety on a moped.*

Working in a group, role play a situation where Johnny tries to convince his parents that he will be responsible if given greater freedom.

Family relationships can be really good because…

- You live closely with members of your family and do lots of things together.
- You can relax and be yourself when you are with close family.
- Members of the same family often share the same characteristics, likes and dislikes.
- They put up with you, even if you are in a bad mood.
- You know your family will always support you whatever happens.

…but they can also be difficult because

- Family members can often be blunt and outspoken about mistakes and faults.
- Family arguments can sometimes be the worst.
- Families know each other really well, but this means they also know how to tease, upset and annoy each other.
- Sometimes members of your family can embarrass you in front of your friends.
- If you are having problems with a family member, you might not be able to walk away if you have to live with them.
- Sadly, sometimes families don't care for each other as much as they should. When family relations completely break down this is called a 'dysfunctional family'.

Family pressure

Sometimes family life may be affected by a particular crisis. In difficult situations it can be particularly important to maintain strong family relationships. Here are some examples:

Family break up: When a relationship ends in separation or divorce this can be very stressful for everyone in the family, particularly the children. Following a family break up, children may have to get used to seeing much less of one parent, perhaps just visiting at the weekends. There may be less money to spend as the single parent tries to manage the household budget on one wage.

Remarriage: A young person may also feel negative pressure if a parent finds a new partner and remarries. Having to adjust to a blended family, with a step-parent and possibly step-siblings, could be stressful.

Bereavement: The death of a close family member is one of the most difficult situations that anyone can face. Children who are coping with bereavement in the family can experience feelings of isolation, shock and distress. Teenagers may become withdrawn, or perhaps take risks with drugs and alcohol, as a reaction to what has happened.

Young carers: Some children are under huge pressure as they have to care for a parent, perhaps because of disability, illness or an addiction problem. Most young carers are between eight and fifteen years old, although some are as young as five. Sometimes a young carer will have to look after a younger brother or sister, or perhaps a grandparent, who is suffering illness or disability. Young carers may have to take on many of the household jobs, and might be responsible for the shopping, cleaning and cooking.

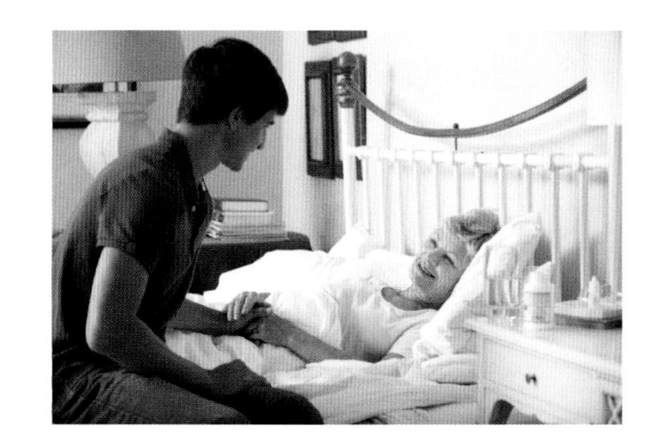

Friendships

Friends are really important, no matter how long a friendship lasts. You may feel that your family does not understand your problems, but a close friend your own age can relate to what you are going through. Friendships also encourage independence from your family and open up opportunities, such as trying a new activity or joining a club. Most people enjoy the company of others; building good relationships with other people can have a positive effect on a person's self-esteem and sense of self-worth.

Teamwork

Discuss the following questions in small groups:

- Which do you think is best – a small circle of close friends or a large group of casual acquaintances?
- Consider the friendships you have now. For how long have these friendships lasted? Does anyone have a friendship going back to P1 (or earlier)?
- Are your friends mostly around your own age and from a similar background? Are these factors unimportant?
- What do you consider to be the ingredients of a successful friendship?
- What personal qualities do you consider important in a friend?
- Do your friends see these qualities in you?

Healthy relationships with friends

Many people would agree that **mutual respect** is a necessary ingredient in a friendship. As with any healthy relationship, **communication** is necessary so that a friendship can develop and become strong. This will lead to a good understanding between friends.

If there is an argument or disagreement this does not necessarily mean that the relationship is unhealthy. As long as friends can communicate with one another and are prepared to listen to each other, they should be able to resolve a conflict. Healthy friendships involve respecting each other's differences.

There is a sense of **sharing** in a healthy friendship, with close friends spending time in each other's company, perhaps taking part in the same activities. Friends often share likes and dislikes, hobbies and interests.

Trust is essential in building a strong friendship. It is important to be able to share secrets with a friend without worrying that they will be passed on to others. Closely associated with trust is **loyalty**. True friends are the ones you know will always stand by you, no matter what happens. In a healthy relationship, friends do their best to keep their promises and don't usually let each other down. Good friends care; they show **kindness** and **support** each other through difficulties.

No relationship is perfect and friends will let each other down and hurt each other's feelings, often without meaning to. This is why **forgiveness** is an important quality in a healthy friendship. The strongest bonds are usually those where friends show the most forgiveness towards each other.

Healthy friendships are those where there is **equality** in the relationship; one person will not attempt to dominate the other by making all the decisions, or telling their friend what to wear and who to talk to. Friends also need to **accept responsibility** for the relationship, by both putting in an effort to make it strong. It is important never to take friends for granted. Through friendships we can learn about the qualities we would expect to see in others and how we can show these qualities ourselves.

Activity

Choose five of the factors listed under 'Healthy relationships with friends'.

- Score each of them out of 10 according to how important you think they are in a healthy friendship.
- Explain your choices in a short paragraph.

Think about

When a friend needs support

A sign of a strong, healthy friendship is when a friend turns to you for support. This could be because they are facing a difficult situation, such as:

- They are unhappy at home, perhaps as a result of parents fighting.
- They have just ended a relationship with a girlfriend or boyfriend.
- They are in trouble at school.
- They have to cope with a health problem, concerning themselves or a family member.
- They have not been accepted for a school team, choir or drama production.
- They are disappointed with their exam results.

What would you do to help a friend in these situations?

Peer pressure

Peer pressure is when a friend, or group of friends, tries to persuade you to do something you are uncomfortable with. While peer pressure can sometimes be positive, all too often it is negative and a young person may feel pressured into:

- smoking, drinking or taking drugs.
- stealing or shoplifting.
- fighting or vandalism.
- truancy or ignoring schoolwork.
- joining in with bullying others.
- having a sexual relationship when they don't want to.

It is important to choose friends carefully as a true friend will not usually put their friends under this kind of pressure. It is also important to know your own mind, be prepared to stand up to people and do what you think is right.

Sexual relationships

There is no correct age to begin dating; everybody is different and individual families will have their own rules. When you decide to start a relationship, it should be because you genuinely care about that person, not just because you want a boyfriend or girlfriend – or because your friends think you should be dating.

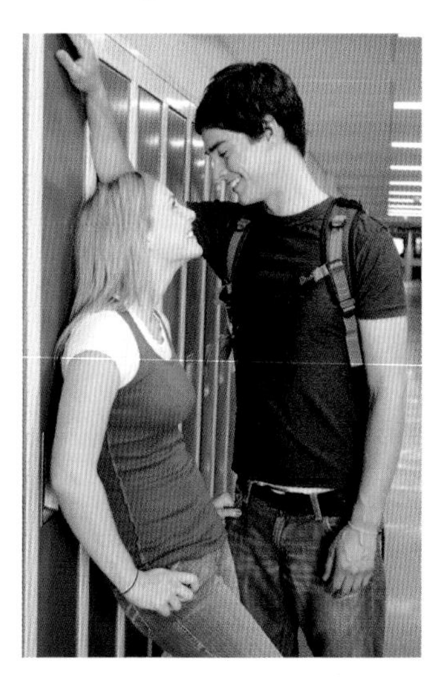

Healthy dating relationships

The ingredients of a healthy friendship – such as **trust, honesty, consideration, loyalty, forgiveness** and **sharing** – will also be present in a healthy dating relationship. However, dating relationships are different as they also include physical affection. Therefore **mutual respect** is especially important in a dating relationship, as no one should feel pressured into intimacy that they do not want or are not ready for.

It probably does not matter to you what your friends look like, but as a dating relationship will involve some degree of **physical attraction**, a dating partner's looks may well be important. In fact, physical appearance is often what leads two people to be attracted to each other in the first place. However, a relationship that is based on physical attraction alone will not last for very long. A strong, healthy relationship will be based on someone's character – that you like them as a person, respect and trust them, find them fun to be with and enjoy their company.

Communication is another important factor in a dating relationship. This does not just mean regular contact with your partner through social media; it means talking to them and sharing your feelings. This is particularly important to ensure that you both know what each other is ready for in the relationship and respect each other's wishes.

Independence is another quality that should be present in a healthy dating relationship. While the couple who are dating will want to spend time in each other's company, it is also healthy to spend some time apart and maintain existing friendships. A dating partner should not be jealous or possessive. This is a sign of an unhealthy relationship.

When a relationship needs to end

If you ever feel anxious about a relationship you are in, or you feel threatened in any way, then it might be time for it to come to an end. Below are some reasons why a relationship should end:

- If the person puts pressure on you to take part in sexual activities you do not feel comfortable with, perhaps applying emotional pressure such as "If you loved me, you would do it…"
- If your girlfriend or boyfriend is verbally or physically abusive towards you.
- If the person you are dating abuses alcohol or drugs, especially if they want you to do the same.
- If your family and friends are concerned about your relationship. Perhaps they have noticed a change in your behaviour since you began dating or have other concerns for your well-being.

Sexual orientation and gender identity

Sexual orientation

The term sexual orientation describes what sex or gender a person is attracted to.

- **Heterosexual** – A person who is attracted to someone of the opposite sex (from the Greek word *héteros*, meaning different).
- **Homosexual** – A person who is attracted to someone of the same sex (from the Greek *homós*, meaning same).
- **Bisexual** – A person who is attracted to both males and females.
- **Pansexual** – A person who is attracted to someone regardless of their sex or gender identity.
- **Asexual** – A person with a lack of sexual attraction to any sex.

Gender identity

A person's sex (whether they are male or female) is determined at birth. Gender identity is what a person feels their gender is and what they identify with. The physical features a person is born with do not necessarily define their gender, as a person can identify with a gender different to the one they were born with (e.g. they were born biologically female but identify as male or they were born biologically male but identify as female). Everyone expresses their gender in a unique and personal way, perhaps through behaviour, hairstyle and clothes.

Some people know from a young age that their gender is different to the one assigned at birth, while others may not work out their gender identity until adulthood. The term **gender dysphoria** is used when someone feels uncomfortable with the gender assigned to them – they feel it does not match their gender identity. **Transgender** is a term used to describe a person who identifies with a gender different to the sex (male or female) they were born with. **Non-binary** is used to describe a person who does not identify with a specific gender.

The effects of sexual orientation and gender identity on people's well-being

Relationships with other people

There is an increasing understanding that there are different types of sexual orientation and gender identity, so, for most people, these have no affect on their relationships with others. However, some people are unwilling to accept those who are different to themselves and some even have negative reactions, for example:

- **Homophobia and transphobia** – Homophobia is a dislike or prejudice against anyone who is homosexual. Prejudice means to 'pre-judge' and therefore any feelings of prejudice are closely linked to ignorance, lack of understanding and fear of the unknown. Transphobia is a dislike of someone because they are transgender.
- **Negative attitudes** – A person may experience negativity or rejection from family, friends, colleagues or members of their community who find it difficult to accept their sexual orientation or gender identity. A person in this situation may feel unsupported, misunderstood, excluded or pressurised to 'change'.
- **Discrimination** – This is where a person receives unfair treatment because of their sexual orientation or gender identity, or because of what others perceive their sexual orientation or gender identity to be.
- **Hate crime** – This is when someone or their property is attacked because of their sexual orientation or gender identity. This can include vandalism, physical or verbal abuse, and any other kind of bullying.

Physical effects

- If a person experiences negative treatment by others due to their sexual orientation or gender identity, this could affect their physical health and well-being.
- If a person is the victim of physical bullying, this may result in pain and injury.
- Concern over negative treatment or physical bullying may also cause them to lose sleep.

Emotional effects

- Negative treatment by others due to sexual orientation or gender identity could also affect a person's emotional health and well-being.
- This negative treatment could cause stress, or feelings of anxiety and depression.
- A person may separate themselves from others, as they feel safer on their own or that no one understands them, which could lead to loneliness and isolation.

Coping with any negative effects

No one should be made to feel that they are 'different', not 'normal' or should change their sexual orientation or gender identity. However, some people are affected by the negative reactions of others. The following strategies can help people cope with any negative effects of sexual orientation or gender identity:

- Remember you are not alone. There are people of all sexual orientations and gender identities.
- There are many websites, forums and organisations offering advice, support and people to talk to about sexual orientation and gender identity.
- Talk to someone you trust. They can listen and offer support.
- People of all sexual orientations and gender identities are protected from discrimination by the law. If you feel that someone is discriminating against you, speak to a teacher or your employer about it.

Unhealthy relationships

Relationships with other people are an important part of life from the moment we are born until we die. Relationships begin with family, then friends, then later on, there may be a romantic attachment. Ideally, these relationships should help to make us better people as well as bring enjoyment.

Unhealthy relationships rarely promote these feelings, but can lead to someone feeling uncomfortable, sad or angry. This doesn't mean that just because you have an argument or dislike the way someone has treated you that a relationship is unhealthy – disagreements happen in healthy relationships too.

Unhealthy relationships are those where positive characteristics (such as trust, compromise and mutual respect) are usually absent. Instead, there may be a lack of trust, insecurity, manipulating behaviour or constant criticism. If there is violence present in a relationship, this is usually a sign that it is abusive.

An unhealthy relationship, whether at home, school or work, is likely to cause stress and anxiety for a considerable part of a person's life. This will have a negative effect on a person's physical and emotional health.

Physical effects

Lack of sleep and disrupted eating patterns could be the result of an unhealthy relationship. This can lead to an inability to focus at work or school, or carry out other responsibilities, such as parenting. The resulting anxiety can lead to a weakening of the body's immune system, resulting in frequent illness. Other health issues include the risk of high blood pressure and heart disease. If someone is in a violent relationship, they may have physical injuries inflicted by a parent or partner. An unhealthy relationship can cause considerable stress. A person in this situation may resort to self-harm, or abuse of drugs and alcohol, as a way of coping with the situation.

Emotional effects

One of the serious effects of an unhealthy relationship is that a person's self-esteem can be lowered. This can lead to stress, anxiety and depression, which will add to the negative picture a person might have of themselves. A person might also find it difficult to accept the love and friendship of a genuine relationship, through suspicion or feelings of their own unworthiness.

Support for people in unhealthy relationships

The following advice may be useful for someone who is in an unhealthy relationship:

- Talk to the other person/people in the relationship and try to work something out.
- Get some advice from family and friends who are not directly involved.
- Contact a professional counsellor or organisation, such as Relate (support for people in all types of relationship), Accord (advice for married couples), or It's Finished (support for anyone dealing with a break-up from a partner).
- If a marriage is heading towards a separation or divorce, then the next step would be to contact a solicitor for advice.
- The PSNI may need to be contacted in a situation involving domestic abuse or physical violence.

Assessment for learning

1. Name one positive factor in a healthy family relationship. [1]
2. Name one positive factor in a healthy dating relationship. [1]
3. Describe two signs of an unhealthy relationship. [4]
4. Explain two ways friends can support each other. [4]
5. Discuss how a counsellor may support a person in an unhealthy relationship. [6]
6. Evaluate the effects of sexual orientation on a person's well-being. [10]

CHAPTER 2D
Personal Safety and Well-Being

Chapter Summary

In this chapter you will be studying:

- **The causes and consequences of risk-taking behaviour.**
- **Assessing and managing risk.**
- **The benefits and misuse of social media.**
- **Different types of abuse and its effect on young people.**
- **Dealing with abuse, exploitation and bullying.**

Risk-taking behaviour

Taking risks is a part of life. A person who decided to avoid all risky behaviour would probably never get out of bed all day, as everything we do involves some risk. However, people need to look after themselves too. They need to be aware of potential risks and know how to manage them.

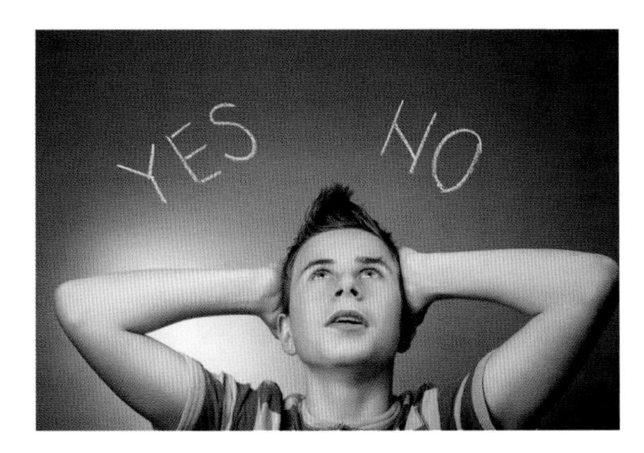

As a teenager, you are probably granted more freedom by your parents or carers than when you were young. You may be allowed to stay out later than in the past, spend more time with your friends and try new activities. This new freedom will allow you to become more independent but it also brings more risks. With greater independence comes greater responsibility, as you have to make your own choices and look after yourself.

Positive risk-taking can be a rewarding experience, if it involves taking on a challenge, such as auditioning for the school play, or taking up a new sport or activity. There is a level of risk involved as you may well be in a difficult or unfamiliar situation, and there is always the possibility of failure. However, the sense of achievement from doing something successfully can boost your self-confidence and self-esteem. People need to take risks in order to work towards their goals.

Negative risk-taking involves irresponsible behaviour and is unlikely to bring any benefits to the person taking the risk or other people who might be involved. Instead it might put them at risk, physically or emotionally. It is usually seen as irresponsible, destructive or anti-social, for example binge drinking, having unprotected sex, anti-social behaviour or driving dangerously.

Causes of risk-taking behaviour

Boredom – Facing challenges, taking risks, feeling excitement – these are all part of living a life that is interesting and fulfilling. Some people, however, feel that their lives are dull and boring. They may turn to risk-taking behaviour for the thrill it gives them.

Attention seeking – Some young people feel lonely and isolated from their peer group and may also feel that parents, carers and teachers don't have any time for them. Taking part in a risky or anti-social activity can be a way to try to get attention.

Peer pressure – Some people are more likely to be affected by peer pressure than others. For some young people, just being with a group of friends makes them more likely to take risks than if they were on their own. Peer pressure can cause a desire to impress others or to be accepted by the group. These feelings may seem more important than considerations of personal safety, harm to others or being in trouble with the police.

Influence of drugs or alcohol – Drugs and alcohol can make a person more reckless and therefore more likely to take risks. After a person has sobered up, they may regret what they have done, as they would never have acted in such a way without the drugs or alcohol.

Addicted to the adrenaline rush – Adrenaline is a hormone that is produced by the body in situations of danger or stress. It causes the heart rate to increase, blood vessels to contract and airways to dilate. These feelings can be very intense and are described as an adrenaline rush. Some people take part in extreme sports (such as skateboarding, rock climbing or bungee jumping) as they love the feeling of exhilaration that comes from an adrenaline rush. However, getting enjoyment from a harmful activity (such as anti-social behaviour) is wrong – there are better ways to do something exciting.

Financial gain – Some people take negative risks by committing crimes, such as shoplifting or breaking and entering into someone's house. The motivation to steal could be a mixture of greed, wanting to impress others and the adrenaline rush.

Teamwork

Working in a group, discuss each of the causes of risk-taking behaviour.

- Have you ever taken risks for any of these reasons?
- Share examples with the rest of your group.
- Do you consider any of these to be a positive reason for taking risks?

Assessing and managing risk

Self-evaluation of risk – A sensible approach to risk-taking involves considering the consequences of doing something. This does not mean scaring yourself and refusing to do anything new, but learning how to assess risks and make the right choices.

A person considering taking part in risky behaviour should ask themselves:

1. *Could this activity harm me physically or emotionally?*
2. *Could it have any long-term effects on my health?*
3. *Could it harm others?*
4. *Is this activity against the law?*
5. *Could I get a criminal record that could affect my future?*
6. *Will taking part in this activity damage my relationships (e.g. with my parents or friends)?*

If an activity can only bring harm to yourself and others, then it should be avoided.

Resist negative peer pressure – Remember that everyone has the right to be treated with respect. This means that no one should be bullied or forced into doing something they are unhappy with, particularly if this activity carries risks to personal well-being or safety.

An effective way to deal with negative pressure is to be assertive – this means being firm about your personal limits without being aggressive. Say 'no' firmly and stick to your decision; true friends should respect your feelings. If the crowd you hang out with seems to be spending more and more time committing petty crime (such as shoplifting, graffiti or vandalism) then maybe it's time to find new friends!

Consider alternative activities – There are plenty of constructive channels for risk-taking, such as sports or outdoor activities. Mountain biking, rock climbing, canoeing or playing a team sport could be a positive way of getting an adrenaline rush. Even though some of these activities might be considered potentially dangerous, taking part with qualified instructors can greatly reduce the risks involved. Of course, not everyone enjoys outdoor pursuits. There are plenty of other exciting new activities to choose from – perhaps something creative, some voluntary work or a part-time job.

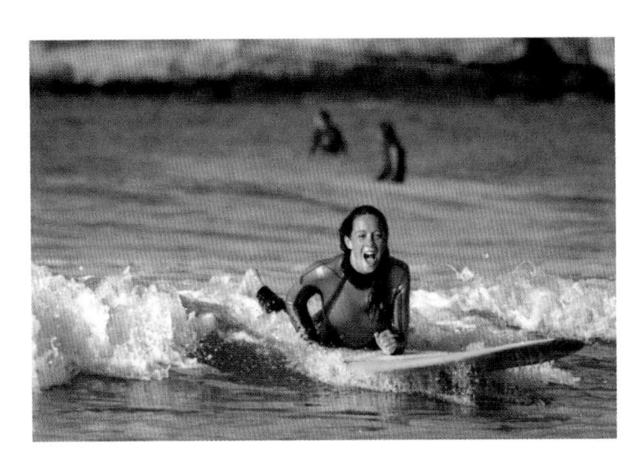

Think about

- Can you think of any other ways in which risk-taking behaviour could be managed?
- Share your ideas with the class.

Activity

Assessing risk

- Working in a group, look at the following scenarios.
- For each scenario, assess the potential risk by asking yourself the following questions:
  1. *Could this activity harm me physically or emotionally?*
  2. *Could it have any long-term effects on my health?*
  3. *Could it harm others?*
  4. *Is this activity against the law?*
  5. *Could I get a criminal record that could affect my future?*
  6. *Could taking part in this activity damage my relationships (e.g. with my parents or friends)?*
- Give each scenario a risk rating from 1–10 (where 1 is low risk and 10 is high risk).
- Finally, decide which scenarios involve positive risk, and which involve negative risk.
- Record your conclusions in a table like the one below.

	COULD IT HARM ME?	COULD IT HAVE ANY LONG-TERM EFFECTS ON MY HEALTH?	COULD IT HARM OTHERS?	IS IT AGAINST THE LAW?	COULD I GET A CRIMINAL RECORD?	COULD IT DAMAGE MY RELATION-SHIPS?	RISK RATING	POSITIVE C NEGATIVE RISK
Having unprotected sex								
Skydiving								
Getting a lift home on a friend's scooter								
Binge drinking in the park								
Rock climbing								
Walking home late at night								
A day at the beach sunbathing								
Taking drugs at a party								
Vandalising a bus shelter								
Auditioning for the school play								

Anti-social behaviour

Anti-social behaviour is any activity that causes harm to an individual or area, such as:

- shouting or swearing in public
- playing loud music at night
- drinking in public places
- bullying or threatening people
- vandalism (e.g. damaging property and graffiti)
- firework misuse
- racing cars around the neighbourhood
- buying or dealing drugs on the street

Consequences

Anti-social behaviour can have a negative effect on others. It can frighten individuals or lead to whole areas feeling unsafe. Graffiti can be particularly distressing if it involves hateful comments about race, religion or sexuality.

For the person behaving antisocially, there are also personal consequences to consider. They could be issued with a civil injunction, Community Protection Notice (CPN) or Criminal Behaviour Order (CBO) as punishment. These require the person to follow certain rules, such as spending time with certain people, staying away from certain places or fixing the damage caused to property. If they do not follow these rules they could face a fine or time in prison.

Assessing and managing the risk

To assess the risk of anti-social behaviour, the following factors need to be considered:

1. ***Personal harm*** – Arson (deliberately setting fire to property to cause damage), firework misuse and reckless driving can harm both the person carrying out the activity and also innocent people.
2. ***Damage to property*** – Vandalism of property can be both upsetting and costly for the owner to repair. It can also create a negative image of the local area.
3. ***A criminal record*** – Anti-social behaviour can have very serious consequences if those carrying it out get into trouble with the law. Future employment and plans to travel overseas can be affected by a criminal record.

There is no safe level for anti-social behaviour and the only way to manage the risk is not to take part in any anti-social activities.

Teamwork

Role play

A meeting has been arranged at a local community centre to discuss concerns over increasing levels of anti-social behaviour in the area. The following people are present:

- A 15-year-old, currently under a Criminal Behaviour Order (CBO)
- The parent/carer of the young person
- A police officer
- A community worker
- A concerned local resident

- Working in groups of five, give each person a role to play.
- Discuss the problem with each group member, keeping to their role.
- Report back to the rest of the class with your conclusions.

Further thinking

Use the Internet to find real life examples of anti-social behaviour damaging people's lives.

Unprotected sex

Even though there is lots of information available about contraceptives, many people have unprotected sex. Some people choose not to use contraceptives, others use them incorrectly. Also, no contraceptive gives 100% protection against either a sexually transmitted infection (STI) or pregnancy. They can considerably lower the chance of this happening, but it must be remembered that there is always a risk involved.

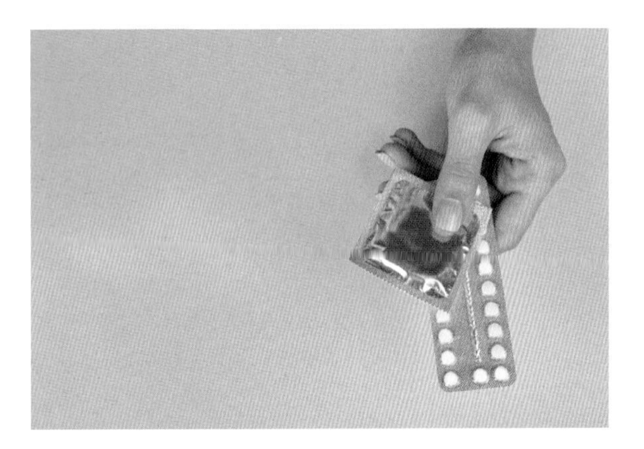

Consequences

Unprotected sexual contact increases the risk of STIs. This doesn't just include full sexual intercourse; STIs can also be transferred through intimate touching of the genitals. STIs have many short- and long-term health risks.

Unless a couple are trying for a baby, sex without the use of contraception could lead to an unplanned pregnancy. If the couple is young or not in a committed relationship, they may not feel ready for the responsibility of bringing up a child.

A sexual relationship involves an intimate connection with another person. The end of a relationship can have a greater effect on emotional health if there has been this level of intimacy.

Assessing and managing the risk

The following strategies can help minimise the risks of unprotected sex:

1. ***Sex education*** – Being properly informed about sexual activity, the risks involved, the contraceptives available and how to use them, all help people assess the risks of unprotected sex and make healthy decisions about sex.
2. ***Abstinence*** – This means not having sex. The only certain way to avoid an STI or unplanned pregnancy is to avoid all sexual activity. Some people practice abstinence until marriage.
3. ***Contraception*** – There are many types of contraception available. Some protect against unplanned pregnancy and STIs (e.g. male condoms), while others only protect against unplanned pregnancy (e.g. contraceptive injection or pill). It is important to choose a contraceptive that protects against both.
4. ***Avoiding alcohol and drugs*** – Drugs and alcohol lower a person's inhibitions and cloud their judgement. This can affect people's ability to make healthy decisions about sexual activity.

Further thinking

- Use the Internet to find out where to get advice on contraception.
- Research the different types of contraception available.

Self-harm

Self-harm is when someone deliberately inflicts pain or injury on themselves, perhaps by hitting, cutting, or burning themselves. Self-poisoning, by taking an overdose, is also an example of self-harm. Self-harm is often used as a way of coping with difficult feelings, overwhelming situations or traumatic experiences.

Below are some of the reasons given by young people to explain why they self-harm:

"It helps me find relief from a really bad situation; I feel in control."

"I feel it is the only way to get my own back."

"Everything goes wrong and it's all my fault; I need to punish myself."

"It's the only way I can get anyone to notice me."

"Sometimes I feel so angry I think I'll explode; it helps me calm down."

Consequences

Self-harm has a negative effect on health and well-being. The physical effects of self-harm can be dangerous and even life-threatening. These include wounds, infection, scars, nerve damage and hair loss. Self-harm may even lead to someone making an attempt on their life. Other physical effects might appear more minor, such as a scratch or a bruise. Regardless of how serious the physical effects appear to be, self-harming is usually part of an underlying problem.

The emotional effects of self-harm may not be as obvious, but they are no less harmful. Some people who self-harm may initially experience positive emotions, such as a sense of control or a release of tension. However, the long-term emotional effects of self-harm can be very damaging, for example:

- A person may feel irritable, anxious or depressed.
- There may be feelings of shame, guilt or stress from hiding the problem from others.
- They may suffer from low self-confidence and low self-esteem. By harming themselves, they are not building positive coping techniques.

Assessing and managing the risk

The following strategies can help minimise the risks of self-harm:

1. ***Realising there is a problem*** – Most people who self-harm try to hide it from the people around them. If you notice any changes in the behaviour of a friend or relative, ask them if they're OK or speak to a member of their family about it. Unexplained cuts or bruises, sadness, low self-esteem or expressing a need to punish themselves could all be signs of self-harm.

   Some people who self-harm are in denial; perhaps they think that if they only self-harm occasionally, it's not really a problem, or if they scratch rather than cut themselves, it isn't real self-harm. The first step is realising that self-harm, in any form, has a negative affect on their health and well-being.
2. ***Talk to someone*** – This is the next step. People who self-harm can really hurt themselves, so it is important that they speak to someone about their feelings. This may be a friend or family member, a teacher or colleague. They should then make an appointment to see their GP, who can recommend coping strategies or refer them to a therapist to discuss their feelings. If someone tells you that they self-harm, it's important to listen and then help them find the support they need.

Info box

It is important to talk to someone if you have ever self-harmed or considered it. You could speak to someone you know or someone anonymous at one of the following organisations:

Contact – www.contactni.com

Childline – www.childline.org.uk

Samaritans – www.samaritans.org

Severe dieting and compulsive overeating

A balanced diet is essential for good health and well-being. There is nothing wrong with changing your diet if you feel your current eating habits are unhealthy. However, both severe dieting and compulsive overeating can be harmful to your health.

Consequences

Surviving on a very low calorie diet in an attempt to lose as much weight, as quickly as possible, is not recommended by doctors, and can be severely damaging to health.

Short term, a person on a severe diet may experience intense hunger, stomach cramps, bad temper, low energy and tiredness, depression and constant cravings for food. There may be very rapid weight loss, which is not a good thing. Not only excess fat is lost, but muscle and water as well.

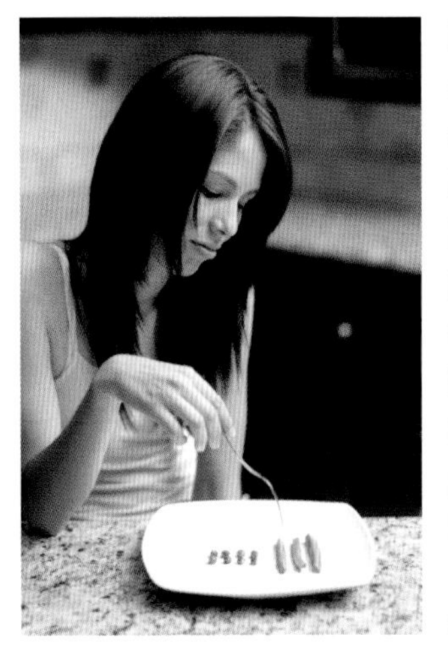

Long term, severe diets can weaken the body and trigger an underlying health issue, such as a heart condition or kidney problems. In extreme cases, where the body is seriously starved of nutrients for a prolonged period, severe dieting can be fatal.

Compulsive overeating (or binge eating) can also be damaging to health. It is a form of food addiction, where the addict has no control over the amount of food they eat. They often eat large amounts of food very quickly, until they feel uncomfortably full. They may experience feelings of shame at their overeating and fear of weight gain. Frequent overeating can lead to obesity, which has a negative effect on health (see page 63).

An eating disorder can develop when someone has difficulty maintaining a healthy, balanced diet. Sufferers struggle to manage their eating habits, eating too much or too little, or a combination of both. These disorders have a negative impact on both physical and emotional health, and at their most extreme, can be fatal. Sufferers need medical intervention and/or expert counselling to help them.

Common eating disorders

Anorexia – This eating disorder is characterised by very low body weight – the result of strict dieting almost to the point of starvation. A person suffering from anorexia will have a fear of gaining weight, even though they are very thin.

Bulimia – This eating disorder involves periods of binge eating, followed by vomiting or misuse of laxatives.

Binge eating disorder – This is when a person eats large amounts of food very quickly until they feel uncomfortably full. Often they will feel guilty afterwards and might starve themselves the next day to compensate.

Other specified feeding or eating disorder (OSFED) – This is when the characteristics of the eating disorder don't exactly match those of anorexia, bulimia or binge eating. It is the most common type of eating disorder.

Assessing and managing the risk

Following the advice below can help to minimise the risks of dieting and/or overeating:

1. ***Seek expert help*** – Anyone who experiences unhealthy eating patterns should seek professional advice. Their GP can refer them to an eating disorder specialist to discuss their feelings towards food and help with healthy diet planning.

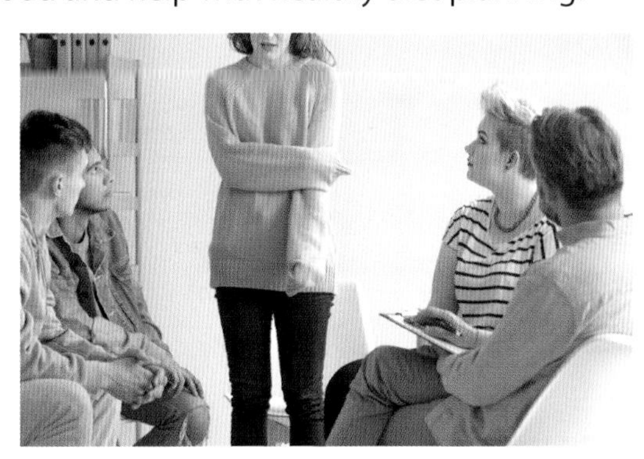

2. ***Make good food choices*** – Healthy eating is essential when trying to follow a balanced diet or lose weight. Choose nutritious food and try to avoid too many 'empty' calories, such as those found in junk foods (see page 61). Avoid the temptation to skip meals (especially breakfast) in an attempt to lose weight faster.
3. ***Follow healthy weight loss guidelines*** – The best way to lose weight is to make healthy, long-term changes to your diet and physical activity. Health experts recommend a steady weight loss of around 1–2 pounds a week, until a healthy weight is achieved. 'Crash' diets, which attempt to bring about a fast weight loss, can be very unhealthy and are unlikely to succeed in the long term.

Teamwork

Working in a group, discuss the following:

- Why do people take the risks of severe dieting?
- Do they have a negative concept of self?
- Do you think the media is responsible?
- Can you think of any other reasons?

Dangerous driving

Dangerous driving includes behaviour that could potentially endanger the driver of the vehicle, any passengers, innocent bystanders and cause damage to property. There are irresponsible drivers of all ages, but young people are often associated with dangerous driving, particularly speeding, vehicle theft and driving under the influence of alcohol or drugs. The passengers themselves can also be a problem, especially if they have been drinking and are encouraging the driver to take risks.

Consequences

Drivers of stolen vehicles or those under the influence of drugs or alcohol often drive recklessly and without regard for the speed limit. This increases the risk of crashing and injury to the driver, any passengers and innocent bystanders.

Driving under the influence of alcohol or drugs is a serious offence, which can lead to:

- a 1 year ban from driving.
- an unlimited fine.
- six months in prison and a criminal record.

A person who causes death while driving under the influence of drugs or alcohol could go to prison for up to 14 years.

Those convicted of vehicle theft or 'joyriding' can also face a fine, points on their driver's licence, a driving ban or imprisonment. A person who causes death while driving following the theft of a vehicle could go to prison for up to 13 years. A passenger in a stolen car can also become a participant in the crime, especially if it can be proved that the passenger knew the car was stolen. If two friends are caught in a stolen car, then both the driver and passenger may be convicted.

Assessing and managing the risk

The following strategies can minimise the risks associated with driving:

1. ***Think carefully before accepting a lift*** – If you get into a car with a driver who you don't think is going to drive safely, particularly if he or she has been drinking or taking drugs, then you are taking a huge risk which could result in serious injury or death.
2. ***Know the limits*** – The official advice from the government is never to drink and drive, as just one drink could increase the risk of crashing. The official limit in Northern Ireland is 35 micrograms of alcohol per 100 millilitres of blood, so it is possible to drink a very small amount of alcohol and still drive legally. However, many drivers follow the government advice of no alcohol at all when driving, as this is the safest option.

Teamwork

Working in a group, assess the risks involved with each of the following:

- antisocial behaviour
- unprotected sex
- deliberate self-harm

Suggest ways in which risks can be kept to a minimum when:

- dieting
- driving or accepting a lift from someone

Assessment for learning

1. Write down one example of positive risk taking. [1]
2. Write down one example of negative risk taking. [1]
3. Describe two causes of risk-taking behaviour. [4]
4. Explain two consequences of severe dieting. [4]
5. Discuss the risks associated with unprotected sex. [6]
6. Evaluate the strategies associated with assessing and managing self-harm. [10]

Social media

Social media is a collection of websites and apps that allow users to communicate, create and share information, pictures and videos with each other. Some of the most commonly used are Instagram, Twitter, Facebook and YouTube but there are many others.

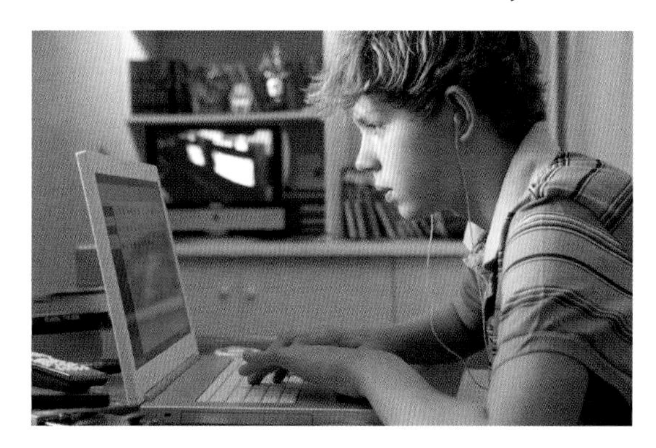

Benefits of social media

There are many benefits of social media, in both personal and business life. People can make and maintain friendships, find romance, look for a new job, keep up to date with members of their family, communicate with people who share a common interest and keep up with the news. It can also be a great way to share tips and ideas.

Websites like YouTube and Pinterest are very popular for sharing information about music, hobbies, cooking and DIY activities. Social media groups can provide a lifeline for many, such as exhausted parents looking for advice or people with rare diseases wanting to contact other sufferers. Charities, voluntary groups, clubs, churches, synagogues and mosques all use social media to keep people informed about fund-raising, times and events.

Social media can help businesses to promote products or services, share opening times and connect with potential customers. It can also be useful in education, perhaps through sharing helpful revision advice or allowing schools to communicate with parents.
It is estimated that 35 million people in the UK use social media platforms, so there has to be many benefits in doing so.

Misuse of social media

Social media sites are now proactive in trying to stop the sharing of dangerous behaviour. For example, they take down graphic images or unsuitable posts. Unfortunately, social media can also be abused and used in ways that it was not originally intended for. Sites like YouTube and Facebook are being used by some teenagers to post information about their risk-taking behaviour, such as dangerous stunts, sexual relationships, substance abuse or violence. This is potentially very harmful if risk-taking behaviour is seen as something to boast about and be made public. Other people may want to copy what they have read about.

There are other areas of concern with social media:

- **Cyberbullying (online bullying)** – This involves posting comments and uploading photos with the intention of upsetting someone. Cyberbullying, unlike other forms of bullying, is not just limited to personal contact with the bully. Victims can be subjected to bullying 24 hours a day, every day of the week. Social networking can expose young people to other forms of harassment and inappropriate contact.

- **Image-based abuse** – This involves intimate photos or videos being shared online without someone's permission. Sometimes the person may have given permission for the image to be taken or they've taken it themselves, but then it is shared without their consent. Sometimes the person may not even be aware that the images were taken. If someone gets images sent to them without their consent this is also image-based abuse. Young people could be exposed to pornography or other inappropriate content.

- **Fraud and identity theft** – With so much personal information now accessible online, it is has become even easier for thieves to steal someone's identity or financial details. Some set up fake social media accounts using other people's photos. They can use this stolen identity to spread opinions or try and sell products to the real person's friends. Child groomers (see page 107) can also use these accounts to exploit children by posing as someone else.
- **Lack of privacy** – Anything posted online creates a 'digital footprint'. Even when users apply the strongest privacy settings on social media, it doesn't always provide complete protection. It is therefore important to be careful what you post online. For example, a joke between friends may not seem funny to everyone, and people can be particularly sensitive about opinionated subjects like politics and religion. Employers might look at social networking sites to see what they can find out about a potential employee, so it's important that they like what they see.
- **Time wasting** – Social networking is currently the most popular use of the Internet and so a lot of time is spent using it. Too much time spent on social media can be an unhealthy distraction, as it can waste valuable working, studying and socialising time.

Activities

Design a leaflet aimed at primary school age children. The purpose of the leaflet is to raise awareness of safe Internet use.

Abuse

Abuse is when a person suffers cruel or hurtful treatment from another person. Abuse can happen anywhere, but it can be particularly traumatic if it is experienced at home or inflicted by a member of the family.

Types of abuse and ways of recognising them

TYPE OF ABUSE	WHAT IS IT?	SIGNS OF ABUSE
PHYSICAL ABUSE	Deliberately causing injury to someone else; can involve hitting, punching or kicking.	Physical symptoms, such as bruises, burns, broken bones; withdrawn and anxious; nightmares and sleep problems.
SEXUAL ABUSE	Being forced or coerced into taking part in sexual activities without consent.	Physical injuries; might be afraid of certain people or try to avoid them; show sexual behaviour that is inappropriate for their age.
EXPLOITATION	Any form of deliberate manipulation or abuse of power (e.g. sexual exploitation or withdrawing money from a vulnerable person's bank account).	*Children:* missing school; staying out late; having unexplained gifts or possessions; signs of unexplained physical harm. *Adults:* signs of physical injury; being withdrawn; having difficulty with finances; being overprotective of money or possessions.
EMOTIONAL ABUSE	Deliberately trying to make someone else feel inadequate and worthless.	Loss of self-confidence and low self-esteem; depression; difficulty making friends.
NEGLECT	Deliberately ignoring the needs of a vulnerable person, such as a child.	Malnourished; poor hygiene, dirty hair and nails; health problems.

Physical abuse

Physical abuse is an intentional act to cause injury to another person. It can involve hitting, punching or kicking someone. Both children and adults can be victims of physical abuse. (Physical abuse also includes bullying, which is discussed on pages 110–111).

Personal strategies to deal with physical abuse

- ***Seek help immediately*** – Don't keep quiet and hope the problem will resolve itself.
- ***Ask family or friends to help*** – Talk to someone you trust and tell them about the abuse. It might be helpful to have a list of people who you could contact in an emergency.
- ***Report the abuse*** – Take pictures of injuries resulting from physical abuse and make sure it is reported to the PSNI.
- ***Seek professional help*** – Being a victim of physical abuse is traumatic and sufferers may need advice, support or counselling. There are a number of organisations that offer help and guidance such as Refuge, Women's Aid, Men's Advice Line and Galop.

Government strategy to deal with physical abuse

The Family Homes and Domestic Violence (N.I.) Order 1998

This is the legislation in Northern Ireland that allows victims of domestic violence and abuse to apply for protection from the person responsible. Following a court hearing, a judge can grant an order to stop or prevent a person from abusing, harassing, pestering, using or threatening to use violence against another person in any way. The court also has the power to attach an 'exclusion zone' to the order. This means the person accused of abuse is not allowed to go to certain areas, such as the street where the victim lives, or the school the child attends. A judge can also make a decision on who has the right to live in a property.

Domestic abuse

Domestic abuse is any type of controlling, threatening, violent or abusive behaviour between people in a relationship.

Sexual abuse and exploitation

Sexual abuse is when someone is forced or coerced into taking part in sexual activities without their consent. This type of abuse can take place in two ways: contact (such as touching or rape) and non-contact (such as showing a child sexual acts, or persuading them to send sexual images or videos).

Consent

Consent is when someone actively and freely agrees to participate in an activity. Consent can be withdrawn at any time.

Sexual assault

Sexual assault is any sexual act that a person did not consent to, or is forced into against their will. It includes any form of sexual violence, for example rape, which is forced sexual intercourse or sexual activity. Sometimes the victim may have no physical injuries or signs of assault.

Personal strategies to deal with sexual assault

Anyone who believes they have been the victim of a sexual assault should report it to the PSNI, as it is a serious crime. There are also many services that can offer treatment or support, or who can make a referral to more specialist help. These include:

- A GP or practice nurse at a health centre.
- Voluntary organisations, such as Women's Aid, Victim Support and the Rape Crisis team.
- A hospital accident and emergency (A&E) department.
- A specialist counselling service for young people.

It is important to remember that any assault is not the fault of the victim. Often sexual assault is carried out by someone known to the victim. However, it is sensible to try to keep yourself safe when going out, especially at night. Make sure you stay in the company of friends and have reliable transport home.

Sexual exploitation

Sexual exploitation is when an abuser uses their relationship or position of authority to take advantage of (exploit) someone and coerces them to take part in sexual activities. If that someone is under 18 years old, this is known as child abuse.

Children who are being exploited may not know that what they are being asked to do is wrong. Some young people are 'groomed' by an abusing adult who gives them presents, offers them compliments or affection and makes them feel special. They often mistake this for a loving relationship but ultimately the abuser wants something in return. They might also be threatened with physical or emotional abuse.

Many child groomers use the Internet, particularly social networking sites, instant messaging and dating apps to make contact with young people, often posing as younger people themselves. This is why it is so risky to meet up with someone that you chat to online and don't know in the real world. Some groomers never meet the children they are exploiting. Instead they persuade young people to send them sexually explicit images or videos, or take part in online sexual activity. Groomers may threaten to send these images or videos to the young person's friends and family unless they take part in more sexual activity.

Child grooming

Child grooming is when someone establishes an emotional relationship with a child and gains their trust in preparation for sexual abuse, exploitation or trafficking.

Personal strategies to deal with sexual exploitation

- Be aware of situations that might put you at risk. Be careful who you are alone with and don't meet up with anyone you don't know.
- Be careful who you chat to online and don't share personal images or information about yourself.
- Do not accept money or gifts from people you don't know very well.
- If you feel you are being exploited in any way speak to a trusted adult.
- Collect evidence of any online exploitation by taking screen shots of conversations or videos.
- Seek expert help, which is available from many organisations in Northern Ireland, including Childline, NSPCC, Childnet and the PSNI.

Government strategy to deal with sexual abuse

Call to End Violence Against Women and Girls: Action Plan (2014)

This document aims to take action on a number of issues involving violence and abuse towards women and girls by:

- preventing violence against women and girls from happening in the first place by challenging the attitudes and behaviours that foster it and intervening early to prevent it.
- providing adequate levels of support where violence occurs.
- working in partnership to give support for victims and their families. This includes the government, voluntary and community groups.
- taking action to reduce the risk to women and girls who are victims and making sure that those who commit these crimes are brought to justice.

Information taken from: 'Call to End Violence Against Women and Girls: Action Plan (2014)', HM Government, https://assets.publishing.service.gov.uk/government/uploads/system/uploads/attachment_data/file/287758/VAWG_Action_Plan.pdf

Prostitution

Prostitution is a form of sexual exploitation. It involves engaging in sexual activities in return for something beneficial, such as money, affection, drugs and alcohol, or somewhere to stay.

Some young people are groomed for prostitution. They may even think that their abuser is their boyfriend or girlfriend. However, they may be physically or verbally threatened by this person, or manipulated into having less contact with friends and family.

Some situations can make a young person more vulnerable to exploitation, such as being distant from the people who would normally care for them, having an addiction problem or being homeless. Usually people who get involved in prostitution rely on the money and find it very difficult to give up.

Personal strategies to deal with prostitution

For anyone who feels that prostitution is their only option, there is help out there:

- The Belfast Sex Worker Service provides health care and support to sex workers.
- For anyone reliant on prostitution for income, Advice NI offers advice on available benefits and how to get out of debt.
- For anyone struggling with addiction, there are relevant support agencies to offer help and advice, such as Addiction NI and Rehab4Addiction.
- For anyone who feels unable to leave their situation due the threat of physical abuse, there are various organisations that can offer help, including the PSNI, Women's Aid and Men's Advice Line.

Human trafficking

Human trafficking is a serious crime that can affect anyone, of any age, gender or nationality. It involves the trade of people, mostly for the purpose of sexual slavery, forced labour, prostitution or being forced to perform criminal acts. The victims are often threatened with violence or manipulated into thinking they have a dream job or life in an overseas country. Victims of trafficking can be very hard to detect and are often afraid or unable to seek help. The victims of human trafficking have many urgent needs, such as medical help, emergency shelter and legal advice.

Invisible Traffick works to promote awareness of human trafficking throughout all of Northern Ireland and Ireland. They have a free and confidential phone line so victims of trafficking can access help and support. Invisible Traffick work in partnership with other organisations and largely rely on the work of volunteers and donations from the public to carry out their work. Visit their website for more information: www.invisibletraffick.org

Government strategy to deal with human trafficking

Human Trafficking: The Government's Strategy (2011)

This document, produced by the UK government, recognises the seriousness of the problem and sets out plans to try and end this practice. This includes measures to prevent trafficking and support for victims. The strategy outlines a number of aims, including:

- To tackle trafficking from end to end: from recruitment to exploitation, ensuring agencies have the right tools and intelligence to reduce the threat, and maintaining effective victim support.
- To identify victims of trafficking and provide support tailored to the victim's needs.
- To strengthen border controls and policing to prevent traffickers entering the country.
- There is also special emphasis on protecting children who are trafficked.

This strategy is supported by the Human Trafficking and Exploitation Act (Northern Ireland) 2015.

Information taken from: 'Human Trafficking: The Government's Strategy', HM Government, https://www.gov.uk/government/publications/human-trafficking-strategy and 'Human Trafficking and Exploitation Act (Northern Ireland) 2015', http://www.legislation.gov.uk/nia/2015/2/contents/enacted

Female Genital Mutilation (FGM)

FGM involves cutting or altering a girl's genitals. The procedure is mostly practiced in parts of Africa, Asia and the Middle East but also occurs in the UK. For some communities, FGM is part of their cultural heritage and many women cannot marry without it. There are no known health benefits from the procedure and there is growing worldwide concern about the practice, which is seen as a human rights issue. There are a number of health risks associated with FGM, including pain and severe bleeding during the procedure; and infections, trauma and complications during pregnancy and childbirth after it.

FGM is illegal in the UK and Ireland. If a young girl living here believes she is at risk, she should talk to a trusted adult, such as a relative or teacher.

Government strategy to deal with FGM

The Home Office (part of the UK government) have produced a resource pack on Female Genital Mutilation. It was developed to help local authorities understand their responsibilities in preventing FGM being experienced by women and girls in the UK. FGM is illegal in the UK and it is also an offence for FGM to be performed abroad on a UK Citizen. The government resource aims to promote the welfare of children and protect them from the harm of FGM. It stresses that everyone has a role to play – parents, teachers, the police and healthcare professionals.

For more information visit: www.gov.uk/government/publications/female-genital-mutilation-resource-pack/female-genital-mutilation-resource-pack

Emotional abuse

Emotional abuse is when a person deliberately tries to make someone else feel inadequate and worthless. For example, a child may be shouted at and bullied so that he or she feels intimidated, ashamed or unfairly criticised. A child who is emotionally abused receives no positive emotional support from parents or carers.

Neglect

Neglect is when parents or carers deliberately ignore their child's needs. There are four types of neglect:

1. ***Physical neglect*** – This is failing to provide for a child's basic needs. A child may be left hungry, dirty, or without adequate clothing or shelter. They may be in potential danger through a lack of adult supervision.
2. ***Medical neglect*** – This is failing to provide health care. It might involve not seeking medical help when a child is ill, neglecting dental care or regular check-ups.
3. ***Educational neglect*** – This is failing to ensure that a child receives an education.
4. ***Emotional neglect*** – This is failing to provide a loving environment where a child feels valued and accepted.

A child who is neglected may also suffer other types of abuse from parents or carers. Neglect is very serious and can have long-term effects that continue into adulthood.

Personal strategies to deal with neglect

If you think you might be being neglected – It may be difficult to know if you're being neglected but if you're worried about anything at all, talk to a friend, a friend's parent, a teacher, a school counsellor or doctor. If you'd rather speak to someone you don't know, you can speak to a counsellor at Childline any time via chat, email or phone.

If you think someone you know is being neglected – There can be many signs that someone is suffering from neglect. They may appear tired, pale or lacking in energy; seem isolated from their friends; or have some hygiene issues, such as dirty clothing. If you notice these signs, or are concerned about anyone, you should speak to someone about it. You could speak to a family member, a friend, a teacher, a school counsellor or doctor. You can also contact the NSPCC or the Gateway Service Team in the Health and Social Care Trusts for advice.

Government strategy to deal with neglect

In 2018, the UK government set out plans to tackle child abuse and neglect. This included a more effective way of sharing information between police, social workers and healthcare professionals. The Home Office and Department for Education have responded to a joint consultation, 'Reporting and acting on child abuse and neglect', which sought views on the best ways to protect vulnerable children from all types of abuse and neglect. As part of this initiative, the government plans to review the current laws on child abuse and neglect.

Dealing with abuse

Any form of abuse is unacceptable and should not be kept secret. However, it can be very difficult for children and young people to speak out, especially if they are so young they think that what they are experiencing is 'normal'.

Victims of abuse, however young, should try to talk to someone they trust, such as a family member or teacher. There are also websites and survivor forums where victims of abuse can share their experiences anonymously. If the abuse is the cause of other issues, such as drug abuse or mental health problems, then it's important that they seek expert help and advice. Finally, a victim may feel that reporting the abuse to the police is the right thing to do, even many years after it has occurred. This may help to bring closure to distressing childhood experiences.

The effects of abuse on young people

Abuse can have a physical and emotional effect on a young person's personal development. These effects can be both short term and long term, as well as affecting both physical and emotional health and well-being.

Physical health and well-being – A child who is abused may well have unexplained injuries, soreness, burns and bruises. A child living in a violent home may be physically harmed by trying to intervene in an incident between other family members. A neglected child may appear to be dirty, tired or poorly nourished and their physical health is likely to deteriorate as a result. A young person suffering long-term abuse may be more likely to abuse drugs and alcohol or to self-harm. In later life, a person may continue to suffer the effects of childhood abuse. Some might find it difficult to build close relationships with others. Others might suffer from mental health problems, such as depression or post-traumatic stress disorder (PTSD).

Emotional health and well-being – A child or young person suffering abuse may become anxious, depressed and withdrawn. They may feel a range of negative emotions, including anger, guilt and fear, or suffer from low self-esteem. Many children are led to believe that the abuse is their fault for some wrong-doing, or because they are not good enough. Some struggle with their behaviour, either at home or at school. Feeling powerless and afraid at home may even lead an abused child to be particularly aggressive towards others outside of the home.

Bullying

Bullying can make a victim feel frightened, humiliated and powerless. They may become reluctant to go to school or work, or even leave the house. For some, the negative pressure can lead to a fall in their standard of work and a loss of confidence in their own abilities.

Why do some people bully others?

Sometimes people bully others for the following reasons:

- They have problems at home, school or work.
- They are the victim of bullying or violence themselves.
- They feel powerless themselves and bullying gives them a feeling of power.
- They feel threatened by their social group and want to feel more secure.
- They are lonely and isolated, with no real friends.

Different types of bullying

There are many ways that bullies can harm other people. Here are some examples:

Physical bullying – This includes hitting, kicking, pinching and punching, or deliberately damaging someone's property to cause upset and distress.

Verbal bullying – This includes insults, teasing and spiteful remarks. This is often about a person's appearance, race, nationality or sexual orientation.

Sometimes verbal bullying takes the form of a 'joke' that others laugh at, but the victim finds upsetting.

Exclusion – This involves encouraging others to exclude someone socially, perhaps by refusing to sit next to someone in class or not speaking to them. It can also include telling lies, spreading rumours and gossiping about someone behind their back, rather than saying mean remarks to someone's face.

Cyberbullying (online bullying) – This form of bullying uses electronic types of communication to harm a victim. It can include abusive or hurtful texts, posts, images and videos. Intimidating others online or spreading nasty rumours is also a form of cyberbullying.

Homophobic or transphobic bullying – This is when someone is bullied because they are lesbian, gay, bisexual or transgender, or because their friends or family are. They can also be bullied for showing traits, appearance or behaviour that the bully *perceives* as lesbian, gay, bisexual or transgender.

Personal strategies to deal with bullying

It is important for anyone who is being bullied to tell someone they trust so something can be done about it. Being bullied can seriously effect a young person's physical and mental health, how they perform at school and make relationships. Bullying can increase the risk that someone will develop anxiety or depression and the long-term effects can continue into adult life.

Here are some suggestions to deal with bullying:

- Just ignore it and walk away; the bully may get bored if they get no reaction.
- Stand up for yourself but do not use violence, which could make the situation worse or get you into trouble.
- Tell someone you trust so something can be done about it. Speak to a parent, carer or teacher, or ask a friend to report the bullying on your behalf.
- Keep a record of all incidents or nasty messages; if you are the victim of cyberbullying, do not delete spiteful messages but keep them as evidence.
- Increase your security settings on social media to try and prevent contact from bullies.

Government strategies to deal with bullying

The Education and Libraries (Northern Ireland) Order 2003 made it compulsory for schools to have an anti-bullying policy. This should include measures to prevent all forms of bullying among pupils. The effectiveness of these measures is monitored through school inspections of pastoral care arrangements.

The Department of Education funds the Northern Ireland Anti-Bullying Forum (NIABF) Its aim is to raise awareness through special events and campaigns, such as anti-bullying week, held in November each year. The NIABF website has many resources and downloads for young people and their carers. These include information on tackling cyberbullying and homophobic bullying.

Assessment for learning

1. Name one type of abuse. [1]
2. Write down one sign that a child may be suffering from neglect. [1]
3. Describe one personal strategy to deal with sexual exploitation. [2]
4. Explain two effects abuse can have on a young person's health. [4]
5. Discuss how social media can be misused. [6]
6. Evaluate how government strategies can help vulnerable people deal with exploitation. [10]

Teamwork

Working in a group:

- Discuss some of the most effective personal strategies for keeping safe from sexual abuse and exploitation.
- Why do you think some people bully and abuse others?
- Do you think the government is taking sufficient action to prevent the abuse, bullying and exploitation of young people? Give reasons for your point of view.

CHAPTER 2E
Responsible Parenting

Chapter Summary

In this chapter you will be studying:

- **The roles and responsibilities of parents, children and young people.**
- **The impact of becoming a parent.**
- **The opportunities and challenges for parents in different situations.**
- **The role of parenting in a child's development.**

Roles and responsibilities in the family

Parents

What does being a responsible parent involve? Taking on the role of parent involves many different tasks, all involving a variety of personal skills and qualities. Here are some of the main things a parent should do:

Provide for their child's basic needs – Children need their parents to provide water, food, shelter, clothing and safety. The family home should be a safe environment, a place of comfort, warmth and happiness.

Look after their child's physical health – Children need their parents to provide regular dental care and medical care if their child is ill.

Look after their child's emotional well-being – Children need their parents to provide a loving environment where they feel valued and accepted. This will involve spending time with them, encouraging any interests and skills they might have, and providing opportunities for social development.

Keep their child safe – Parents should never mistreat or harm their children through abuse or neglect. They should also do all they can to protect them from abuse from others.

Teach their child good morals and values – Parents should make sure that their children learn good morals (such as the difference between right and wrong) and values (such as kindness, respect, honesty and forgiveness). This will help them grow up to be good citizens.

Be responsible for their child's behaviour – Parents should set consistent boundaries for their children. They should reward good behaviour and discipline bad behaviour (within reason).

Listen to their child – Parents should try to create an atmosphere where they can talk about anything that is worrying them.

Show respect for their child's privacy – This is particularly important for teenagers.

Ensure that their child goes to school – until they are at least 16 years old.

Encourage responsibility – Parents should allow children to make decisions for themselves and encourage them to learn from the experience.

Be a good role model – Children need to have a good example to follow.

It is therefore a huge responsibility to be a parent. While nobody expects parents to be perfect, they should try and do their best for their children.

Children and young people

In most families, everyone has a role to play. From a very young age, children can be expected to have some responsibilities. These will change and develop as the child becomes older, more independent and more responsible. For example:

Taking responsibility for yourself – Even young children can start to take responsibility for themselves by looking after their personal hygiene, such as brushing their teeth or washing their hands before eating.

Sharing in the household duties – Even very young children can help with simple household tasks, such as tidying up their toys or putting away items of clothing. They may be limited in what they can do, but will grow up knowing that it's important for every family member to make a contribution (and not only when forced to or in return for money). Older children and teenagers should be able to share the household tasks, such as hoovering, cooking or cutting the grass.

Behaviour towards others – Showing respect for other family members is everyone's responsibility. Children should be taught how to treat other family members, such as brothers and sisters, parents and grandparents. As children grow older, they will be expected to take on more responsibility and this might include looking after other members of the family.

Respecting the rules of the house – All families have their own rules. For young children, this might include a set bedtime or amount of screen time. For teenagers, there may be rules about staying out late or the amount of time spent studying. Young people have a responsibility to respect rules made by the adults in the family.

Playing a part in decision making – Young children may have a limited role to play in decision making, but can still be asked their opinion. This might be something very simple, such as an activity for the weekend. Older children could be asked to contribute to more important discussions, such as whether to have a pet and who is going look after it.

Teamwork

Rules of the house

Working in a group:

- Discuss what rules are needed for family life to run smoothly. You need to consider the responsibilities of both adults and children in the family. Maintaining good relationships between everyone is also important.
- Decide on your list of rules then write them on a large sheet of paper.

Roles and responsibilities within different family structures

FAMILY STRUCTURE	ADULTS IN THE FAMILY	CHILDREN / YOUNG PEOPLE IN THE FAMILY
	May have to:	*May have to:*
NUCLEAR FAMILY	• discipline and set acceptable standards. • play a positive role in the development and up-bringing of children in the family.	• respect their parents' wishes. • help out with household chores. • make an effort to get on with siblings. • play an active role in being a part of the family unit.
SINGLE-PARENT FAMILY	• bring up the child on their own. • carry out all adult responsibilities around the house on their own. • be the only wage earner.	• be more responsible and mature. • provide more help to their parent around the house. • recognise that there is only one income and money might be limited. • help to take care of younger siblings.
EXTENDED FAMILY	• care for their parents or in-laws as well as their children (parents). • help out with child care (grandparents).	• help look after grandparents or older relatives. • be more responsible and mature. • accept that space in the house is limited, for example, having to share a bedroom.
GRANDPARENT FAMILY	• take on extra responsibilities, such as going back to work to bring in extra income to raise their grandchildren.	• respect the possible age limitations and generational differences of their grandparents. • adjust to a limited income. • help out with physical work around the house.
STEP-FAMILY/ BLENDED FAMILY	• adjust to a new partner and settle in to a new way of family life. • cope with their children being unhappy with the new arrangements. • accept responsibility for their partner's children.	• be open to change and a different way of family life. • be tolerant and understanding when making relationships with step-brothers and step-sisters. • accept that things might be difficult at first when adjusting to new family members.
FOSTER FAMILY	• help children cope without their family members and settle into their new environment. • teach children the family rules and what is acceptable behaviour. • find strategies to manage children who have emotional or behavioural issues.	• cope with not being with their parents and possibly their siblings. • be adaptable and able to accept change. • behave well and respect the rules of the new family.

Think about

- What other family structures can you think of?
- List the responsibilities in each structure for children, young people and adults.

Young carers

It is a positive experience for children in a family to take on responsibility, even when they are young. However, some children have to take on more responsibility than others, such as caring for a parent, grandparent or sibling, perhaps because of disability, illness or an addiction problem.

Most young carers are between eight and fifteen years old, although some are as young as five. Young carers may have to take on many of the household jobs, and might be responsible for the shopping, cleaning and cooking. They may also have to give physical care, such as bathing and feeding the person who is ill. A young carer might have to cope with some difficult or stressful situations at home; for example, a parent who has been drinking heavily, or a sibling who is experiencing severe pain.

The impact of becoming a parent

Being a parent is a full-time, demanding job, with very little time off, especially in the first few years. There are a lot of challenges to be faced emotionally, socially and financially.

Emotional impact

For anyone who is about to become a parent, there will be a significant emotional impact, regardless of the circumstances. Even for two people in a stable relationship, that were trying for a baby, knowing they will be bringing a new life into the world is a serious responsibility. However, if the future parent(s) are not in a stable relationship, young or unprepared for the pregnancy, there will be an even greater emotional impact.

Many women feel a bit low, upset, anxious or stressed for a couple of weeks after giving birth. This is very common and is a result of changes in hormones during pregnancy. However, if these feelings last for longer, or start later, the mother might be suffering from postnatal depression. Postnatal depression can be overwhelming but there is a lot of support available. Like any form of depression, the NHS recommends visiting a GP if anyone experiences symptoms of depression for most of the day, every day, for more than two weeks.

Becoming a parent can also have a very positive impact on emotions. There might be feelings of excitement and looking forward to the challenges of parenthood. For a couple raising a child together it is a new stage in their relationship together. For young parents particularly, becoming a parent can also bring greater maturity with the new responsibilities that have to be carried out.

Social impact

Having a baby can lead to many changes in a parent's life, especially to their relationships and social life. These changes can have a very significant impact if the pregnancy is unplanned – perhaps an older couple having to adjust to a new baby when their family has grown up or teenagers facing a pregnancy for which they are not ready.

Pressure on relationships – Having a baby can put pressure on relationships for all couples, regardless of their age or whether the pregnancy was planned.

New parents usually find they must cope with lack of sleep, added responsibilities at home and fewer opportunities to spend time together. If the baby is their first child, it can also be stressful adjusting to the role of being a parent.

For older parents, a new arrival may put pressure on relationships within the family, especially if the other children in the family are teenagers or have already grown up. Similarly, if a young person has a baby while living with their parents, this can put pressure on relationships with the rest of the family.

Relationships that start during teenage years have a greater chance of breaking down than relationships that begin later in life. Statistics[1] suggest that 90% of teens who get married because of pregnancy will be divorced within six years.

Restrictions on social life – When a couple or individual takes on the role of parent, this involves new responsibilities, which can put restrictions on social life. Even before the baby is born, there may be new restrictions on the mother-to-be because of the need for a healthy lifestyle. This means eating a healthy diet; taking the correct supplements; exercising moderately; getting plenty of rest; and avoiding smoking, drinking alcohol or taking drugs. The blood supply of the unborn baby is linked directly to that of the mother through the umbilical cord, so any poisons pass straight to the baby.

Once the baby is born, childcare arrangements have to be considered before planning to go out with friends, participate in sport or any hobbies. These restrictions apply to parents of all ages and can leave them feeling isolated. Teenage parents, especially single parents, may feel particularly isolated and perhaps even excluded from society. Some may find it difficult to continue with their education, find suitable employment or take part in any training schemes.

Social stigma – Despite research to the contrary,[2] some teenage mothers are negatively stereotyped as irresponsible or promiscuous, and some same-sex parents face prejudice about their suitability to raise a family.

Financial impact

Having a baby and raising a child to adulthood can be very expensive. Some people will economise to reduce spending, perhaps by buying second hand equipment or borrowing expensive items from family and friends. Others will spend more.

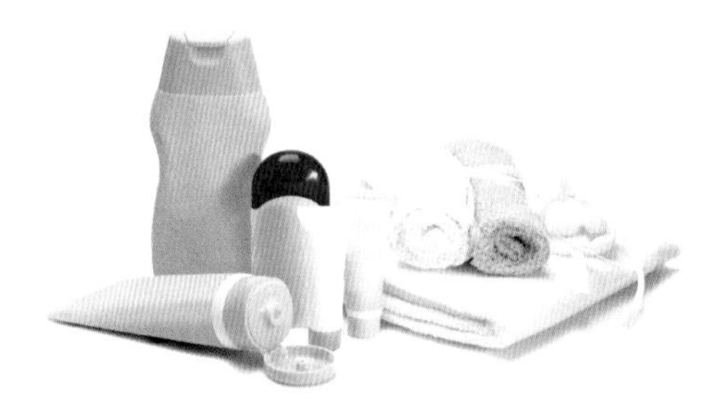

- Before the baby is even born, at least £2000 could be spent on essentials such as a pram, a car seat, changing and feeding equipment, baby monitors and clothes. This figure does not include decorating the nursery, which can cost an extra £1000 or more.
- There are many additional items that need to be bought in the baby's first year. Money might be spent on nappies, infant milk formula, baby food, clothes, toys, a cot, a baby walker, safety gates, a play pen and many other items.
- The most recent Cost of a Child report[3] from Child Poverty Action Group reveals that the basic cost of raising a child until the age of 18 is £150,753 for a couple and £183,335 for a lone parent. These figures are based on what the public thinks is a minimum standard of living.

[1] Source: Aggieland Pregnancy Outreach, https://pregnancyoutreach.org/marriage/

[2] Source: Kyla Ellis-Sloan, 'Teenage Mothers, Stigma and Their 'Presentations of Self', University of Brighton, www.socresonline.org.uk/19/1/9.html, 28 February 2014; and 'The kids are OK: it is discrimination, not same-sex parents, that harms children', MJA, www.mja.com.au/system/files/issues/207_09/10.5694mja17.00943.pdf, 23 October 2017

[3] Source: 'The Cost of a Child in 2018', Child Poverty Action Group, www.cpag.org.uk/content/cost-child-2018

Where does the money go?

Many families spend over £500 during the first month of a baby's life. This includes an average spending of:

- £23.52 on nappies.
- £243 on clothing.
- £53.51 on feeding equipment.
- £183.51 on toys and furniture.

There is also equipment to buy, which can be expensive. For example:

- a new cot can cost from £70 to £700, but according to Baby Child's study the average is £129.50.
- a new pram can cost from £100 to over £2000.
- a new car seat usually costs between £100 and £150, but can cost as much as £400.

It brings the total for year one of having a baby to around £11,498.

Source: Information from 'What is the average cost of a baby?', the money advice service, www.moneyadviceservice.org.uk/blog/what-is-the-average-cost-to-have-a-baby

Further thinking

- Use the Internet to help you make a list of the essential equipment that would need to be purchased:
  - before a baby is born
  - during the first year
- Find out the average cost of these items new and second hand.

Assessment for learning

1. Write down one responsibility parents have towards their children. [1]
2. Write down one responsibility children have towards their parents. [1]
3. Describe one responsibility of a young carer. [2]
4. Explain two emotional impacts of becoming a new parent. [4]
5. Discuss the financial impact of having a baby. [6]
6. Evaluate the social impact of a couple becoming new parents. [10]

Opportunities and challenges of parental responsibility

Being a parent is for many people the most rewarding and enjoyable part of their life. However, it can also bring many difficulties, challenges and frustrations.

Carers

Carers are people who offer foster care to babies and children, when the children's parents are unable to look after them. The children become temporary members of a carer's family and live in the carer's home. Foster care can be long or short term, but it's not permanent, unlike adoption. If a carer becomes attached to the foster child, they might find it difficult to give the child up. The children fostered can be of all ages and some may come from difficult home circumstances. Some might have emotional or behavioural issues, which can be challenging. However, foster care can be extremely rewarding and carers have the satisfaction of knowing they helped a child whose family is going through a crisis. This can help to boost their self-confidence and feelings of self-worth.

Adoptive parents

Adoption is a legal procedure where all the responsibilities of the child's 'birth parent(s)' are transferred to the adoptive parent(s). Unlike foster care, it provides a permanent family for children whose own parent(s) are unable to bring them up. It can give adopted children a real sense of belonging to a family and provides a stable home life, perhaps after some time spent in care.

For the adoptive parent(s), providing a home for a child can be extremely rewarding. It may allow them to raise a child or children when perhaps they were unable to have their own. Parent(s) might also think about adopting a child when they already have children of their own. This could be because there are medical issues preventing them from having any more children, or because of a conscious choice to extend their family through offering a child a home. Adopting in these circumstances impacts the whole family, whether existing children are still at home or grown up.

Like foster care, the adopted children can be of all ages and from all home circumstances. Some may have suffered trauma, neglect or abuse which can result in a range of difficulties. This can make family life challenging for the adoptive parents and wider family. Another big challenge is the long and complicated procedure of adoption. However, having such patience shows that the adoptive parent(s) are likely to be patient parent(s).

Single parents

Some people become single parents following a separation, divorce or the death of their partner. Others might choose to be single parents and don't want the child's father or mother in their life. Single parents can become especially close to their child or children, as they are the only parent. There are no arguments about what is best for the child and no other parent to undermine decisions that are made. However, a single parent will probably have more responsibilities, be under more pressure, and have to manage all the household tasks and bills by themself. This can all cause stress. They may also have a reduced social life and possibly feel lonely.

Same-sex parents

More and more same-sex couples are becoming parents, largely due to advances in reproductive technology. This can involve the challenge of finding a suitable surrogate or egg donor. Same-sex parent families are often carefully planned, sometimes at great financial expense, usually making them very committed parents. However, some same-sex parents still face social stigma and worry that their children will be negatively affected by the prejudice of others.

Young/teenage parents

There are many opportunities, but also a number of challenges, facing younger parents raising a family. Young parents in their teens and twenties may have more energy and stamina than older parents. There is also less of an age gap and generational differences between them and their children. The grandparents may also be relatively young and therefore able to take an active role in helping with childcare.

Younger parents have to take on family responsibilities earlier in life than friends of the same age who don't have children. However, they may also find that their children have grown up and left home earlier too. Younger parents may have greater opportunities to pursue hobbies, careers, or education later in life than older parents.

However, raising a family can be challenging for young parents, especially those in their teens. One issue to be considered is accommodation. The best option might be to continue living at home even though a lot of patience and understanding will be needed to prevent strained relationships. Family support can be crucial, regardless of whether the young parents are living at home or not. Childcare can be very expensive and this may be impossible for someone on a tight budget. Family members might be able to help by childminding from time to time. Younger parents may also find that their social life is more restricted now that they have family responsibilities.

It is during teenage years that most young people start to make plans for their future careers – making subject choices for GCSEs, deciding whether to go on to sixth form study or get a job, or perhaps considering college or university. Having a baby during this time is going to change a young person's priorities. Future plans for education or a career may have to be put on hold or carried out on a part-time basis. Even though career plans may be difficult for teenage parents, many young people are determined to make a success of their education and have a promising career alongside caring for their family.

Older parents

Many people are having children later in life than their parents and grandparents. Some are moving in with their partners or marrying later. Some are choosing to pursue study or a career before starting a family. Others are remarrying and starting a family with their second partner. There are many reasons but as a result, there are more older parents than in the past.

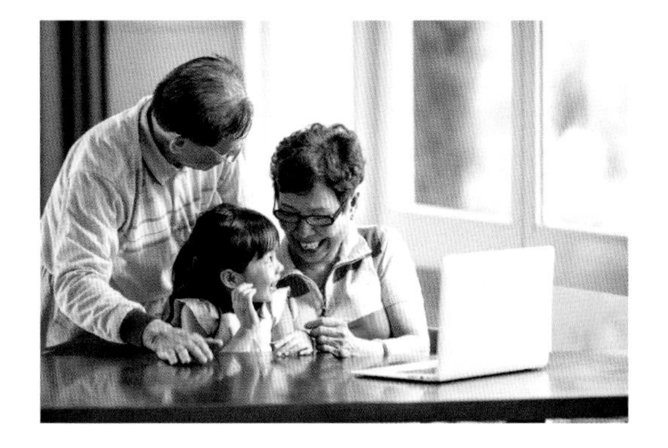

Older parents are often mature, with life experience, are in a stable relationship and have financial security. However, they may find the sleepless nights more difficult than younger parents, or struggle to find the energy needed for young children. They might find it difficult to relate to their child when (s)he becomes a teenager. Their children might also have fewer years with their parents before they pass away.

Further thinking

- Use the Internet to find out the average age of first-time mums in Northern Ireland.
- How has this average age changed over time?
- Why do you think this is?

Step-parents/ blended-family parents

Step-parents usually take time to consider parenthood, as their relationship grows with the child's parent. Blending families can give step-parents the opportunity to have a larger family, or have a child with their new partner. However, having a larger household may also present financial challenges. There could also be bonding issues and arguments if the child resents having a step-parent. There could be further challenges if the step-parent already has children, in getting along and treating all the children in the family fairly.

The role of parenting in a child's development

Children learn from the influences around them. Parents, and other adults who play a role in caring for a child, are a young child's first teachers and have an important impact on how they grow and develop.

Physical

Parents should ensure that a child's basic needs are met, so they can be physically healthy. These include a balanced diet, regular meals and opportunities for exercise. Parents should also provide a warm, clean and safe environment in which to grow up, lessening the risk of illness and accidents. Medical care should be provided when needed.

Social

Parents are expected to provide opportunities for social development. These include encouragement to make new friends and taking the child to places where they can meet other children, such as parent and toddler groups, and the local park. As children grow older, they should be encouraged to join clubs and teams where they can pursue interests and meet socially with peers.

Emotional

Parents should help their children to be aware of their emotions and cope with them in positive ways. From a young age children should be taught that emotions such as fear, anger or disappointment shouldn't lead to violent or destructive behaviour. A parent should encourage their child to recognise what their strengths are and what they need to improve on. Children should be given the opportunity to solve problems for themselves and learn from their mistakes.

Intellectual

Parents should encourage their child to learn through play, by providing stimulating and educational toys. This is a very important part of a child's development, which begins at birth. When a child starts school, parents should take an interest and support the work of the teachers. A child may also be encouraged to play an instrument, learn a language or take up a hobby.

Moral

Parents should teach their children good morals: the difference between right and wrong. They should also teach them good values, such as the importance of kindness, respect, honesty, generosity and forgiveness. It is important for parents to be consistent in their approach, set boundaries, reward good behaviour and discipline bad behaviour (within reason). They should also try to teach by example. If the family follows a religion, moral development can also involve teaching that religion's values.

Assessment for learning

1. Write down one responsibility for an adult in a blended family. [1]
2. Write down one reason children might be brought up by a single parent. [1]
3. Describe one difficulty facing step-parents . [2]
4. Explain two benefits of adopting a child. [4]
5. Discuss the opportunities of becoming a foster parent. [6]
6. Evaluate the role of parents in a child's development. [10]

CHAPTER 2F
Making Informed Financial Decisions

Chapter Summary

In this chapter you will be studying:

- **Managing a budget and the consequences of poor budgeting.**
- **Making financial decisions.**
- **Protecting against fraud and identity theft.**
- **The advantages and disadvantages of consumer choices and comparison websites.**
- **Financial advice and consumer protection.**

Managing a budget

What is a budget?

A budget is a plan for spending and saving. It involves asking yourself:

- How much money do I have available?
- How much do I expect to earn or be given?
- What should I spend my money on?

Some expenses are essential while others are not. Having a budget is all about prioritising how your money should be spent, so you can meet obligations to other people and use your money for your own benefit.

A budget can be either short term or long term. A short-term budget will involve managing your finances (your money) effectively for the next week or month ahead, perhaps making sure that you have money to spend if you go out with friends at the weekend. A long-term budget might involve saving for a summer holiday or an expensive item, such as a new phone.

Needs and wants

When making a budget, it's very important to consider the difference between needs and wants.
A need is something necessary for survival, such as food, clothing and shelter. A want is something you would like to have, such as a new phone or a better car. These items can enhance a person's life but they are not absolutely necessary.

Some items can be both a need and a want. For example, food is needed for survival, but a meal in a very expensive restaurant could be considered a want rather than a need. Similarly, clothes are essential, but they do not have to be the latest fashion or have a designer label; these clothes are wants not needs.

A person's lifestyle or the society in which they live can influence whether an item is a need or a want. Many people would consider a smartphone to be an essential part of their life. However, in some parts of the world, electricity is regarded as a luxury.

Why have a budget?

Effective money management can make all the difference between being in control of your life or feeling stressed out and worried about how you are going to cope.

There are many advantages to having a budget. It can help you:

Spend money wisely – A budget can show you exactly where your money goes. This can help you to decide whether money is being well spent or wasted, and whether you need to change what you are spending most money on.

Achieve money goals – Money is a tool that can help you reach a certain goal, whether it is to own the latest phone, watch or shoes, or pay off the mortgage. A budget can help you to use this tool effectively so that goals are reached.

Stay out of debt – Having a budget is all about planning ahead, being aware of what expenses are coming up and making sure that there is money available to cover them. A person who plans their spending carefully is more likely to avoid getting into debt, as they will not be forced into borrowing money to meet essential expenses.

Save money – Even on a very small income, it's possible to save money with careful budgeting. Savings can help with money management, when unforeseen expenses occur that have not been budgeted for. Putting savings into certain bank accounts means they can grow by gaining interest.

Activity

1. Create a pie chart showing what you spend money on each month.

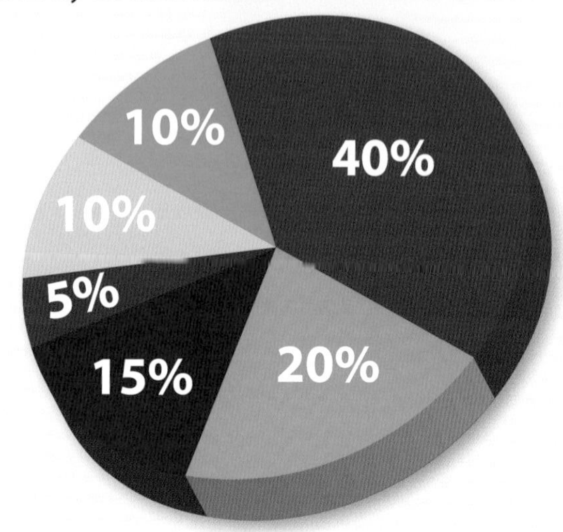

2. Work out a budget for yourself that balances your monthly income with your expenses and also allows you to save for something that you really want to buy.

The family budget

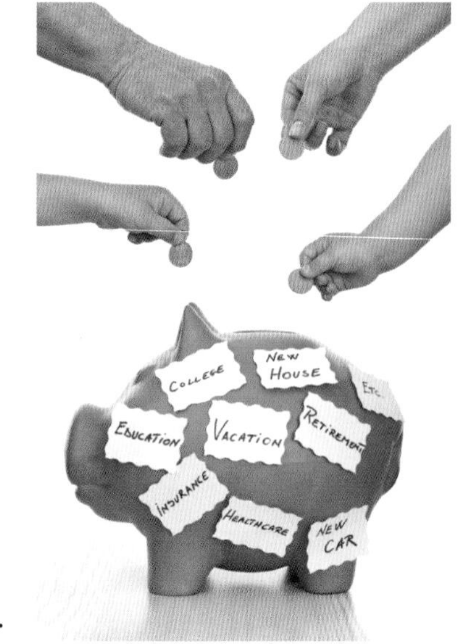

It is important for each family to have a budget and manage their money efficiently. In a typical family, there will be short-term expenses to budget for, such as the weekly food bill, and long-term financial commitments, such as paying the rent or mortgage, or the repayments on a loan.

Family income

A family's income may come from the following sources:

Employment – When an employee works for an employer, he or she will get wages in return. In many families, the main income is the salary from the work of one or both parents, either part-time or full-time.

Self-employment – A person who is self-employed makes their own income by working for themselves, rather than working for someone else and being paid a wage.

Investments – Some people make an income from their savings. Some investment schemes will pay out a regular amount of interest while others give a lump sum at the end of the period of investment.

Benefits – There are a variety of government benefits that people are entitled to depending on their circumstances.

A family will need to budget its income against outgoing expenses, which will probably be a mixture of needs and wants.

Family expenses

A family's expenses might include:

Housing – This is often the largest expenditure in the family budget as it usually includes paying rent or a mortgage, as well as bills for the maintenance of the house. With a rented property, these bills will probably be smaller since some of the upkeep will be the responsibility of the landlord.

Household bills – Paying for electricity and fuel to heat the home, such as gas or oil, will take up a large part of the family's income. Other household bills might include:

- insurance for the contents of the house and for the building itself (if owned rather than rented).
- paying rates. This money goes towards public services such as health, education, infrastructure and rubbish collection.
- repayments on any loans and credit agreements, such as credit card bills.
- line rental, TV licences, and phone and Internet contracts.

Food – Another large expense for most families, this includes the money spent in the supermarket, any lunches purchased at school or restaurants close to work, and any takeaways or meals out in restaurants.

Clothing – This is another potentially large expense, especially with school uniforms, work clothes and trying to budget for the clothing that family members want as well as what they need. Some families give 'luxury' items of clothing or shoes as presents to help with the cost.

Transport – Most people need transport to get to and from work, school, the shops or to visit family and friends. Many people use public transport and spend a lot of money on bus and train tickets or passes. Many people also travel by car, and maintaining a car, or possibly two or three, can become very expensive. As well as the bills that can be planned for, such as road tax, fuel, insurance and regular servicing, cars can be a source of unexpected expenses from breakdowns and accidents.

Children – The expenses associated with children change as they grow. Babies can be expensive as they need nappies, new equipment and a constant supply of new clothes. Older children may need an expensive school uniform or equipment for a hobby or sport that they enjoy.

Entertainment and holidays – While these can be considered as wants rather than needs, many people expect to spend money on leisure activities or a holiday as a reward for working hard the rest of the year. Many families make it a priority to have money available for an annual holiday. Entertainment could include going out, as well as subscriptions to streaming services.

Savings – Some families regard savings as important, perhaps to have a 'nest-egg' for retirement, or to help pay for further education for the children.

The consequences of poor budgeting

One of the benefits of having a budget, and keeping to it, is that it gives someone an overview of their spending as a whole. This means it's easier to see where over-spending occurs and whether a reduction can be made. With poor budgeting, one financial set-back, such as an expensive car repair, can cause someone to borrow money and get into debt. Being in debt might lead to the following problems:

More debt – A person in debt might be tempted to borrow more money to pay their existing debts. Accumulating more debt is likely to make the situation worse, especially if the money is borrowed from a loan shark, payday loan or multiple credit cards.

Legal problems – A person could be taken to court for non-payment of debts, particularly if these debts are associated with a business. Even if a person does not end up in court, a history of debt can affect their credit rating, making it difficult to borrow money in the future.

Loan shark – This is an unscrupulous money lender who offers an unsecured loan at a high rate of interest.

Payday loan – This a short-term loan, lent at a high rate of interest. It can give quick cash in an emergency, but can be a very expensive way to borrow money, especially if it is not repaid quickly.

Bailiff – Also known as an enforcement agent, this is an official who removes someone's possessions when they owe money. These items are then sold to repay debts.

Loss of property – If the payments on a mortgage or secured loan are not made, then a person may lose their home. If a person is in debt but does not own their home, then the courts can authorise bailiffs to remove any valuable possessions from their property.

Health problems – Being in debt can cause enormous stress and have an effect on mental health. A person who is worried about their financial situation can experience feelings of inadequacy, shame and despair about the future. Constant worry can also have an impact on a person's physical health and well-being.

Relationship problems – Debt, stress and all the problems associated with it can put a strain on relationships. Some family members might experience feelings of anger, disappointment or resentment towards each other. This strain can sometimes lead to relationship breakdown.

How to cope with debt

The following strategies might help someone manage their debt:

HOW TO COPE WITH DEBT

- Work out a realistic budget and keep to it.
- Try to use cash or debit cards instead of credit cards.
- Talk to creditors and try to renegotiate the terms of a loan, mortgage or credit agreement. An Individual Voluntary Agreement (IVA) could be agreed with creditors to pay off any debts over a set period of time.
- Avoid borrowing more money, unless a friend or family member is offering you an interest-free loan.
- Seek some professional financial advice (see page 133–134).
- Prioritise your debts and clear the most important ones first.

How to be money smart

Some tips to help you be smart with money…

- Make a budget – and stick to it.
- Make sure you know the difference between a 'need' and a 'want'.
- Cut down on non-essential spending.
- Shop around and make sure you are getting the best price.
- Save money – use a savings account and try to earn some interest.
- Be smart about advertising and only buy something because you want to.
- Only spend what you have – do not borrow from your friends unless it is an emergency.

Think about

- Can you think of any other tips on how to be smart with money?
- Apart from poor budgeting, can you think of any other reasons why someone might get into debt?

Assessment for learning

1. Give one source of income for a family. [1]
2. Give one expenditure for a family. [1]
3. Describe two ways to cope with debt. [4]
4. Explain two benefits of having a budget. [4]
5. Discuss how poor budgeting can impact the whole family. [6]

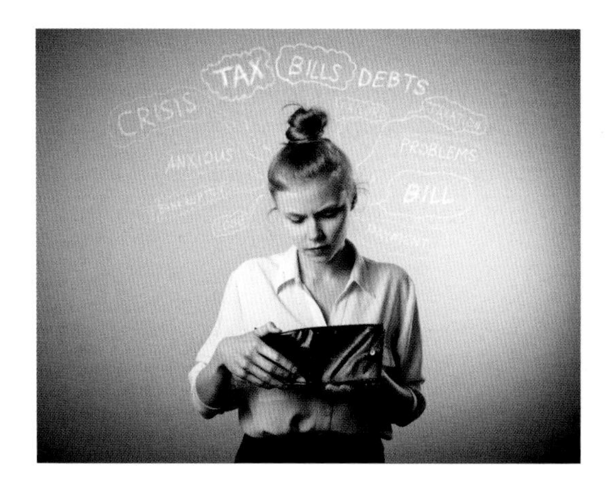

Making financial decisions based on research, advice and the credibility of information

When making any decision that involves spending money, it's important to do some research, take advice and decide what is going to work best for you. There is no shortage of advice available on the Internet, from the companies providing the product, comparison websites and customers posting reviews about their purchases. Smart consumers need to weigh up how credible (reliable) the information is before making any financial decisions.

Online shopping

This is a very popular way to shop, from the weekly shop to one-off special purchases. There can be much more variety than in high street stores and even better deals. Also, there is no time spent travelling to the shop and no queuing at the tills. However, online shoppers need to compare prices and research products thoroughly, as they can't actually see or handle the item before buying. Other disadvantages can include the added cost of postage and the risk that the item might not arrive on time or at all. For these reasons, it's important that customers find out the cost of posting before purchasing anything, ensure the websites they're using are reputable and that there's some sort of buyer protection. Many websites also allow shoppers to view feedback on sellers and their products. This indicates how satisfied customers were with their purchases and the customer service of the seller.

Personal loans

A personal loan gives someone the opportunity to borrow a large sum of money from a lender such as a bank, building society or finance company. This could be for a variety of reasons, such as a new car, a new bathroom, an extension to the house or a holiday. The loan has to be paid back with interest.

There are many types of personal loan, varying in the amount borrowed, interest to be paid and the length of time to pay it back. Generally, the longer the borrower has to repay the loan, the lower their monthly payments will be, but the more the loan will cost overall.

With so many types of loan available, from so many lenders, careful research is needed to make sure that borrowers get the best loan for their individual circumstances. Comparison websites allow borrowers to compare various personal loans in one place. However, there are also some disadvantages of using these websites, as you will see on pages 132–133.

What is meant by interest on a loan?

Sometimes a person will lend money as a favour, for example, to a friend or family member, and they will only want the original amount of money paid back to them. However, most loans are made with the intention of earning money for the lender, so the borrower has to pay back more than the original amount of the loan. The extra money paid on the loan is called 'interest'.

Internet banking

All the high street banks and building societies offer online banking services and some online banks do not have high street branches at all. Online banking is very convenient, as people can manage their money anywhere, 24/7. Many people keep track of their finances through an app on their phone or tablet, or via the bank or building society's website. Most wages, benefits and other payments are also paid electronically. However, there are concerns about the security of Internet accounts. If a criminal can access a customer's online bank account, they may be able to steal their money, commit identity theft or fraud.

Consumers need to decide if the convenience of Internet banking outweighs the possible risks. To do so, they need to research the benefits of online banking, the potential risks involved and the advice on how to protect themselves. Some of the basic ways that customers can protect themselves against fraud are explained on pages 129–130 but there is a lot more information available online.

Current account

This is the most popular form of bank or building society account. With a current account, customers can access their money at any time using their debit card or online banking. This easy access means that large amounts of cash don't need to be carried around.

There are many types of current account available, all offering various benefits and disadvantages. There is a lot of information available online and in branch from account providers, and each bank will be happy to recommend their most appropriate account. However, potential customers will have to shop around the competing providers for the best account for them. Independent websites, such as Money Saving Expert, can be useful sources of information. They often compare the different deals across various banks and offer impartial advice on the best accounts for different types of customer.

Saving schemes

The type of savings account a customer chooses will depend on their goals. Generally, the longer they're prepared to put their money away for, the more interest they can get. However, a customer might suffer a loss of interest if they withdraw from a long-term savings account at short notice or incur an early access charge, so it's worth considering how much flexibility they need. Again, careful research is needed. It is worth noting that financial trends can change from day to day, so up-to-date information is essential.

ISAs

An ISA is an Individual Savings Account, offering tax free savings of up to £20,000* in the current tax year. There are various types of ISAs, so consumers need to work out which one is right for them. This could depend on whether they need to access their money at short notice, want to manage their account online or want to take the risk of an ISA based on stocks and shares. There is a lot of information available online from ISA providers, but, like personal accounts, the banks providing them will only recommend their own accounts. Websites such as www.gov.uk offer some independent advice.

* Figures current 2019/2020.

Further thinking

Imagine you are a financial adviser. Three clients come to you for advice on the following financial decisions:

Client 1 – *"Is it safe to install an app on my phone for Internet banking?"*

Client 2 – *"What is the best kind of ISA for me to save money in?"*

Client 3 – *"Should I get a credit card?"*

- Use the Internet to research advice for each financial decision.
- Select the most relevant sources of information for each client and weigh up how reliable they are.
- Finally, write an email to each client, recommending the most useful sources of information for their financial decision. Don't forget to explain why you think each source is reliable.

Payment methods

Deciding how to pay for goods or services is an important decision when managing finances. When, in the past, people would have saved up to buy something, now they are more likely to pay using credit. When something is bought on credit, you have the item immediately, but must pay for it at a later date. Buying with credit can have many advantages over using cash – but there is also the potential to overspend and get into debt.

Paying by cash is often the easiest way to make purchases and works extremely well for many different transactions, particularly when the amount of money involved is relatively small. However, paying by cash does have limitations, especially in an age where we are relying more and more on banks, building societies and plastic cards.

PAYING WITH CASH	BUYING ON CREDIT
✓ There is less temptation to overspend and get into debt, as when the cash runs out, you must stop spending. ✓ Paying by cash is best for small items. ✓ It can be easier to keep track of spending and stick to a budget.	✓ Credit is convenient, as you don't need to carry a lot of money when buying expensive items. ✓ Credit can help if you need money quickly for an emergency. ✓ Credit is convenient when shopping online.
✗ Cash can be lost or stolen. ✗ You can't take advantage of a special offer or pay for an unforeseen expense unless you have enough cash in reserve.	✗ Credit usually costs more than cash, as there is interest to be paid. ✗ It can be easier to get into debt with credit, as you can buy things you can't afford.

Debit cards

A debit card has direct access to the card holder's account, usually a current or savings account with a bank or building society. Debit cards are similar to cash as the money is taken directly from the bank account, and if there is no money in the account then the transaction is declined. Many people prefer a debit card to cash as it is more convenient. Debit cards can be used in shops, restaurants and garages and also for online shopping. However, with a debit card there can be the temptation to overspend or waste money on an impulse buy.

Credit cards

A credit card allows the card holder to borrow money in order to buy goods and services. When a person uses a credit card to make a purchase, the money is not automatically withdrawn from their bank account. In the first instance, the card provider pays for the purchase. At the end of the month, a statement is sent out, detailing the purchases and informing the card holder how much money is owed. If a person chooses to pay by instalments then interest will have to be paid on the amount that is unpaid. The amount of interest can vary, so careful research needs to be carried out before committing to a credit card. A store card is a form of credit card. They may offer rewards and discounts when used in store, but may have a higher interest rate than other credit cards. As with debit cards, some people find it tempting to overspend when using a credit card.

Contactless payments

These are a fast and convenient way to pay for purchases costing £30 and under. Debit and credit cards, keyfobs, watches and mobile devices can all be touched against a contactless terminal. No PIN is needed to make a payment, although you may be asked for a PIN from time to time for security purposes. Again, like with debit and credit cards, some people find it tempting to overspend when using contactless, particularly as contactless devices don't always produce a customer receipt to help keep track of spending.

Fraud and identity theft

Identity theft happens when criminals access enough information about someone's identity (such as their name, date of birth and address) to commit identity fraud. They can then buy goods or services for themselves, which are paid for out of the victim's bank account, or move money from the victim's bank account into another account. Sometimes criminals take paper statements from someone's rubbish. Sometimes they phone or email, pretending to be from a legitimate organisation and request bank account details.

How to protect yourself

People who make payments with cards, and who use the Internet for shopping and banking, need to be aware of the possibility of fraud and how to protect themselves. The following strategies can help protect you against fraud:

- Shred any paper bills or documents relating to your cards. Do not put them in the rubbish bin. If possible, just have online statements.
- Bank accounts and credit card statements should be monitored regularly to check they are accurate, and that there are no unauthorised payments. If you notice anything suspicious, you should inform your bank immediately.
- If you receive an email or phone call from your bank or card provider, don't give out any information unless you have asked them to contact you. If you think the call or email is genuine, ring them back on contact details you already have for them or make contact through their official website.
- Shield your PIN when making a payment in a shop or using an ATM.

- When using contactless payment, ensure you are the only one to handle your card and the contactless device. Do not hand them over to anyone else.
- For online banking, have a secure password that can't be guessed easily. If possible, install the free security software offered by most banks on your computer.
- When shopping online, make sure that the website has a secure section for payments. Before typing in payment details, make sure there is a Secure Sockets Layer (SSL), a technology that encrypts (scrambles) data so your details are safe.
- Where possible, use an e-payment service such as PayPal for payments. Repeatedly typing in debit and credit card numbers online increases the risk of theft.
- If you have a credit card, use it instead of a debit card for online payments. Some credit cards offer

protection against fraud and it is more difficult to recover lost funds on a debit card.

- Do not use public or unsecured Wi-Fi when accessing Internet banking, shopping online or for anything that involves personal details.
- Protect yourself against scams by ignoring any emails that contain spelling mistakes or errors, ask for personal details or are from addresses you don't recognise. Never open any attachments unless you are certain of what they are.
- Watch out for emails that seem too good to be true, perhaps offering you a share in an inheritance, compensation for a recent injury or a tax refund. This could be a phishing email. This is a method used by criminals to try and access usernames and passwords, which they can then sell on.
- Be wary of investment scams. Typically, 'cold callers' will phone or email, offering an opportunity to invest money in a scheme that can't fail. Unsuspecting victims are often encouraged to act quickly or they will miss out on the offer. Some people have lost their entire savings to investment scammers. Remember, never share your personal details over the phone or through email.

Assessment for learning

1. Write down what a personal loan is. [1]
2. Write down what an ISA is. [1]
3. Describe two advantages of using a debit card to make purchases. [4]
4. Explain two advantages of having a current account for banking. [4]
5. Using the information in the Source and your own knowledge, analyse some of the strategies to protect against identity theft. [6]
6. Evaluate the advantages of buying on credit. [10]

Source

Identity theft is becoming a serious issue. Criminals are becoming skilled at stealing personal information and using the victim's details to order goods, open a bank account, get a credit card or obtain a loan.

There are may ways for consumers to reduce the risk of identity theft. They can shred any bills or paper documents, cover their PIN when using an ATM, and make sure they are the only one to handle their contactless cards.

They can protect themselves by only buying goods on secure websites, never giving out their personal details without checking the request is genuine, and being suspicious of emails or phone calls that seem too good to be true.

Consumer choices

It is important for a buyer to think about what is best for them and not to be influenced by the latest offers. Through advertising there is tremendous pressure on people to spend their money. Here are some key questions to consider:

Should I consider quality or price?

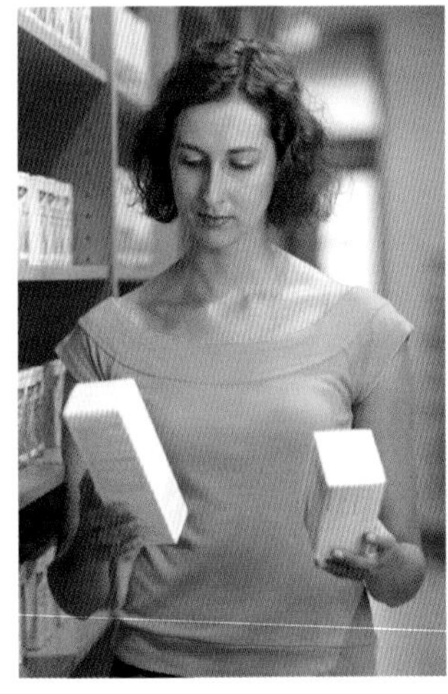

When shopping, the price of an item is very important; if money can be saved on one thing, it means more can be spent on something else. However, it's sensible to check the details of the product as it could be that the low price is an indication of low quality. The same applies when buying products online, especially as you can only see a picture of the item for sale. The bargain earphones or trainers may turn out to be an inferior copy of the branded product you thought you were buying. Sometimes buying a cheaper alternative, even if it is not as good quality, can be the right decision. For example, it might not matter if the product is not high quality if it is used only occasionally.

When considering quality or price, a final decision can also be affected by someone's budget and what they can afford to spend on the item.

Is it better to buy or rent?

This is a very important consideration, especially when it comes to housing. As property is so expensive, most people can't afford to buy a house or apartment outright. There are two main alternatives – either to buy through a mortgage or to rent.

A mortgage works in the same way as a loan. The money to buy the property is lent to the buyer by a bank or building society, and this has to be paid back with interest. As the sum of money involved will usually be very large, a mortgage can take up to 25 years or longer to pay back. There are many different types of mortgage available, aimed at meeting the different needs of home buyers. The table below shows some of the advantages and disadvantages of buying or renting property.

	BUYING A HOME	RENTING A HOME
ADVANTAGES	✓ You will own the property (once the mortgage is paid off). ✓ Buying property is often considered to be a good investment, as house prices usually increase over time. ✓ Being a home owner can help to improve your credit rating. ✓ If you own your home, you can do what you like with it. Any alterations or improvements are up to you and often add value to the property.	✓ Renting is usually less expensive, especially initially. There are no legal fees when taking out a tenancy agreement and the deposit is much smaller than for a mortgage (usually one month's rent). ✓ The landlord is responsible for any repairs and maintenance. ✓ Rent generally stays the same price each month. ✓ Renting gives more flexibility, as it is much quicker and easier to move home. Tenancy agreements are usually for less than a year, whereas selling a house can take months or even years.
DISADVANTAGES	✗ Buying your own home is expensive. You will have legal fees to pay and need a large deposit for your mortgage (usually a percentage of the value of the house). Also any repairs and maintenance are your responsibility as the home owner. ✗ The monthly mortgage payments may vary depending on the rate of inflation. Repayments that seemed manageable when taking out the mortgage can become difficult to manage if interest rates rise. ✗ There is no guarantee that property prices will rise or even stay the same. If the value of the house decreases, you are still committed to mortgage payments for the original price. You could end up paying more for your home than it is worth. This is called 'negative equity'. ✗ A mortgage is a secured loan. This means that if a buyer can't keep up with the repayments, the bank or building society has the right to sell the house to get their money back.	✗ You will not own the property. ✗ You might have to move home when your tenancy agreement expires, even if you would like to stay. ✗ If you would like to own a property in the future, it can be difficult to save for a deposit when spending money on rent each month. ✗ You might not be allowed to decorate or alter the home to your own taste.

Should I buy new or second hand?

Buying second hand can be a great way to save money and many people are happy to buy nearly-new items at a fraction of their original cost. Second-hand sales are booming online, via websites such as eBay and Gumtree, and even on social media. Vintage clothing is much sought after and on the high street, charity shops are extremely popular.

If you have to buy something expensive that you will not need very often (such as a rucksack, for a one-off trip) then a cheaper second-hand item might be best. Similarly, if you decide to learn a new sport or to play a musical instrument, starting out with second-hand equipment would be cheaper and you could always buy new at a later date if you enjoy the activity.

Some careful considerations need to be made before buying second hand:

- Did the item originally have a guarantee? Can I be reasonably certain that it's not going to break or develop a fault? These are particularly important questions if buying an electrical item.
- The item may appear to be in good condition, but is there any way of telling if it's had heavy use?
- Do you know and trust the person you are buying from? A second-hand crash helmet might seem a bargain, but not if it's been in an accident and will give you only limited protection.

Further thinking

Patrick is 24 years old, single, and earns a decent wage as a sales representative. He wants to buy a car and needs something reliable, as he will be using it for work as well as leisure activities. Patrick has £5000 in a savings account. However, he can't decide whether to spend this money on a second-hand car or borrow more money so he can buy something new.

- Use the Internet to research the advantages and disadvantages of buying a new car rather than a second-hand one.
- What advice would you give to Patrick in his situation?

Activity

Give an example of a situation where it might be best to buy:

- an item that is cheap, but not very high quality.
- a more expensive item that is better quality.
- something that is new and comes with a guarantee.
- a second-hand item.
- online.
- in a shop.

Using comparison websites

For most people, it's important to make sure that they are getting good value for their money and the best service or product available for their needs. The Internet provides a wide range of information and consumer websites have become popular for gathering the relevant information together in one place. They are particularly popular for comparing car and home insurance, and energy supply, such as electricity, gas and oil.

Comparison sites help consumers to compare products based on price, special features and reviews by other users. They can help people save a lot of money on their bills each year, but it's important to remember that comparison sites are also making money. Many rely on commission from big companies to fund their business.

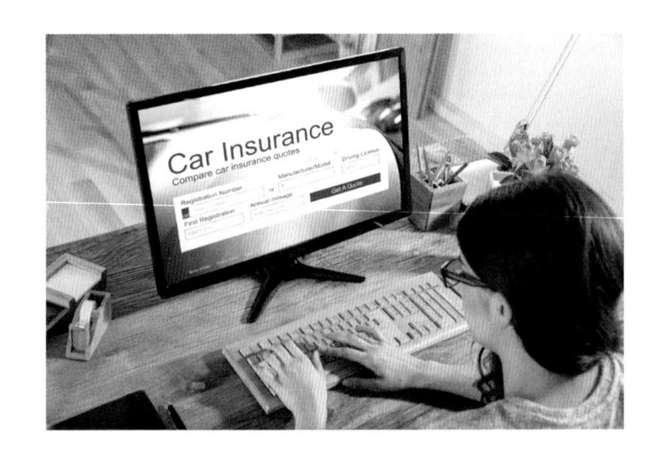

Advantages of using price comparison websites:

- **Save money** – You can choose the lowest price available on a comparison website, as you can sort the quotes by price. If you are trying to cut your home heating bills, some comparison sites allow you to search for the best package, depending on where you live.
- **Convenient and time efficient** – Comparison websites provide an easy way to see lots information without having to trawl through different websites yourself. This saves you time.
- **Wide variety and choice** – You can compare results and prices across a number of different comparison websites. There are so many sites to choose from, all asking for slightly different information and with different companies providing quotes, that there is no shortage of information.
- **Smaller companies** – Comparison websites often include plenty of smaller companies that are less well-known but could be a lot cheaper.

Disadvantages of using comparison websites:

- **Not all companies use them** – There are some insurance and energy providers who don't use comparison sites, as they want customers to go to them directly for a quote. There may be a better deal for you than the one you see on a comparison site.
- **Some comparisons are just based on price** – Some companies put up a very low quote, so they appear at the top of the results page, but when you look into it the deal is not as good as it seems. There may be extra services included with a slightly more expensive deal.
- **Commission charges** – Comparison websites are a business and their aim is to make money. There can be a built-in commission charge for using the website, which is avoided if you go to the company directly. Some comparison sites get paid a one-off fee if someone switches their insurance or energy provider, so they have an incentive to get customers for a particular business.
- **Availability in Northern Ireland** – Not all comparison websites cover Northern Ireland.

Sources of financial advice and consumer protection

With so many financial decisions to make, it's reassuring to know that there are a number of places offering advice. There are also laws in place to try and protect consumers from dishonest companies and traders.

Financial advice

- **Free financial advice** – There are a number of organisations offering free financial help, including Advice NI, websites such as Money Saving Expert, and charities such as Turn2us.
- **Friends and family** – Many people prefer to turn to family and friends for financial advice, rather than seeking professional help. There may be advantages in talking to someone who knows you well, or perhaps getting an opinion from a person close to you before speaking to a professional. However, it's important to evaluate any advice given to make sure it's right for you.

- **Independent financial advisers** – Professional financial advice can help people decide which product best suits their needs. An independent financial adviser (IFA) can help with choosing the right mortgage, deciding on the best way to invest a sum of money, or planning for retirement. IFAs give unbiased advice from all the different companies available but they will charge for their services.

- **Advisers at a local bank** – Many banks offer financial advice for their customers, especially if they are considering an investment, mortgage or loan. Many people choose to speak to their bank for advice as they feel the financial adviser will be trustworthy and knowledgeable. It can be reassuring to work with a business where they already have an account. However, banks can only advise on the products they offer. There might be a more suitable product with another bank or company.

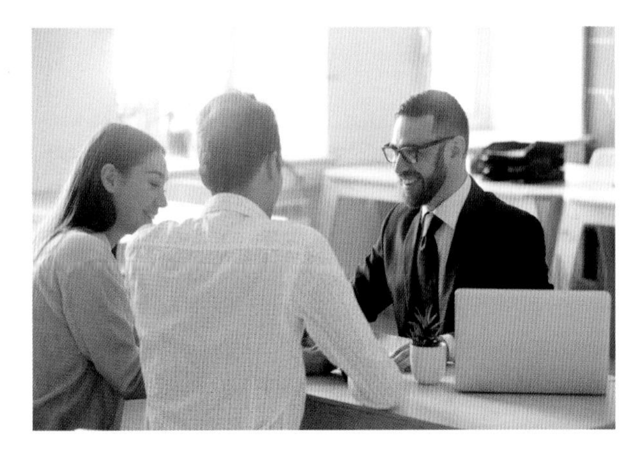

- **Online research** – There are many websites that offer free and unbiased financial advice, such as www.unbiased.co.uk and www.financialadvice.co.uk. Which? (www.which.co.uk) is an organisation that campaigns on consumer issues, reviews products and offers independent financial advice on many topics. It charges a small subscription for some of its services.
- **NGOs** – Some voluntary organisations offer specific advice to the groups of people they help. For example, Age UK offers finance advice for those who are over 50; Shelter, the housing and homelessness charity, offers free advice on housing, debt, benefits and health issues. Advice NI (see page 52) offers advice on welfare reform, benefits, debt and housing.

Consumer protection

Consumer Rights Act 2015

This acts covers the following:

- **Product quality** – Items must be as described, fit for purpose and of satisfactory quality.
- **Returning a product** – Customers have a right to return goods within 30 days for a full refund, if they are faulty.
- **Repair or replace** – If goods become faulty outside the 30-day period, the retailer is obliged to repair or replace the item.
- **Digital content** – This act defines digital content as "data which are produced and supplied in digital form". Just like any other product, digital content must be as described, fit for purpose and of satisfactory quality. Customers have a right to reject goods with a digital element within 30 days for a full refund, if they are faulty.
- **Supply of a service** – 'Services' cover a wide range of activities from minor repairs to a major home improvement and also includes work carried out by professionals, such as solicitors, travel agents and accountants. All services must be carried out with reasonable skill and care and for a reasonable price.
- **Delivery rights** – The seller is responsible for the goods until they are in the possession of the buyer. Complaints about undelivered goods should be made to the retailer, even if it is the courier who may be at fault. If a retailer has not delivered within 30 days, customers have the right to cancel the order and get a refund.

Consumer Protection from Unfair Trading Regulations 2008

This act bans:

- **unfair commercial practices.** This includes any practice that:
  - falls below the good-faith standards of skill and care that a trader would be expected to exercise towards customers.
  - affects the consumers' ability to make an informed decision about whether to purchase a product.
- **misleading advertisements and aggressive sales practices.** Traders are not allowed to:
  - claim something about a product that is untrue.
  - omit or hide important information about a product.
- **31 unfair sales techniques.** These include cold calling, doorstep calling and pressure selling.

Consumer Credit Act 2006

This acts covers the following:

- **Protection** – It gives customers protection when entering into a loan agreement. It also gives them the right to a 'cooling off' period of 14 days. During this time, they have the right to change their mind and cancel a credit agreement.
- **Credit worthiness** – A credit provider must assess whether or not a potential customer can afford (and is likely to pay) repayments on the credit card or a loan they are applying for. They can do this by applying to a credit reference agency to check the customer's credit history, and other details.
- **Information** – The customer must be made aware of the following when entering into a credit agreement:
  - the interest charges and APR.
  - the total amount payable.
  - the amount and timings of the repayments.
  - the identity of the creditor.
  - the type of credit.
  - the nature and length of the agreement.

Assessment for learning

1. Write down one source of financial help for consumers. [1]
2. Write down one disadvantage of using a comparison website. [1]
3. Explain two advantages of renting property. [4]
4. Explain two ways that consumers can be protected when buying goods and services. [4]
5. Discuss the impact of online shopping for consumers. [6]
6. Evaluate the use of credit when purchasing goods. [10]

CHAPTER 3A
The Impact of Globalisation on Employment

Chapter Summary

In this chapter you will be studying:

- **The following ways that global economic changes affect Northern Ireland:**
  - **changing employment patterns.**
  - **migration.**
  - **the growth and impact of new technologies.**
  - **skills shortages in the workforce.**
  - **emerging careers resulting from globalisation.**

The global economy

This will involve a consideration of the resources that are available (such as land and workers) and the demand for a product.

In the past, there were limited opportunities to buy and sell overseas. Today, fast and efficient transport systems and electronic communications make worldwide trade part of our everyday lives. This is all part of a process known as **globalisation**. Globalisation can bring enormous benefits to our lives, but it can also have some negative impacts on the local economy and employment.

Imports refers to the products, services or raw materials that are brought into a country.
A country's **exports** are the products, services or raw materials that are sold abroad. Northern Ireland imports and exports a wide range of products, services and raw materials. Some of its exports include meat, dairy and bakery products, ready meals and convenience foods, laboratory equipment, quarrying machines and generators, computer software, and medicines. Imports into Northern Ireland cover a very wide range of products, from computers to confectionery, and vehicles to vegetables. Some imports to Northern Ireland are in the form of raw materials used in local manufacturing, while others are the finished product that has been made overseas.

Teamwork

Working in a group, discuss the following statement:

"Globalisation is creating a shrinking world."

- What do you think this means?
- Do you agree or disagree?
- Can you think of any examples?

The implications of the global market for Northern Ireland

The impact of globalisation and worldwide trading has both opportunities and potential drawbacks for Northern Ireland.

Advantages:

- **More variety** – One of the main advantages of imports is that it provides a much wider variety of food, clothing and other goods, such as electrical items. The climate in Northern Ireland is unsuitable for growing many of the items that are part of daily life – imagine having no tea, coffee, bananas or sugar!
- **Competitive prices** – Often goods that are imported from overseas are cheaper than locally produced ones, even when the cost of transportation is taken into consideration. Competitively priced products from abroad can encourage local producers to try and reduce their prices.
- **An increase in profits** – Firms in Northern Ireland might find that competing on the world market is very successful and gives their business a boost. This could have very positive results, such as an increase in trade and the employment of local people.
- **An increase in employment** – Successful businesses might be able to expand, as increased sales lead to higher levels of production. This expansion can also lead to the creation of new jobs and a reduction in unemployment.
- **Political reasons** – The government sometimes offers financial incentives to encourage businesses to market their products abroad. Foreign trade can promote good relations with other countries throughout the world, and develop opportunities for exports and joint ventures.
- **A skilled workforce** – Global trading can lead to an investment in advanced technology and training for businesses in Northern Ireland. This could lead to a more skilled and motivated workforce.

Disadvantages:

- **Small businesses** – Some Northern Ireland businesses may encounter drawbacks as a result of globalisation. Perhaps they are simply too small to operate on a global scale and it may not be possible to compete with larger businesses.
- **Language barriers** – New staff may have to be recruited or existing staff trained to speak other languages.
- **Currency** – Fluctuations in currency exchange rates can affect the price of imports and exports, and must be taken into account by a business thinking of trading overseas.
- **Transporting goods** – Businesses may need to spend some time researching suitable transport arrangements before entering the global market. It may be that the cost of transporting the goods will make it too expensive for buyers overseas.

- **Official documentation** – Businesses will have to be familiar with the regulations and documentation needed for trading with countries overseas. This may take time, effort and cost money, so careful consideration will be needed to decide whether the extra business potential can justify this.
- **Existing customers** – If a business is putting a lot of effort and resources into developing overseas trade, then there may be less focus on the market at home. If existing customers are lost, this could be very serious if global trading turns out to be unsuccessful.

Further thinking

- Using the Internet, find as many different examples of imports to Northern Ireland as you can.
- What would your life be like without these items?

Changing employment patterns

Traditionally, many people's careers began when left school or university, and they stayed with their chosen profession until they retired, perhaps with promotion or added responsibilities along the way. However, for an increasing number of people today, their career path will not be like this, as employment patterns are changing.

Today, many people have to be flexible, possibly moving to a different area to stay in work or having jobs in a number of different industries. Working from home is also becoming more common for many people, as are flexible working hours and fixed-term contracts. Here are some reasons why employment patterns are changing:

Advances in information technology (IT) and the use of computers

In general terms, people's occupations reflect the society they live in. For example, there has been significant growth in the IT industry as computer technology is playing an increasingly important part in our lives. Advances in IT have also led to changes in employment trends. Many people now use the Internet for shopping, so this has changed the way many retailers carry out their business. Some retailers find it's no longer economical to maintain a shop at all, as customers prefer to browse on their computer screens in the comfort of their own homes. Many people would prefer to choose and book their holiday online rather than visit a travel agent. These changes mean that less people might be employed in occupations where face-to-face contact is needed with customers but more people will be employed in jobs such as website design. For many occupations there is no longer any need for employees to actually go into the work, as their job can be carried out from home, using a computer or phone.

Changes in lifestyle

Widespread use of computer technology has to led to many people **working from home**. For businesses there are a number of benefits of having employees working from home: they can use their workspace differently and may be able to reduce costs, such as money spent on electricity. Many employees prefer working from home as it's more flexible and can fit in with childcare arrangements. There is also no need to spend as much time and money on commuting if work is carried out from home.

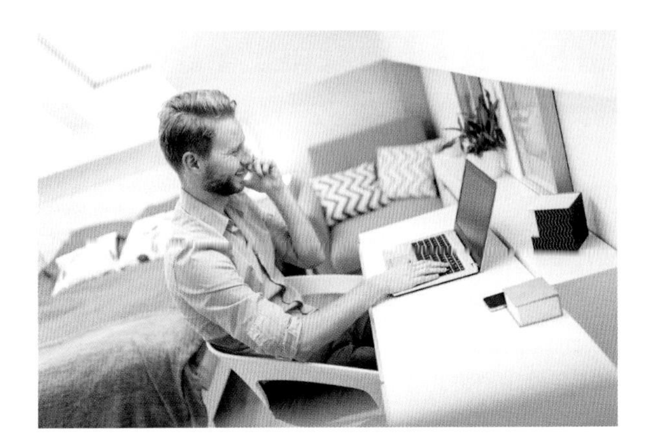

In the past, many women stayed at home to bring up a family, whereas today many women continue their careers by sharing childcare with their partners or family members, or with the help of external childcare. This leads to increasing numbers of nurseries and day care centres for pre-school age children to fulfil this demand, and with it more opportunities for careers in **childcare**.

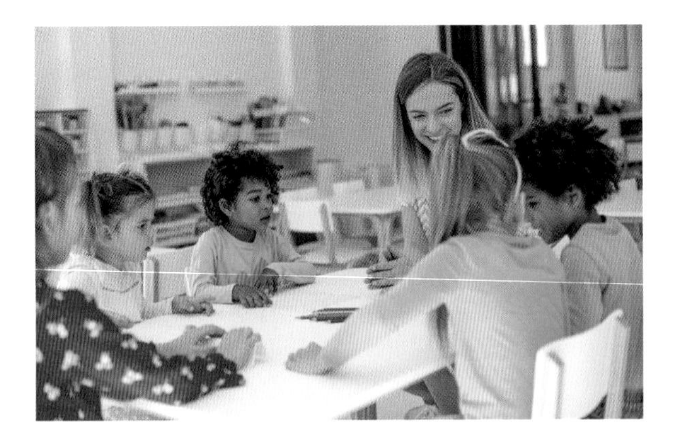

Many people now work **flexible hours**, rather than the traditional 'nine to five' office hours. We have become more of a 24-hour society, with many of the larger supermarkets and some garages open around the clock. This means that employees will need to be flexible, but also have the opportunity to work shifts that fit in with their other commitments. Different employees will have different needs, for example, a parent might prefer to work during the day when the children are at school, but a student might be available for evening work. More people are also working **part time**, perhaps to fit in with family arrangements or other commitments, or maybe because they have more than one part-time job.

Short-term contracts are another feature of this more flexible attitude to work. An employer may use a short-term contract if they think the work might be temporary, rather than commit to a permanent contract. An example of this might be seasonal work, such as retail work leading up to Christmas, or to employ someone to carry out a particular task, such as a research project. Short-term contracts give flexibility to the employer and some employees welcome the opportunity to do a range of different tasks, building up their skills and experience. However, for some employees, it can mean uncertainty over the future.

The need for retraining

People who have been working for a few years may find that the skills and knowledge they acquired when training are quickly becoming outdated. This is especially true with computer skills, as technology is moving so rapidly in this area. Employees have to accept that retraining is now an important part of any career to keep up with modern technology.

Some people may have to retrain and learn new skills because jobs in some of the traditional industries are being lost. There are now fewer workers in primary and secondary industries (such as farming or ship building) but an increasing number of people in the service sector (such as restaurants and entertainment). Some manufacturing jobs in Northern Ireland are declining as locally-made produce can't compete with cheaper imports.

Companies moving abroad

Some locally-based companies might decide to relocate their business overseas, to have a better chance of their business being successful. The reasons for this may include:

- There is less tax to pay to the government.
- The local people are prepared to work for lower wages.
- Supplies and raw materials can be purchased more cheaply.
- The running costs of the business are much lower overall.

This will have an effect on the local job market, as when a business moves overseas, the existing employees might be made redundant and left facing unemployment.

Further thinking

Working in a group, use the Internet to research the following:

1. Job advertisements
    - What types of work are available in your local area and in Northern Ireland as a whole?
2. Local companies that have chosen to relocate overseas
    - What type of businesses are they?
    - Why have they moved abroad?

Present your findings to the rest of the class.

Migration

Not everyone is fortunate enough to find suitable employment in their local area – for many people finding work means moving, perhaps even to a different country. Traditionally, far more people have left Northern Ireland than have arrived looking for work. In recent years, the situation has changed and there are now a significant number of people choosing to live and work in Northern Ireland.

Migration
Migration is the movement of people from one country to another. It can be permanent or temporary, and take place over long or short distances. Short-term migration might be seasonal, as people move looking for more favourable conditions. Seasonal migration can affect people who are looking for work, as temporary opportunities become available, for example, agricultural work during summer and autumn harvest, or retail work during December.

Emigration
Emigration is when people leave a country to live elsewhere. This can be permanent or temporary.

Immigration
Immigration is when people move into a country from another country. This can also be permanent or temporary.

Immigration is when people move **in**to a county.
Emigration is when people **e**xit (leave) a country.

Migrant worker
A migrant worker is a person who travels to a different area for work. They don't necessarily intend to stay in their destination country, although many do choose to stay.

Immigration into Northern Ireland

Immigrants and migrant workers are becoming increasingly significant in Northern Ireland. They include people from China, India, Poland, Portugal and the Philippines. Many of the people who immigrate to Northern Ireland want a better life for themselves and their families, and they are determined to work hard to achieve this. They make a positive contribution to the growth of the economy and ease work and skills shortages in many areas of employment, including health care, food processing, agriculture and hospitality. They also bring many benefits to cultural life. However, some immigrants experience negative attitudes towards them, not only in the workplace but also in the rest of society (see 'Challenges of immigration' on page 13).

Emigration from Northern Ireland

In the past, many people have emigrated from Northern Ireland to live in places such as America, Australia and other parts of the UK. There are many reasons why people choose to emigrate from Northern Ireland. Some people move for personal reasons, such as moving to the country their partner is from or to join family members who live elsewhere. Many people chose to leave during the Troubles, to avoid sectarianism and violence. Some people leave Northern Ireland for university and don't return. Others feel that Northern Ireland lacks employment opportunities and move overseas to find a better job with higher pay and therefore enjoy a better standard of living. Some return when they have earned sufficient money or advanced their career.

Emigration can have a positive effect as it takes some people out of the job market, helping to ease unemployment. However, if the people who are leaving are those with training and skills then the result can be a 'brain drain'. This means there are many unskilled workers but posts for people with specific skills can't be filled.

The growth and impact of new technologies

New technologies are changing the workplace, having an impact on both the work that is carried out and the way in which it is done. It can make the workplace efficient and effective, but employees at all levels have to be confident using the technology. A business also needs to decide at what point to upgrade to the latest technology or whether this may be impractical as too many staff will have to be retrained. Some businesses do not need the latest technology to help them move forwards and be successful.

Advantages of technology for a business...

- **An increase in productivity** – new technology can allow jobs to be completed more quickly.
- **Fewer employees are needed** – Many jobs that needed employees can now be automated.
- **Higher profits and a higher income** – This is due to the increase in efficiency and production, combined with the need for fewer staff.
- **Advanced communications** – These include the use of email, mobile phones and computer systems.
- **A more competitive business** – Some of the savings made through the new technology can be used to lower prices and attract more customers.

...and some disadvantages...

- **New skills** – Employees may have to be retrained so they can operate the new technology.
- **Maintenance** – The new equipment may be difficult to maintain. If it breaks down, the whole work schedule could be affected.
- **Costs** – The new technology may be expensive to install at the start, even though it may save money in the long term.
- **Time** – It may take time to reorganise the workplace to set up the new technology. A business working to very tight deadlines may find this is impractical.

Teamwork

Working in a group:

- Create a spider diagram listing the different technologies that you use every day (at home and at school).
- Discuss the impact that these technologies had on your everyday lives.

Some examples of technology in business

- **Retailing** – Most retailers use the Internet to promote their products, and online sales make up a large portion of their income. Many retailers also use computer software to keep a check on stock levels.

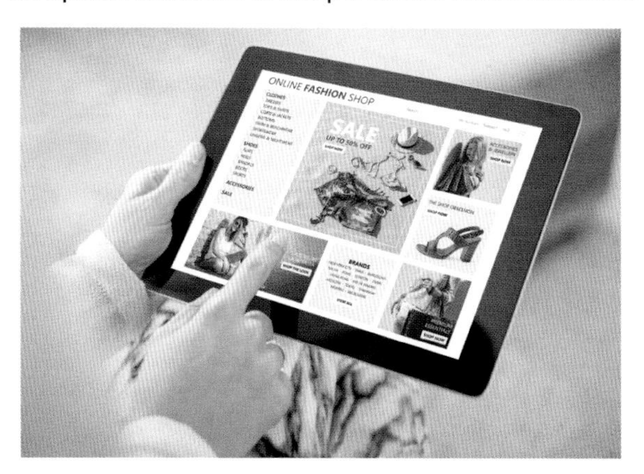

- **Manufacturing** – New technology has helped manufacturers to make products more quickly and cheaply. This includes machine tools and design software. Most also use computer software to keep in contact with suppliers and customers.
- **Agriculture** – Many farmers are now using satellites and digital technology to support precision farming. This involves collecting data to find out which part of their land is best suited to certain crops, perhaps because it's drier or sunnier. The data can also inform farmers what fertilisers and pesticides a particular piece of land needs. Many dairy farmers are now using robotic milking systems to make their work more efficient. The robot can milk a herd of cows, check the milk and record data about individual cows.

- **Travel and tourism** – Technology is playing an important role in transforming the travel and tourism industry. Many people are no longer using high street travel agents to book a holiday but choosing to book themselves online. This has helped to reduce costs and improve efficiency. The use of social media and online reviewing of tourist attractions and accommodation can help customers make informed choices about their holidays and excursions.

The impact of technology on employment

Technology is changing employment, whether the workplace is a dairy farm, office or restaurant. This has created both opportunities and challenges for businesses in Northern Ireland.

Changing skills

The growing use of technology and development of new equipment has led to the creation of many new areas of employment. Businesses need to employ people who are trained to use these new technologies, and also need to motivate existing staff to acquire new skills. Employees need to be flexible and willing to retrain so they can use new equipment.

Redundancies and unemployment

Technology leads to more tasks becoming automated and less need for people to be employed to do them. This is one of the reasons why using new technologies can save businesses money. An example of this is in the banking sector, where the introduction of Internet banking led to many large banks closing their high street branches. Therefore, does this mean that as computers and machines are replacing human workers there is going to be more unemployment? The situation is not quite as simple as this and the introduction of new technology doesn't always lead to redundancies. Improved technology can reduce costs, and therefore prices can be more competitive. This could lead to an increased demand for a product, which might require more employees being hired.

The Internet and businesses

There are many ways in which a business can benefit from using the Internet to market its goods, especially if the business wants to trade overseas.

- **A global market can be reached** – Traditional ways of marketing a product, such as a newspaper advertisement or a poster on a billboard, are expensive and usually limited to large companies. The Internet opens up new possibilities for businesses to reach customers from all over the world.
- **There is the scope to offer a wide range of products and services** – Businesses can use the Internet to promote a variety of different services as well as simply advertise goods for sale. For example, a customer can choose a holiday destination, research available flights and book their holiday online.
- **Business hours are increased** – With the Internet, a product can be bought straightaway, so business hours are increased to 24 hours a day, 7 days a week throughout the year. Online feedback from customers can help a business to improve its services and be more successful.
- **Particular groups of customer can be targeted** – Through market research, businesses know what 'type' of person is more likely to purchase their product. Potential customers can be targeted, depending on the websites they use.

Employees with disabilities

New computer technology is now being developed for the workplace to help employees who are disabled. This is called **assistive technology**. Many jobs today require IT skills, yet for some disabled people this can be a barrier to employment as standard equipment can be difficult for them to use. Assistive technology can make computers accessible for a person who is disabled, or simply make their working life easier. Here are some examples:

- A person who is physically impaired may find it difficult to use a standard keyboard or mouse, but there are many alternatives available. These include one-handed keyboards or screen pointers that can be controlled with almost any part of the body.
- Special screen reading software has been developed to help people who are blind to use computers. Words on the screen are converted into speech and a braille readout can also be produced on a special display under the keyboard.

Assisted technology is a good example of a workplace technology that is opening up new opportunities for a section of the population who may not have always been well-accommodated in the world of work.

Skills shortages in the workforce

The increase of new technology across all job sectors is having a significant impact on employment and recruitment. There are exciting new career opportunities in many developing areas, but this has led to the issue of skills shortages. Across the UK, companies urgently need to recruit talented people to fill highly-skilled roles and this situation is even more acute in Northern Ireland. Skills shortages are also more apparent in companies that use the most advanced technology in the workplace.

A skilled workforce is vital in meeting the challenges of the global economy, so what action needs to be taken to address the problem?

- The skills that are being taught in schools need to meet the needs of modern businesses. The STEM subjects (Science, Technology, Engineering and Mathematics) are the most under supplied and forecast to be the most in need due to the anticipated growth in the IT and manufacturing sectors. Careers services have an important role to play as a link between schools, colleges and businesses.
- The government, industries, schools, colleges and universities need to work together. Schemes need to be considered that will attract students to train in the areas where there are skills shortages. Governments should cooperate with industries to identify areas where they are lacking skilled workers.
- Companies can try to minimise skills shortages by assessing what training is needed for their workforce now and what might be needed for the future. If an investment is made in training staff this will increase the level of skills within the company.

Emerging careers resulting from globalisation

There are new careers resulting from the increase in technology in the workplace and also from the impact of globalisation. It is anticipated that the economy of Northern Ireland will strengthen over the coming years, with the following areas playing an extremely important role:

Information technology (IT)

IT, particularly software development, database development, systems architecture and Internet specialist skills, is at the heart of every organisation and is central to our daily lives: for example, mobile communication, gaming, touch screen technology and satellite navigation devices.

Creative and digital media

Digital is everywhere and is at the heart of the UK economy, underpinning growth through both the development of new technologies and the provision of services to businesses and consumers. All national trends and forecasts predict continued demand for high level skills in the sector. Careers are available in mobile technology, digital entertainment and computer gaming.

Agri food

Food and drink manufacturing includes the processing of meat and poultry, dairy, fish and shellfish, fruit and vegetables, and the production of bakery items and drinks. Areas of work include bakery, distillery, creamery and ready meals production. Careers in this sector include laboratory technicians, food scientists and machine operatives.

Business and financial services

There are several different industries within the finance, accountancy and financial services sector. Careers in this sector include accountants, insurance brokers and pensions advisers.

Advanced manufacturing and engineering

This sector includes careers requiring CAD (computer-aided design) and CNC (computer numerical control) skills, mechanical and electrical engineering skills, and strategic marketing. Careers in this area include machine operatives and design engineers.

Renewable energies and recycling

European and global agreements on more energy-efficient technology are creating demand for new engineering solutions. Mechanical engineers are at the forefront of designing everything from better forms of green energy and zero emission engines to the latest breed of nuclear power stations. Careers in this sector include mechanical engineers, biochemists, researchers and development managers.

Health and life sciences

The health and life sciences sector is one of Northern Ireland's most important sectors. The sector combines all elements of science and technology that contribute to the discovery and development of products for the health care and well-being of humans and animals. Careers in this area include pharmacy technicians, occupational therapists and health care administrators.

Further thinking

Working in a group:

- Choose one industry in Northern Ireland and research what jobs are available.
- What skills are needed for these jobs?
- Are there many opportunities within this sector of employment?

Assessment for learning

1. Name one product that is imported into Northern Ireland. [1]
2. Write down what is meant by the word 'emigration'? [1]
3. Describe two areas of employment where growth is expected in the future. [4]
4. Explain two reasons why some companies choose to move abroad. [4]
5. Discuss some of the reasons for skills shortages in the workplace. [6]

CHAPTER 3B
Preparing for Employment: Recruitment and Selection

Chapter Summary

In this chapter you will be studying:

- **The skills, qualities and attitudes required for a successful career.**
- **The importance of lifelong learning in achieving your personal and professional potential.**
- **Ways employers assess candidates' suitability for a job.**
- **Preparing for an interview.**
- **Self-evaluation and reflection on interview to improve future performance.**

Skills, qualities and attitudes required for a successful career

There are a number of skills and qualities that employers look for. Having the right qualifications is vital, but personal qualities are also very important. Once a person is employed, it is also important to make sure that skills are kept up-to-date as the world of work is always changing.

Skills for success

Transferable skills are not related to a specific occupation. They are the skills a person has gained through various jobs or voluntary work, hobbies and sports, and other life experiences. Transferable skills are important, whether a person is starting a new job, changing career, facing redundancy or re-entering the world of work after a long absence, perhaps to raise a family.

Many of the transferable skills that employers are looking for fall into one of the following categories:

- **Essential skills**, including literacy, numeracy and IT.
- **Creative and problem-solving skills**, showing that an employee will be able to handle a variety of different tasks and situations in the workplace.

As well as education and experience, many employers are also looking for a range of **personal skills** or **competencies** (the things a person is good at), such as teamwork, using your initiative, and communication. These skills are now seen as being increasingly important to help both business and relationships run smoothly.

Qualities for success

A person's relationship with their colleagues can be very important in creating a pleasant working environment. Good relations in the workplace can help everyone to do their job better and make going to work every day enjoyable. This is one of the reasons why personal qualities are so important. In addition to this, the workplace today can be very competitive. A person with a variety of skills will have a competitive edge. These qualities include commitment, loyalty and working well with others.

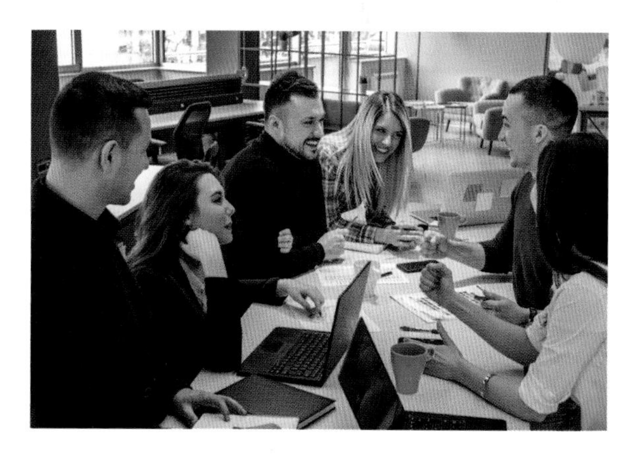

Teamwork

Think about your own skills and qualities.

- Make a copy of the table below but leave out the examples unless you think they apply to you.
- List the skills and qualities you have in the first column and those you would like to have in the second.

Working in a group, discuss your lists.

- Do any of you share some of the same skills or qualities?
- Discuss how you might go about gaining the skills or qualities you would like to have. If you can think of any solutions, write them in the third column.
- If any of the skills or qualities you have feature on anyone else's 'Skills or qualities I would like to have' list (or vice versa), you might be able to help each other out!
- Remember, some skills and qualities can be gained through further training, such as qualifications. However, others are more to do with attitude, such as adaptability and willingness to learn.

Skills and qualities I have	Skills and qualities I would like to have	How I could gain the skills and qualities I would like to have
I'm good at English and can express myself well on paper.	I would like to be more confident when speaking in front of people.	Practice! I could start by volunteering to read aloud more often. I could then move on to doing presentations to the class with a group of other people, so I only have to say a few lines. Maybe by the end of the year I might be able to stand up on my own and give a short speech to the class.

Attitudes for success

As well as skills and qualities, a successful career can also depend on having the right attitude towards your colleagues, your employer and about the work you are doing. Having the attitude for success might include:

- **A willingness to learn and improve** – A willingness to learn, improve and make the most of your abilities are all important qualities. This might involve keeping up with current changes and being prepared to undertake retraining or develop existing skills.
- **The ability to be flexible and adapt to new situations** – In a work environment, you may need to work independently and also as part of a team. You might also have to take on various roles at different times, perhaps when your company is busy or a colleague is off sick or on annual leave. A successful employee will be able to adapt to changing situations.

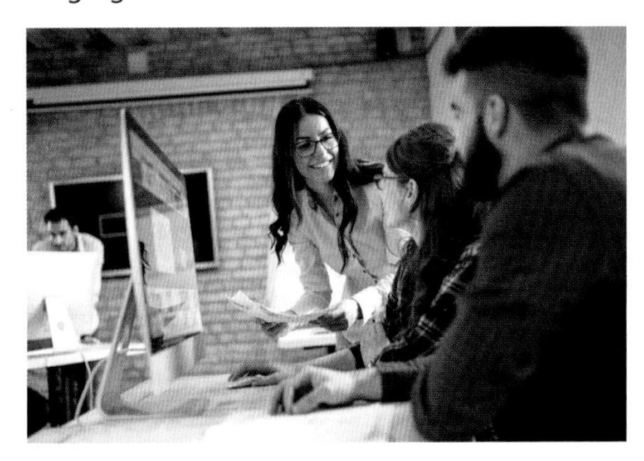

- **Being prepared to take responsibility for your own career** – A successful employee will be self-motivated about improving and developing their career skills and capabilities. This may involve taking on additional study or training in your own time, as well as that offered by your employer.
- **Commitment to your work and employer** – Having the attitude to succeed involves making a serious commitment to your work. This can involve the personal qualities of dependability, responsibility, honesty and integrity.
- **Positivity and resilience** – A positive attitude gets the work done and motivates others, while making the workplace more pleasant. Resilience is an important quality that enables someone to 'bounce back' from difficulties and be determined to find a solution to problems.

Think about

What do you think are the most important skills, qualities and attitudes valued by employers? Give reasons for your opinion.

The importance of lifelong learning

Learning is not just for school, it is a continual process that takes place throughout a person's life. Once someone is in employment, the learning process will also involve professional development and acquiring new work-related skills. This is known as lifelong learning. The successful employee is someone who is flexible and well-equipped to face change, with relevant skills and up-to-date training. Investing some time in learning new skills means equipping yourself for the future, as you will have a better chance of gaining promotion or changing careers.

The advantages of lifelong learning

Here are some of the advantages of lifelong learning in the context of work:

- It can develop existing skills and provide new skills.
- It can provide greater job satisfaction and the motivation to succeed at work.
- It can provide qualifications and experience that can help to secure promotion.
- All these factors can lead to greater self-esteem.

However, it's worth remembering that there is a level of commitment involved in lifelong learning. Deciding to study for further qualifications or learn new skills may not be easy, and takes time and effort.

Here are some important questions a person will need to consider:

- How much will it cost, and will my employer help meet some of these expenses?
- Will I have to sacrifice time spent with friends and family?
- Will my new skills or qualifications lead to career development or promotion?
- Do I have the time for this new course, without becoming too stressed or fatigued because of existing commitments?

What is a career plan?

A career plan is a road map that helps someone reach their destination – their chosen long-term goals. Career planning doesn't stop once they get a job – like learning, it's a lifelong process. It's important for a person to grow and develop in their chosen occupation and this may involve retraining or changing jobs. A career plan is important because it helps a person take control of where they are going in the world of work.

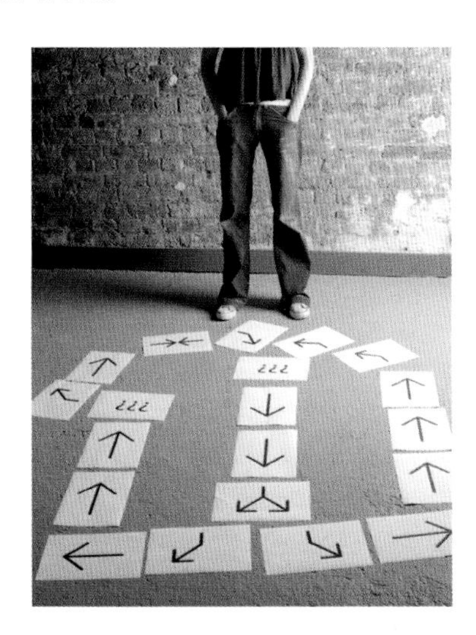

Activity

Make a career plan for yourself.

- Go back to when you first started to think about a career or make choices, such as which subjects you chose to study for GCSE.
- Go as far forward as you possibly can.
- You might like to present your plan as a flow diagram or road map showing where you intend to go.

Ways employers assess candidates' suitability for a job

A person's application for a job will say a lot about them, not just through the information they choose to give, but the way they present it. An employer might assess personal qualities and skills through:

- an initial telephone call.
- correspondence through letter or email.
- an application form.
- an interview.
- an assessment, such as a presentation or test.

Work experience

Many schools include work experience in their curriculum, often through a work placement. This is the opportunity for people to spend some time in a place of employment discovering more about a career or job, and the skills and qualities needed. Any work experience, paid employment or voluntary work should be included in a CV or on an application form, as any previous experience can help an employer to assess the suitability of a potential employee.

Curriculum Vitae (CV)

A Curriculum Vitae is a summary of a person's education and employment history, giving details of qualifications, training and experience. A CV can be an initial way of showing a potential employer that they have the right skills and qualities for the position they are applying for. Employers might ask for a CV to be submitted to support a job application, to help them decide if candidates are the sort of people they are looking for.

Making an application

When a job is advertised, the first stage in an application is usually to look at the details of the role online or request further information by telephone or email. The information usually includes 'essential' and 'desirable' criteria. This refers to the skills, qualifications and experience that the applicant must have in order to apply (essential), and some of the qualities the employer might like to see (desirable). It's important for candidates to read this very carefully before making an application, to decide what evidence can be used to show that these criteria are met.

Some places of employment have their own application form for applicants to fill in. The details asked for are often similar to the information on a CV. As with the CV, it's important that an application form is filled in carefully and clearly, without spelling mistakes, and uses good punctuation and grammar.

Application forms may have a space to give a personal statement outlining why the applicant is interested in the position, why they are suitable for it, and how they meet the advertised criteria. It's especially important to write this carefully and include as much relevant information as possible. If an application requests a CV, there will probably need to be a covering letter as well. In this letter, an applicant could include a brief personal statement about their suitability for the post.

The importance of careers advice

A careers teacher in school or college can help students to make decisions about their future careers in some of the following ways:

- Students can discuss their likes and dislikes, and their personal capabilities. Their careers teacher can then give advice on the jobs or courses that might suit them best.
- Careers teachers will be knowledgeable in all aspects of post-16 and post-18 courses, and can suggest a course or career that is realistic. A teacher will be aware of what exams each student is working towards and what they could aim for next.
- Careers teachers can give impartial advice to students so they are equipped to make their own decisions about their future.

Preparing for an interview

There may be hundreds of applications for a job and from these a very small number will be shortlisted for interview. It's therefore very important for a candidate to make the right impression at this stage in the recruitment process. This can be assisted by careful preparation beforehand.

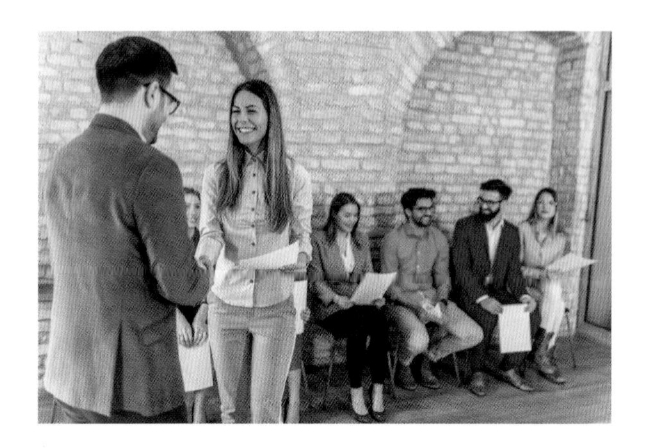

Researching the job and employer

Interviewers expect candidates to know what their company does, so it makes sense to find out as much as possible about their organisation. This will include their line of work, customers, areas where they operate and the ethos of the company. Applicants who have this knowledge may find it helpful when answering questions in the interview. It's also important to ensure they know exactly what the role involves, so it's vital to read the job description carefully.

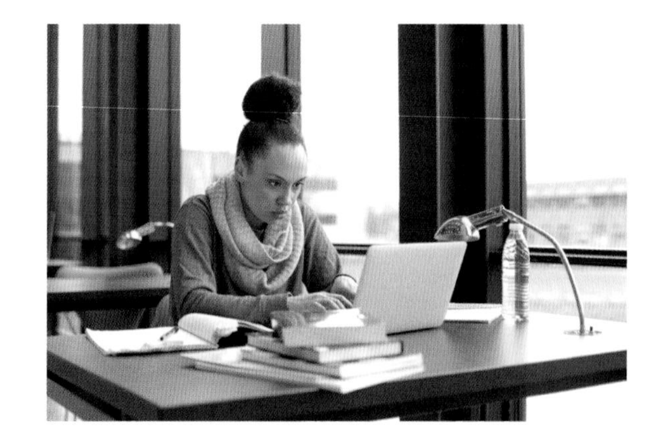

Preparing responses to potential questions

A potentially successful candidate will consider what they know about the company, the job and the skills they are looking for. The next stage is to think of some possible questions that might be asked and prepare suitable answers. The format of an interview can vary, from one-to-one to a group interview. Some interviews may require candidates to give a presentation, complete a test or take part in a role play. It's important to know what to expect and to be well prepared.

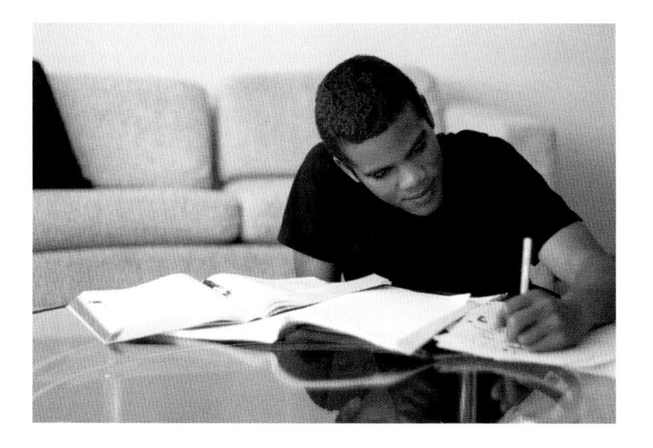

Providing examples to demonstrate experience

When asked questions, candidates should try to answer clearly and accurately, drawing on any relevant experience. Giving examples as evidence, rather than simply giving yes or no answers, is an effective interview technique. Before the interview, it might be useful for a candidate to prepare a list of their most relevant skills, qualities and experience. Each question can be an opportunity to share some of this information with the interviewer (as long as the information is relevant).

Participating in a mock interview

A mock interview is a useful way for candidates to prepare for a real interview. Practising beforehand with a friend, family member or teacher allows them to try out answering questions in a way that highlights

relevant skills and experience. The mock-interviewer might be able to give the candidate feedback on their performance.

Plan ahead

There are practical matters to take into consideration, to avoid the stress of a last-minute rush. These include planning how to travel to the interview and what to wear. For example, a suit might be appropriate for some interviews, but something more casual might be suitable for others. It is essential to be well organised, gathering all the important information needed, such as certificates, qualifications or other examples of work, and putting them in a folder. It's best for candidates to plan to arrive at least 15 minutes ahead of the interview time.

At the interview

It is very important to create a good first impression at the interview. To give a favourable impression, it's useful to be aware of body language, such as making eye contact, smiling, and not slouching or fidgeting. How an applicant dresses at their interview is also important and can help to create a positive image. An interview is also a two-way process and the person applying for the job has to assess whether they really want it. There will probably be the opportunity to ask questions at the end of the interview and this can be another opportunity to make a positive impression.

Self-evaluation and reflection on interview to improve future performance

In the world of work, most people will probably attend interviews many times throughout their career, perhaps for a new job, a promotion or to undertake further education. Whether or not the outcome is a success, there is a lot to be learnt for future interviews by taking the opportunity to evaluate your performance and decide what you could have done differently. By learning from your successes and mistakes, you will be better prepared the next time. This will lead to you becoming more confident and successful at interviews.

Here are some questions you could ask yourself after an interview:

1. Did I arrive on time?
2. Did I speak calmly and confidently?
3. Did I display a confident and positive attitude?
4. Was my non-verbal communication effective?
5. Did I maintain eye contact?
6. Did I answer the questions asked and was I able to keep to the subject?
7. Was I well prepared and knowledgeable about the company and its work?
8. Was I able to emphasise my strengths, skills and the positive contribution I could make?
9. Did I handle difficult questions with ease, or did I struggle?
10. Did I ask useful questions about the role?

Give each one an honest rating out of 10 and see what areas need to be improved for next time.

Interview skills and techniques are important throughout a person's working life. For many people today, a career doesn't mean working in the same position until you retire. There will probably be career changes along the way and new opportunities.

A change of employment may be worth considering in the following situations:

- **A change in lifestyle** – Perhaps a single person now has a partner and a family, and wants to work more 'child-friendly' hours.
- **Work has become boring** – It might be time to learn new skills or study for a qualification that will open up more opportunities.
- **The job situation has become insecure** – People in a particular area of work could be facing redundancies. Retraining for a different line of work might be sensible.
- **Not enough opportunities for promotion** – Perhaps a person feels they are not progressing fast enough in their current career. Earning more money may not necessarily bring greater job satisfaction, but having greater responsibility might.

Assessment for learning

1. Name one skill needed for the workplace. [1]
2. Name one personal quality that an employer might value in an employee. [1]
3. Describe one way that personal qualities can be important in the workplace. [2]
4. Explain two ways that a CV can help an employer assess a candidate's suitability for a job. [4]
5. Discuss how a potential employee can make a good impression at an interview. [6]
6. Evaluate the importance of lifelong learning in a person's career. [10]

Teamwork

- Use the Internet to find a job you would like to apply for. This could be something you would like to do as a career or a temporary part-time job for the summer holidays.
- Working in a group, practice your interview skills.
- Take it in turns to be the candidate being interviewed for your chosen job. The others in your group are the interview panel.
- Give each other feedback on how well the interviews went.

CHAPTER 3C
Rights and Responsibilities of Employers and Employees

Chapter Summary

In this chapter you will be studying:

- **The employment contract, and terms and conditions of employment.**
- **Employer and employee responsibilities and the impact of these not being met.**
- **The code of conduct in the workplace.**
- **Developing positive working relationships.**
- **The causes and consequences of employees' work-related stress.**
- **Ways of dealing with work-related stress.**
- **The roles of trade unions and their impact in the workplace.**

During the industrial revolution, many people had to work in factories for long hours, in appalling conditions, for very little pay. There were no adequate regulations to ensure that workers received rest breaks or didn't work excessively long hours. Accidents were common and people were often treated very badly at work. This highlights how crucial employment rights and responsibilities are so that employees are protected from risk and exploitation.

The employment contract

An employer has a number of areas of responsibility towards an employee. Some of these are contained in the contract of employment, while others come from laws passed by the government. A contract of employment is an agreement between the employer and employee. This contract is made as soon as a person accepts a job and an employee is entitled to a written contract within two months of starting work.

The contract will set out the terms and conditions of employment, such as:

- the starting date of the employment and whether the work is temporary or permanent.
- the salary.
- the hours of work, holiday pay and entitlement to sick pay.
- where the employee will be working.
- the period of notice needed to end the employment.

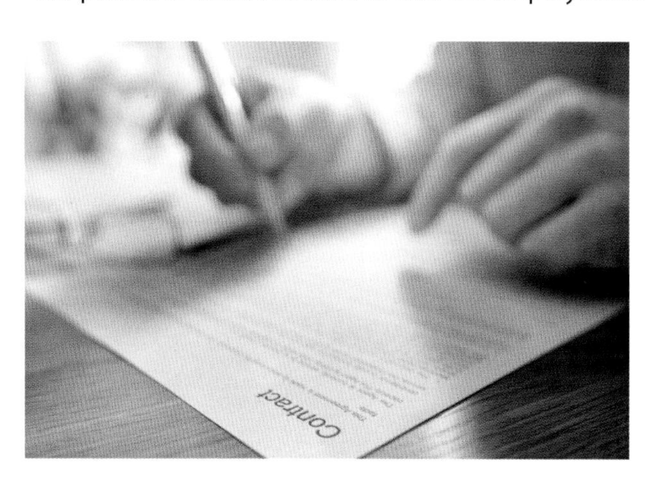

The details that are written down are called the express terms of a contract. There are also implied terms. For example, an employer is expected to have a duty of care towards an employee. This means that they should do everything that is reasonably possible to protect the health, safety and well-being of their employees. An important element implied in a contract of employment is the idea of mutual trust and confidence – the employer and employee both have to be able to trust each other.

Salary – The contract of employment will provide exact information about the rate of pay. This shouldn't be below the National Living Wage[1] or at odds with the Equality Act 2010. Whether salary will be paid weekly or monthly should be outlined in the contract. It must also explain what arrangements are made for sick pay. By law, an employee can receive up to 28 weeks of Statutory Sick Pay (SSP) through the National Insurance contributions scheme.

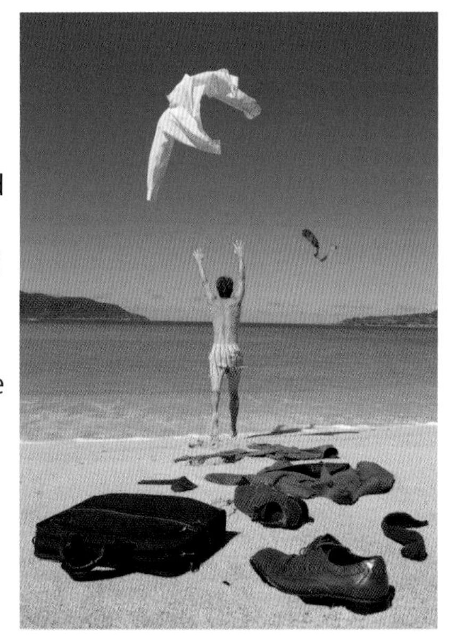

Holidays – These will be detailed in the contract. Most full-time adult workers are entitled to a minimum of 5.6 weeks of annual leave. In addition to this, employees can take reasonable time off to perform public duties, such as jury service, local councillors attending council meetings, and members of a school's board of governors attending school committee meetings.

Exceptional circumstances – If an employee has suffered a bereavement of a close family member, then it is expected that they should have at least three days compassionate leave. This may not be written into a contract of employment, but it is an area where an employer is expected to show a duty of care towards employees.

Career development – This is another area where an employer has a duty of care towards an employee. It is widely accepted that lifelong learning is crucial and an employer shouldn't stop staff from having access to training. This could be through sessions held in the workplace or by making sure that employees have the opportunity to go to organised classes outside of work.

Activity

Create a spider diagram to show the reasons why it is important for an employee to be given a contract of employment for a job.

The responsibilities of an employer

An employer has a duty of care to protect the health, safety and well-being of their employees. There are some basic work rights that everyone is entitled to, from their first day of work. Employers are responsible for making sure that the following are available to their employees:

- the National Living Wage.
- working time rights (such as breaks and holidays).
- health and safety protection.
- the right to join a trade union.
- protection from discrimination, bullying or harassment.
- equality of opportunity in the workplace.

In addition to these obligations, employers should also encourage a working environment where staff feel valued. They should provide adequate training and the opportunity for career development. Employers should consult employees on issues that may affect them and ensure employees can easily raise any concerns they might have.

Employers should also consider requests for flexible working arrangements and try to accommodate these where possible. They must grant maternity/paternity leave and pay, and allow staff to return to the same job afterwards.[2]

[1] National Living Wage for workers aged 25 and over. National Minimum Wage for workers aged 24 and under.

[2] For maternity leave, this is provided that the employee has been on leave for 26 weeks or less.

Further thinking

Visit the following website to find out about the Real Living Wage:
www.livingwage.org.uk/what-real-living-wage

- What is the Real Living Wage?
- What are the difference between the National Living Wage and the Real Living Wage?
- How can businesses benefit from paying the Real Living Wage to their employees?
- Find examples of employers who are paying the Real Living Wage.

Health and safety

Health and safety is all about reducing the risk of injury or illness because of their work. Health and safety is the responsibility of everyone in the workplace but it's the employer who has a legal duty to make sure that the health and safety laws are kept.

The Health and Safety at Work (Northern Ireland) Order 1978 is the main legislation that applies to all workplaces in Northern Ireland. The **Health and Safety Executive for Northern Ireland** is responsible for making sure these regulations are carried out and can inspect places of work.

Under this legislation, employers must decide what could potentially injure an employee or lead to ill health, as a result of their work. This is known as a **risk assessment**. These assessments can help employers to focus on what the health and safety issues *could* be in their workplace.

The law does not expect employers to eliminate all risks, but to protect their employees as far as possible. Employers must also make sure that all their staff are trained in health and safety procedures, how to use equipment provided by the workplace, know where to receive first aid treatment and are clear about what to do in an emergency.

The responsibilities of an employee

Rights and responsibilities should always be a two-way process. In the workplace, an employee has rights that must be met. In return, an employee also has responsibilities towards their employer and co-workers. Some employee responsibilities will be outlined in their contract and these must be kept. However, the law also says that an employee has certain duties and obligations, even if they are not mentioned in their contract.

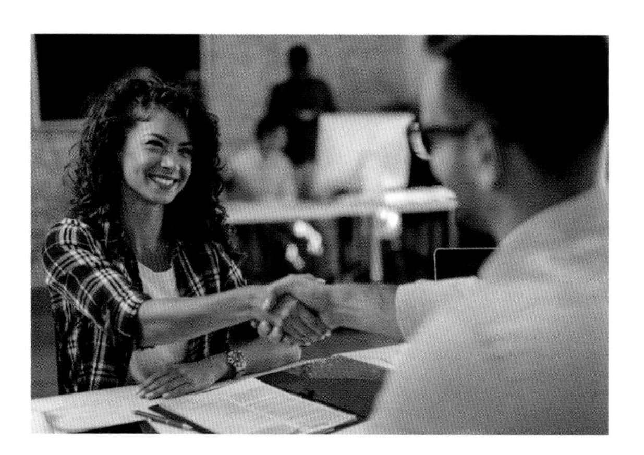

What can an employer expect from an employee?

- **Loyalty** – Employees shouldn't pass on any confidential information about their employer. Employees also have a duty not to compete in business against their employer while working for them as an employee. If an employee has to use the employer's property, then they should look after it carefully.
- **Honesty** – Employees have a duty to be honest. This includes not telling lies or withholding information (such as criminal convictions) in their application, not taking bribes related to their work, and not stealing from their employer. Taking goods or materials home from work, unless they have permission to do so, counts as stealing.
- **Reliability** – Time keeping is an important issue. Even the most conscientious worker can face a transport problem occasionally, but an employee shouldn't be continually late for work or take longer breaks than necessary. If an employer often has to

find people to cover for an employee because of their poor punctuality, they are not likely to be a good investment! Unwell employees are entitled to time off work, but this shouldn't be abused. Employees are expected to take time off sick only if they are genuinely too ill to work.

- **Good work ethic** – Employees should work to the best of their ability and try to have a positive attitude to work. Employers like workers to have a good work ethic and do their best to complete tasks within a realistic time frame. An employee who makes little effort to meet deadlines could cost their employer money or even lose them business.

Think about

Do you have a part-time job? If so, do you think you show any of these qualities at work?

Health and safety

Health and safety in the workplace is the responsibility of everyone. An employer has a legal duty to meet the necessary regulations, but all employees have responsibilities, too. These responsibilities include:

- taking care with their own health and safety.
- taking care not to put other employees or members of the public at risk through their behaviour.
- cooperating with their employer and making sure they follow the health and safety policies for their workplace.
- following the training they received when using any equipment in work.
- telling their employer if there is a medical reason why they may not be able to do their job properly, especially if they drive or operate machinery as part of their work.
- not misusing any equipment that has been provided to keep people safe.

Activity

- Using a computer, design a health and safety leaflet suitable for new employees in a workplace of your choice.
- Your leaflet should outline the health and safety responsibilities of both the employer and the employee.
- Remember to tailor your leaflet to the workplace you have chosen.

A code of conduct in the workplace

A code of conduct sets out how an organisation expects everyone to behave in the workplace. It applies to both employers and employees, and it helps to establish clear boundaries about what is and what is not acceptable at work. New employees are usually given a copy of the code of conduct and might be asked to sign a document stating that they have received and read it. A code of conduct can make life easier for everyone in the workplace. For example, if there is a dress code, employees know what to wear to work and can dress appropriately.

A code of conduct will vary according to the nature of the business and the ethics of the organisation. However, here are some of the guidelines that are typical in many workplaces:

- **Respect for identity and diversity** – Remarks about a person's race, ethnic origin, religion or sexuality are inappropriate, whether said in jest or to intentionally bully and intimidate. Everyone in the workplace should be treated with respect.
- **Responsible behaviour** – This could involve the sensible use of tools and equipment, and not causing harm to themselves, a colleague or property. Responsible behaviour in a code of conduct may also prohibit the misuse of alcohol and drugs in the workplace.
- **Dress code** – If an occupation or workplace has a uniform, then employees will be expected to wear this correctly. For some jobs, the dress code may include essential safety items, such as hard toe boots or hard helmets. If employees wear their own

clothes, it can be helpful to have examples of what is meant by 'smart' or 'business' dress to avoid any confusion. A dress code may also include a ban on clothing such as trainers, sportswear or any item of clothing with an offensive slogan.

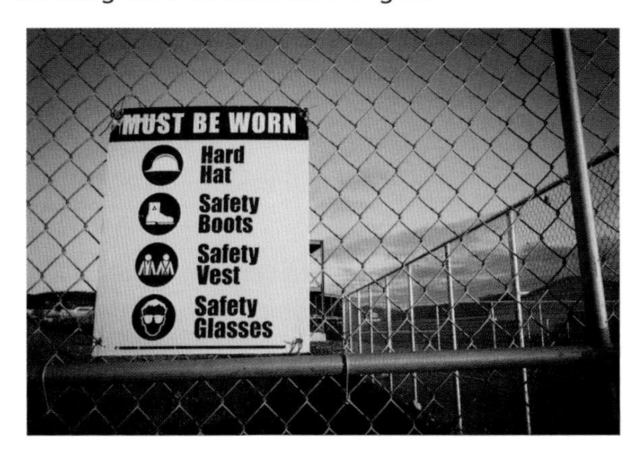

- **Social media use** – A code of conduct for social media use outlines for employees what is safe, professional and appropriate online behaviour. This is especially important if social media is used as part of an employee's work, rather than simply being a social activity during rest breaks.
- **Mobile phone use** – Some organisations don't allow their employees to use mobile phones at work, as they could be a distraction or a health and safety risk. For example, a code of conduct may state that phones are not to be visible and should be on silent during work hours, or that work mobile phones should only be used for genuine business purposes.

- **Maintaining confidentiality** – It is important for employees to be trusted with confidential or sensitive information relating to the organisation or its clients. A code of conduct may say that an employee is not to use any information for personal gain or financial benefit, or not to pass it on to anyone else.

The impact of not meeting responsibilities

Employers

It is important for employers to meet the responsibilities expected by their employees. Failing to meet the basic work rights or duty of care for their employees could result in employees:

- feeling unhappy or undervalued.
- becoming less productive or refusing to work.
- making a complaint or raising a grievance.
- making a claim of discrimination or unfair treatment.
- claiming compensation if they are injured or ill as result of work.

This could lead to the employer's organisation:

- being investigated by a public authority or statutory organisation, such as the Equality Commission for Northern Ireland.
- being prosecuted.
- facing negative publicity.
- being impacted financially, for example, if it has to pay legal fees or compensation, or if negative publicity affects their business.

Employees

It is important for employees to meet the responsibilities expected by their employers. Not doing so can affect everyone in their organisation. For example, if someone is lazy or a poor timekeeper, this can have a negative impact on the overall productivity of the company, and even affect profits. It can also lead to poor relationships with other employees, who may feel they have to do extra work to compensate.

If employees don't meet the responsibilities expected by their employers, they may have broken the terms and conditions of their contract, which could result in some form of disciplinary action. There are two types of consequence for this:

1. **Internal action** – This action is usually taken for issues of **reliability** and poor **work ethic**. The first stage might be an informal warning, where the matter is discussed with the employee. If the problem continues, or there are other issues, then formal disciplinary action could follow. This might include a verbal warning, written warning, or could even result in dismissal.

2. **Legal action** – If matters can't be handled internally, legal action may need to be taken. This is most common for issues of **loyalty** and **honesty**, for example, an employee passing on confidential information that damages the company or stealing from their employer. In severe cases, legal action could result in an employee being sued for damages or even imprisoned.

Developing positive working relationships

It is important to have good relationships in the workplace, as they can lead to happier and more productive employees. Positive working relationships, including respect for colleagues and successful ways of managing conflict, could be achieved through the following:

- **Participating in staff training** – Employees will have their own strengths and weaknesses in their workplace skills. A staff training programme can help all staff to develop the individual skills they need to improve. If there is something that everyone needs to know, such as how to operate a new piece of machinery, then staff training can provide everyone with the relevant skills. When employees are trained to do their work effectively, this can help to reduce conflict in the workplace.
- **Complying with equality employment legislation** – It is important for employees to know that their rights at work are respected. This can lead to positive working relationships and help to minimise conflict between employers and employees. Some examples of employment legislation in Northern Ireland are:
  - ***The Sex Discrimination (Northern Ireland) Order 1976 (amended 1998)***, which ensures that an employer cannot treat a person less favourably because of their sex.
  - ***The Race Relations (Northern Ireland) Order 1997***, which protects all racial groups in the workplace.
  - ***The Disability Discrimination Act 1995***, which protects people from discrimination if they have a disability that is long term and affects their ability to do day-to-day activities.
- **Complying with workplace policies** – The previous section on code of conduct in the workplace shows how potential conflict and poor relationships can be avoided if everyone knows what is expected of them at work. Policies should be communicated clearly in the workplace and respected by everyone.
- **Sharing good practice** – Everyone has something that they are particularly good at in work. By sharing this with others, everyone can increase their skills and capabilities. Sharing best practices with colleagues helps to build relationships and trust, and can also help to reduce duplication of effort.
- **Promoting a positive working atmosphere** – This can be achieved by having a positive attitude towards work and developing resilience when there are set backs and problems. Employees who celebrate each other's success, show gratitude and help each other at work can create a pleasant workplace where everyone works to the best of their capabilities. In such an atmosphere, any conflicts that do arise between employees are more likely to be resolved swiftly and have a satisfactory outcome.

Assessment for learning

1. Name one law that protects employees from discrimination. [1]
2. Name one law that is concerned with health and safety in the workplace. [1]
3. Describe two guidelines that might be found in a workplace code of conduct. [4]
4. Explain two ways that an employer can show a duty of care towards employees. [4]
5. Discuss the consequences for employees who do not meet their responsibilities in the workplace. [6]
6. Evaluate the importance of an employee receiving a contract of employment. [10]

Work-related stress

Feeling under pressure is part of everyday life and people often say they feel stressed when they have too much to do or other people are making demands on them. To a certain extent, stress can be positive and these feelings can help deadlines to be met and tasks to be completed. However, if stress causes a person to feel totally overwhelmed and unable to cope, this is a cause for concern. Work-related stress is becoming increasingly common. An estimated one in five people suffers from work-related stress, with half a million people reporting that they have become ill as a result.[1]

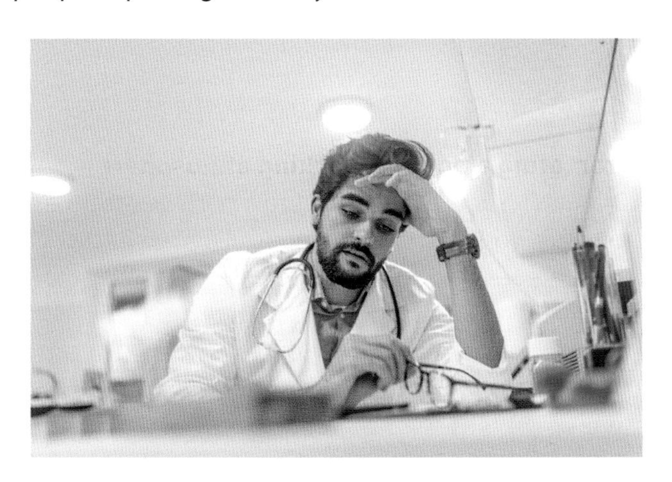

[1] Figures from HSE, cited in 'Tackling stress', National Education Union, https://neu.org.uk/advice/tackling-stress

The causes of employees' work-related stress

Some common causes of work-related stress include poor communication, a poor working environment, and employees doing a job that they have not had the proper training for. Stress may also be caused by an unhealthy work-life balance, which usually occurs when someone feels their work is too demanding on their time, leaving limited opportunities for leisure. Bullying or discrimination in the workplace can also cause stress and the anti-discrimination laws described on page 31 are designed to protect people in this situation. If a person has a disability and suffers stress because workplace conditions are difficult for them, an employer has a duty help them, for example by making adjustments.

The consequences of employees' work-related stress

There are many consequences of work-related stress for both the employee and the employer. People who are suffering from stress may become irritable, short-tempered or anxious. They may feel exhausted but be unable to sleep well because they are worried about work. They may suffer from frequent colds or infections as the body is unable to cope with the demands placed upon it. This might mean that employees need to take time off work, which can cause more stress if they are worried about falling behind. People suffering from stress may find it difficult to concentrate and make mistakes in their work. It can also negatively affect an employee's productivity and job satisfaction.

For an employer, all this can mean increased costs if there are more absences from work, a less productive workforce and a greater turnover of staff.

Ways of dealing with work-related stress

- **Improved planning and organisation** – A person suffering from work-related stress can help themselves by making sure that time at work is as productive as possible. For example, there could be a more efficient way of doing something or perhaps responsibility could be shared with others.

- **Discussion with employer** – An employee should discuss their concerns with their line manager or human resources manager, perhaps with a view to exploring a more manageable workload.
- **Advice from outside agencies** – There are organisations that can offer support and counselling for work-related issues, such as a trade union. GPs can also offer advice.
- **Counselling** – Some employers offer counselling services for employees. This can help employees identify what is making them stressed and make them feel more valued.
- **Taking care of yourself** – It is important for anyone suffering from stress to look after their body and mind by eating well, getting enough sleep, keeping fit and avoiding drugs and alcohol. Making sure they have enough time to themselves each week for leisure activities (a healthy work-life balance, see pages 72–73) can also be beneficial.
- **Absence from work** – It may be necessary for an employee to take time off work in order to recover from stress, or even consider an alternative job or career change.

The roles of trade unions

A trade union is an organisation made up of members (a membership-based organisation) and its membership must be made up mainly of workers. Trade unions have the following roles:

Protecting employees' rights

A trade union represents the rights of employees in the workplace, ensuring that employers meet their legal obligations and responsibilities, such as paying employees at least the National Living Wage, respecting working time rights, and providing health and safety protection. If someone makes a formal complaint against a person in the context of their job, then a trade union will represent the employee. There are different trade unions for different professions and the unions specialise in the issues that affect their particular workers.

Promoting positive working relationships

Trade unions have an important role to play in making workplaces better environments for both employers and employees. They do this by promoting positive working relationships between the two. They can work with employers to negotiate salaries and secure favourable working conditions on their members' behalf. This is particularly useful if there is an issue with either.

Trade unions try to develop close working relationships with employers. This sometimes takes the form of a partnership agreement between the employer and the trade union, which identifies their common interests and objectives. If a major change was needed in the workplace, such as a large-scale redundancy, then trade unions would be involved in the discussion.

Providing benefits to their members

Trade unions can provide additional benefits to members outside of the workplace, such as legal and financial advice. Trade unions may also provide education facilities and consumer benefits, such as discounted rates on mortgages and insurance.

Promoting health, safety and well-being in the workplace

Trade unions promote health, safety and well-being in the workplace by making sure that employers follow health and safety regulations. Trade unions have the right to carry out workplace health and safety inspections, can give valuable advice to employers about potential hazards and can provide assistance in carrying out risk assessments. They can also listen to concerns from workers and investigate possible hazards and dangerous incidents at work.

Positive impacts of trade unions in the workplace

Trade unions have had a significant impact in most workplaces, by protecting employee's rights, negotiating salaries and securing favourable conditions of employment. If workers feel happy and protected, with secure contracts, sick pay and other benefits, then there is less turnover of staff. This is good for employers who have a more stable and reliable workforce.

Negative impacts of trade unions in the workplace

However, trade unions can also have some drawbacks. Trade unions are there to represent workers, but they also cost employees money, as membership fees have to be paid. All members of a trade union must be united, so if the majority of members decide to go on strike to pressurise their employers, all members must strike, even if they don't agree. Members who refuse to do so may be fined by their union. Strike action can cost companies money and have a negative effect on these businesses. If this causes a business to close, this could result in redundancies. Powerful trade unions can negotiate for higher wages but if wages are forced too high, this could also cause unemployment.

Assessment for learning

1. Name one responsibility that an employee has towards an employer. [1]
2. Name one responsibility that an employer has towards an employee. [1]
3. Describe two causes of work-related stress. [4]
4. Explain two ways of coping with work-related stress. [4]
5. Discuss how a positive atmosphere can be created in the workplace. [6]
6. Evaluate the role of trade unions in the workplace. [10]

Further thinking

Use the Internet to find out the name of a trade union that represents each of the following professions:

Nurses • Physiotherapists • Engineers • Electricians • Teachers

Choose one profession and research the benefits and drawbacks of being in a trade union.

CHAPTER 3D
Social Responsibility of Businesses

Chapter Summary

In this chapter you will be studying:

- **The ways that businesses can demonstrate social responsibility.**
- **The benefits to businesses of being socially responsible.**

How businesses can demonstrate social responsibility

Social responsibility is when the government, groups and individuals in society act in a way that benefits everyone. There is the underlying idea that there is the obligation to behave in an ethical way, which also involves taking environmental concerns into consideration. There is a growing awareness that businesses and workplaces have an important role to play in taking social responsibility.

Addressing environmental issues

There are some environmental issues of particular concern to businesses and a range of positive action that they can take to show social awareness:

- **Promoting energy efficiency in the workplace** – Saving energy can save money for a business. For example, bills could be reduced by investing in energy efficient appliances; encouraging employees to turn off lights and computers at the end of the day; and turning off the heating at the weekend.
- **Using renewable energy** – Most of the energy used in the UK comes from non-renewable fossil fuels, such as coal, oil or gas. Businesses could investigate using a source of renewable energy, such as solar, wind or wave power, which could reduce the amount of greenhouse gases that are produced. Many scientists believe that global warming is being advanced by greenhouse gases.

- **Being responsible about waste** – All businesses produce waste, so dealing with it responsibly is important. They could **reduce** waste by buying fewer single-use items and purchasing goods with less packaging. Using emails as much as possible can reduce the use of paper, as can printing on both sides for documents. A simple example of how

businesses can **reuse** is to provide water fountains where employees can refill their own water bottles, instead of using plastic cups or buying bottled water. Reducing and reusing are the best options but **recycling** is also important. Recycling bins should be prominent in the workplace and employees should be made aware of what items should go into them. There are financial benefits in reducing, reusing and recycling too. Businesses can reduce the amount of landfill tax they pay and might also attract customers by showing that they are environmentally friendly.

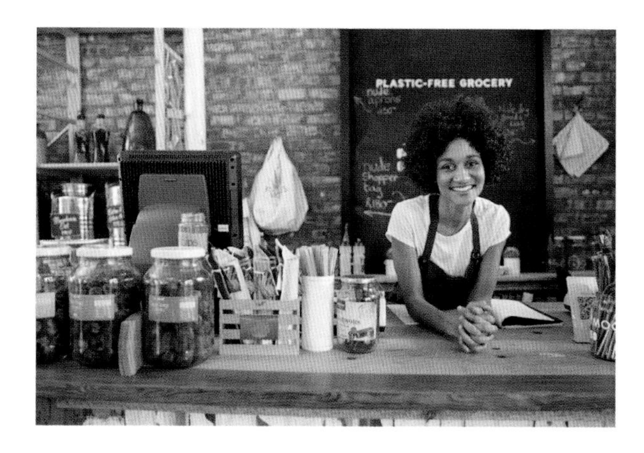

- **Buying responsibly –** Businesses could try to buy goods that have come from a sustainable source and choose suppliers that use less packaging and create less waste. They could also use goods that have been produced locally, which would cut down on the fuel needed for transport and help to boost the local economy. If businesses do buy from overseas, they could make sure that the products they buy have been fairly traded and don't involve the exploitation of people.

Further thinking

- Choose a local business in your area.
- Find out what work it does and how it operates.
- Does the business take any action to address environmental issues?
- Suggest some ways that it could reduce, reuse and recycle.

Supporting the local community

By getting involved in the local area, businesses can improve community relations and also motivate their staff to show social responsibility. This can lead to team participation and help to build interpersonal skills. It can also be beneficial for businesses to get involved in an activity related to their product or service, to improve their public image. For example, a restaurant could provide food to a local charity working with the homeless, while a local building firm could offer free labour or materials to community projects. There are many ways that a business can show social responsibility in their local area, such as:

- **Sponsoring local sports teams or local projects** – This might involve providing sports kit or equipment for a team, or perhaps funds for a special event, such as a competition or tour. A business might get involved with local projects, such as a clean-up event or supporting a local charity. Employees may be encouraged to volunteer in community projects or fundraise for a local charity.
- **Voucher schemes** – These schemes are often operated by supermarkets. For a set amount of money spent on shopping in the store, a discount voucher is given. Other vouchers can be collected to exchange for equipment (such as computers, instruments or sports gear) for schools or youth groups.
- **Scholarship programmes** – Many businesses use their money to help students gain qualifications without the financial burden. Some businesses will pay a student's tuition fees without expecting anything in return, apart from good publicity. Others will require the student to work for them in the holidays or for a period of time after their

course finishes. An apprenticeship helps students gain qualifications while also being paid a wage. It involves the student working for an employer for part of the week and also attending college for one or two days. A degree apprenticeship combines full-time paid work and part-time university study. The business will sponsor the young person by paying the tuition fees for their course and a wage.

- **Work experience placements** – Work experience placements are a valuable way for school and college students to gain an insight into the world of work or the demands of a particular career. A business needs to invest time and effort into making the experience a positive one for the student. Being known as an organisation that supports the interests of young people can boost a business's public image.
- **Encouraging the use of local products** – When businesses source local products, this can benefit the local economy and the environment. The products are also more attractive to potential customers and it's another way for businesses to improve their public image.

Further thinking

Choose a large multinational company.

- Find out what work it does and how it operates.
- Does it show social responsibility towards the environment and/or the local community?
- Can you suggest any other ways that it could show social responsibility?

Benefits to businesses of being socially responsible

Many people are starting to realise the importance of businesses acting responsibly towards employees, the community and the environment. When businesses show social responsibility, it's good for the local community, good for the environment and also for the business itself. Some of these benefits include:

Increased publicity

By being active in the local community, businesses can raise their profile in a positive way. If a business sponsors a local sports team or project, then this is an opportunity to display their company name and logo on a banner, sports kit or other equipment. Consumers may start to link a brand or name with a good cause and if it's one they support, they will be more likely to buy the product. If a business has a reputation for acting on environmental issues, this can also help to create a positive image. For example, Tesco are working in partnership with WWF (World Wide Fund for Nature) to encourage customers to eat more sustainably.

Improved sales

Having a social awareness may attract more customers and therefore the business will make more profit. Many people are aware of the need to use their purchasing power in a responsible way and are happy to support businesses who share this aim. Some customers are willing to pay more for a product if they know it has been ethically produced or if some of the profits are going to a good cause.

Costs are lowered

Environmental initiatives, such as recycling or energy efficiency, could work out cheaper for businesses, therefore saving them money. Some employers now offer incentives to employees to be environmentally friendly at work. A worker who is wasteful with resources is not helping the environment and costing their employer money.

Better community relations

A company that is active in the local area will be viewed positively by the community, again leading to increased sales and rising profits. A responsible business that has a good reputation in the local area will also be more attractive to potential investors, leading to the possibility of the business developing.

Attracting potential employees

A business that has a positive image can also gain a reputation as a good company to work for. With an increased awareness of social responsibility, many people want to be employed by a company that shares their ideals. By being socially responsible, a business can attract employees who believe in protecting the environment, supporting the local community or supporting a good cause.

Teamwork

Role play

Work in groups of about six for this exercise, with each person in the group taking on one of the following roles. Role play the meeting, with each person taking a turn to present their view.

The new shopping centre

A small town is to be the focus of a new development – a shopping centre. A large supermarket is keen to open one of its stores there and will be main retailer. The supermarket and shopping centre will bring jobs to the area and make a greater choice of products available locally to residents. However, a row of old cottages will have to be demolished, as well as a small area of woodland, to build the new shopping centre. Feelings about the project are mixed in the town and a meeting is held in a local community centre to hear people's views.

The people

- **Jack** has owned and run Jackie's Corner Shop for the last 30 years. He is very concerned about the new supermarket, fearing it will force him out of business.

- **Ms Smith** is the public relations officer for the supermarket. It's her job to promote the new venture as much as possible and ensure good relations with the local community. The last thing she wants is any bad publicity or local people protesting as the building work is about to go ahead.

- **Nancy** is fed up with being stuck at home now her children are in primary school. She would love a part-time job and welcomes the idea of the new shopping centre.

- **George** has lived in the cottages all his life. He does not want to move and thinks a new shopping centre is the last thing the town needs. He is also concerned that local businesses will lose their livelihood.

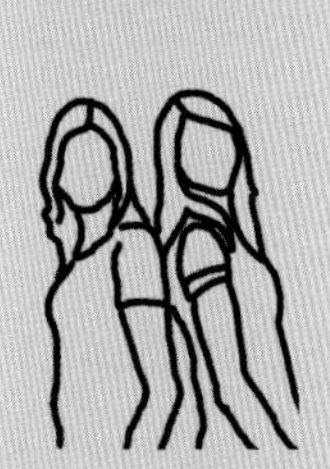

- **Aisling** and **Ciara** are teenage sisters who think it will be brilliant to have some decent shops locally without having to spend a fortune on bus fares. They are also hoping there might be Saturday jobs available in one of the new shops.

- **Kevin** runs a market garden business, supplying local greengrocers with fruit and vegetables. He has mixed feelings about the new centre. If his local buyers go out of business it will affect him badly. On the other hand, the supermarket has promised to buy local produce so the opportunity to sell to them might be very good for his business.

Assessment for learning

1. Write down one way that a workplace can promote energy efficiency. [1]
2. Write down one advantage for a business of using local products. [1]
3. Describe one benefit of a work experience placement. [2]
4. Explain two ways that businesses can address environmental issues. [4]
5. Using the information in the Source and your own knowledge, analyse the benefits of businesses showing social responsibility in the local area. [6]

Source

Many organisations, large and small, are realising the importance of ethical business practices. Showing social responsibility in this way is good for the planet, employees, customers and the local community. Many businesses are finding ways to reduce their impact on the environment by managing waste responsibly and being careful with their consumption of natural resources. Businesses can also play a positive role in local communities by promoting employee volunteering and getting involved in fundraising for projects in the area.

CHAPTER 3E
Exploring Self-employment

Chapter Summary

In this chapter you will be studying:

- **The importance of an entrepreneur carrying out research before starting up a business:**
  - **researching the need for a product or service.**
  - **funding options for the business.**
  - **marketing and promoting the product or service.**
  - **product or service placement.**
- **The advantages and disadvantages of being self-employed.**
- **The support provided by the government and non-government agencies for new and developing businesses.**

The qualities of an entrepreneur

An enterprising person is usually highly-motivated and creative, often setting up projects and seeking new opportunities. If a person with these enterprising qualities goes into business, then the result is likely to be an **entrepreneur**.

An entrepreneur has an idea for a new venture and sees an opportunity that others do not recognise. They are willing to take responsibility for any risks involved and for the final outcome of the enterprise.

Starting up in business

Thousands of people start their own business each year. Some do it because they have had a great idea and have spotted a gap in the market, while others like the idea of being their own boss. Another reason is the possibility of making lots of money. Whatever the reasons for starting a business, it's very important to make careful plans and prepare thoroughly.

Careful research is required in the following areas:

The need for the product or service

An entrepreneur must consider if there is a gap in the market for the product or service they have to offer. If there are others already in business, an important question is: What is its unique selling point and how will it be able to stand out from its competitors? Researching the need for the product or service will also include the potential target group: Will it have universal appeal or will it be targeted at a particular group of people?

Products and services

People require different products and services to satisfy their needs and wants. A **product** is an item that is bought by a customer, such as a phone or pair of shoes. A **service** is an activity that is carried out for a customer, such as childcare or computer repairs.

Funding options for the business

It is important for an entrepreneur to research funding options when considering a new business venture. There may be a considerable outlay needed to purchase materials and equipment, have a website professionally designed and buy or hire transport. Rent for business premises may also need to be covered. The funding might come from an entrepreneur's personal savings, a loan from a bank, or backing from investors willing to support the new product or service. There are also government agencies that can offer advice, support and financial backing, depending on the size and nature of the business.

Providing the product or service

Careful thought needs to be given to the design of the product or service. It is important to have something that will have an impact and is instantly appealing to potential customers. Thought will need to be given to features and functions, whether it's to be a basic, low cost item, or very high tech with plenty of gadgets. When offering a service, rather than a product, similar principles apply: Will the service be aimed at customers who want a basic service and low prices? Or is it aiming to attract people who are prepared to pay more for something if they feel they are getting top quality service?

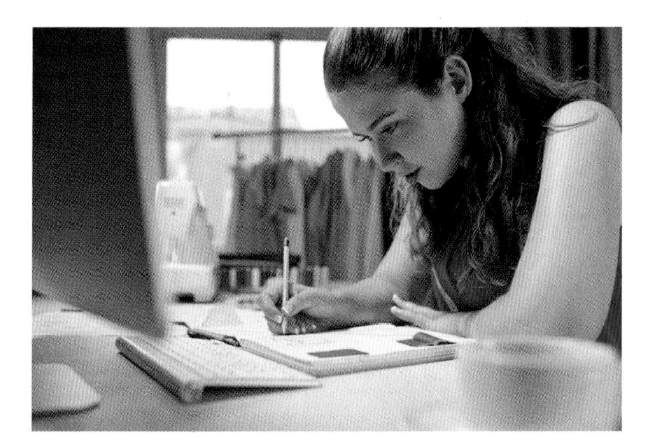

Marketing and promoting the product or service

The next stage is to market the goods or service. The 4 Ps are often used to provide a basic starting point for new businesses:

- ***Product*** – What is the product and how does it meet the needs of its potential customers? Any special or unique qualities need to be considered. At this stage, a name for the business, product or service will need to be decided on.
- ***Price*** – The price at which a product or service is sold is a crucial factor in whether it will sell. Careful thought will need to be given to the cost of production, what profit margins are expected and the price of similar products already on the market. It is essential to find out what potential customers are prepared to pay in order to price something effectively.

- ***Place*** – This refers to where and how customers will buy a product or use a service. With many businesses, this will mean premises, such as a shop or hairdressing salon, whereas an electrician or garden designer will carry out their business at the customer's own home. With increased use of the Internet for buying and selling, 'place' can mean home delivery following a purchase made online.
- ***Promotion*** – This is about communicating with customers so they will want to buy from the business. How will this be done and what form of advertising will be used? To promote successfully, a business needs to know about your customers. A local fast food outlet might post an attractive menu through the letter box of homes in the area, while a more specialist product might be advertised in a magazine. Most businesses now promote their products or services on a website or social media.

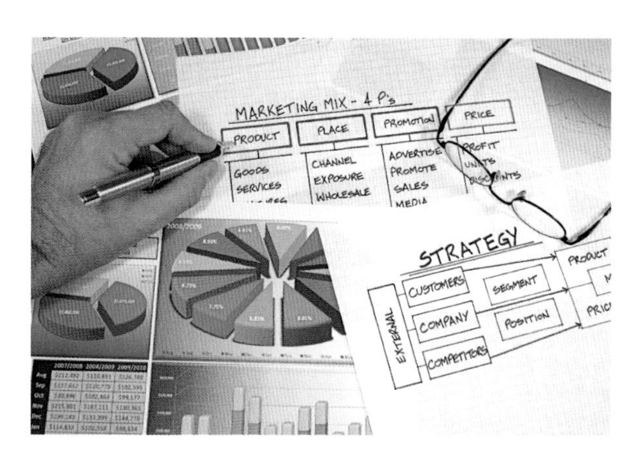

Product or service placement

The final consideration involves where the goods or services are going to be made available to customers, to ensure maximum success with sales. The product may need to be transported from its place of manufacture to where it will be sold, so careful research will be needed on the best method.

If a business is offering a service, important questions will include: Where will it do business with its customers? Will they come to the business or will the service need to go to their home? Some manufacturers don't sell their own products directly to customers but sell to a sales outlet. This means they are not just selling goods from their own premises. For example, it's common for mass produced items, such as snack foods and magazines, to be sold through a large number of sales outlets. More specialised items may use a much smaller number of outlets.

 **Teamwork**

Working in a group, discuss the following questions:

- Why are some business ventures unsuccessful?
- What can make the difference between success and failure?

 **Teamwork**

Start your own business

You and your friends are going into business – you have a brilliant idea!

- Research your idea by working through the questions: What? Where? Who? Why?
- Produce a design for your goods or service and an advertisement to promote it.
- Determine how you will market your product by deciding on product, price, place and promotion.

Present your idea to the rest of the class.

Self-employment

A person who is self-employed makes their own income by working for themselves, rather than working for someone else and being paid a wage. Self-employment might mean a person works entirely alone, perhaps with members of the family helping out, or with a friend or business partner. Some self-employed people run their large successful businesses with a number of employees.

The opportunities of self-employment

- **You are your own boss** – The chance to make your own decisions about your working day, rather than be told what to do, appeals to many people.
- **You work your own hours** – Of course there may be customers to consider, appointments to be kept and deadlines to meet, but self-employment gives the possibility of more flexible working hours.
- **When you work hard at something you are doing it for yourself** – Some people feel that this is a big incentive and motivator with self-employment.
- **Self-employment is a challenge** – Self-employment is hard work and certainly not an easy option, but the challenge is what makes

it attractive to some people, as is the sense of achievement if it brings success.

- **The work is not repetitive** – In some salaried occupations, the same task is repeated over and over. With self-employment, one person may well do everything, so the work can be very varied.
- **You can be more creative and imaginative** – Some people like to try out new ideas and self-employment usually gives more freedom to express your creativity.
- **No one can make you redundant** – Self-employment is usually considered a risky option, but some people consider themselves to be more secure than if they were working for someone else.

The risks of self-employment

- **You may have to work long hours** – Many people who work for an employer can leave at a set time. This is not usually the case if you are self-employed. Work time may easily extend into leisure time.
- **Your income is uncertain** – With a salary you know how much to expect each month and can budget accordingly. Income from self-employment may be erratic, especially at the beginning.

- **You don't get paid for holidays or days off** – Employees are entitled to paid leave and sick pay if they are unwell. If a self-employed person takes time off, this could mean there is no income.
- **Equipment has to be maintained** – Most businesses, however small, need some sort of equipment, transport or machinery. Having to pay for repairs or replacements could eat into the profits.
- **Supplies have to be bought** – With self-employment there are much greater financial outlays than with salaried employment. Essential supplies may need to be bought before the work can be carried out, and payment received.
- **You might miss the social contact** – Although being employed is not just a chance to gossip with workmates, there is an important social side of working with others. People who are self-employed may miss out on this.
- **You have to organise your own taxes and National Insurance** – Employers take care of this for their employees. Self-employed people have to sort this out for themselves, unless their business is large enough to have an accountant.

Think about

Can you think of any other advantages or disadvantages of being self-employed?

Support for businesses in Northern Ireland

Examples of the support provided by government and non-government agencies for new and developing businesses:

The Department for the Economy

"The focus of [the department's] Enterprise Policy is on promoting enterprise and entrepreneurship and creating the necessary conditions that will enable businesses across all sectors of the economy to start and grow".

The Department for the Economy is a government department in the Northern Ireland Executive. Responsibilities include economic policy development, enterprise, innovation, energy, telecoms, tourism, health and safety at work, learning and research, skills training, and promoting good employment practice.

The Department for the Economy has four agencies:

1. **The Northern Ireland Tourist board** is responsible for promoting and marketing Northern Ireland as a tourist destination. This will increase the contribution tourism can make to the economy.

2. **The Health and Safety Executive for Northern Ireland** is responsible for promoting and enforcing health and safety at work. It carries out inspections of workplaces to make sure regulations are being followed.
3. **The Consumer Council** is responsible for protecting and promoting the interests of consumers in Northern Ireland.
4. **Invest Northern Ireland** is responsible for business support in Northern Ireland.

Information from: www.economy-ni.gov.uk. Contains public sector information licensed under the Open Government Licence v3.0.

Further thinking

- Visit www.economy-ni.gov.uk and choose three organisations that the Department for the Economy work with. Write a few sentences describing how they provide support for businesses in Northern Ireland.
- Visit www.economy-ni.gov.uk/about-dfe and research how InterTradeIreland and Tourism Ireland Limited are providing opportunities for businesses. Write a few sentences describing their work.

NI Business Info

"The official online channel for business advice and guidance in Northern Ireland"

NI Business Info gives comprehensive advice on starting, running and growing a business. Its website gives information to potential entrepreneurs on the following areas:

- **Before you start your business** – Advice on things to consider before starting a business and start-up support in Northern Ireland. The website for NI Business Info also gives a number of ideas for a start-up business, such as a pop-up shop, social enterprise or taxi service.
- **Start your business** – Advice on business structure, such as sole trader, business partnership or self-employed. Information is also given on finance and choosing the right premises for the business.
- **Running your start-up business** – Advice includes managing business finances, understanding tax and VAT, and how to protect business ideas.
- **Grow your start-up business** – The next step in expanding a business might be trading with other countries. Advice is given on importing, exporting and trading outside Northern Ireland. Strategies are suggested for other opportunities for growth, such as spotting new business opportunities.

Information from: www.nibusinessinfo.co.uk

Enterprise Northern Ireland

"The voice of enterprise for those supporting and developing small business in Northern Ireland."

Local Enterprise Agencies are independent, non-profit making companies set up to support small businesses and help to develop the local economy. Enterprise Northern Ireland (ENI) is the organisation that represents this network of local groups across Northern Ireland. ENI's vision is to contribute to the development of the Northern Ireland economy by supporting entrepreneurship and business enterprise. They do this at three levels:

- **Supporting** – ENI represents the interests of local enterprise agencies and small businesses. It makes sure the Northern Ireland Executive is fully briefed on relevant issues.
- **Networking** – ENI provides a range of services for members, such as networking events and continual professional development. It provides opportunities for entrepreneurs to learn from others in a similar situation.
- **Delivering** – ENI delivers programmes for businesses, such as Go For It, Social Enterprise Programme and Business Boot Camp. The programmes help small businesses access financial help through start-up loans.

Information from: www.enterpriseni.com

The Prince's Trust

"Youth can do it".

In the UK, around one in five young people are not in work, education or training. The Prince's Trust gives practical and financial support to the young people who need it most. They help to develop key skills, confidence and motivation so young people can gain qualifications, find employment, set up a community project or even start their own business.

The Prince's Trust runs programmes that encourage young people to take responsibility for themselves – helping them build the life they choose rather than the one they've ended up with.

The programmes offered by The Prince's Trust include:

- **Start your business** – This programme helps young people aged 18–30 to be their own boss, through the Prince's Trust training, mentoring and funding. There is also an online course to develop the skills needed for setting up in business.
- **Get a job** – Young people aged 16–30 can access free 'on the job' courses to help gain valuable experience. This programme gives the opportunity to work with top employers, such as the NHS and HSBC, and improve CV and interview skills.
- **Build your confidence** – A range of programmes is available for young people aged from 16–25 to develop skills and boost confidence. This might include spending 12 weeks gaining skills and experience on a community project to transform the local neighbourhood.

Information from: www.princes-trust.org.uk

Further thinking

Use the Internet to research sources of finance that might be available to an entrepreneur.

Assessment for learning

1. Write down what is meant by the term 'entrepreneur'. [1]
2. Name one quality of an entrepreneur. [1]
3. Describe two of the agencies that make up the Department for the Economy. [4]
4. Explain two areas of research for an entrepreneur starting up in business. [4]
5. Discuss how government and non-government agencies can support new businesses. [6]
6. Evaluate the opportunities and risks of self-employment. [10]

CHAPTER 3F
Personal Career Management

Chapter Summary

In this chapter you will be studying:

- **Career planning as a lifelong process:**
  - **reviewing and evaluating learning, progress and achievements.**
  - **setting goals and targets.**
  - **taking action.**
- **The personal skills, qualities and attitudes required for a chosen career.**
- **The benefits of making informed career choices.**
- **Developing decision-making strategies.**
- **External influences and their impact on young people's attitudes to education, training and employment.**

Career planning as a lifelong learning process

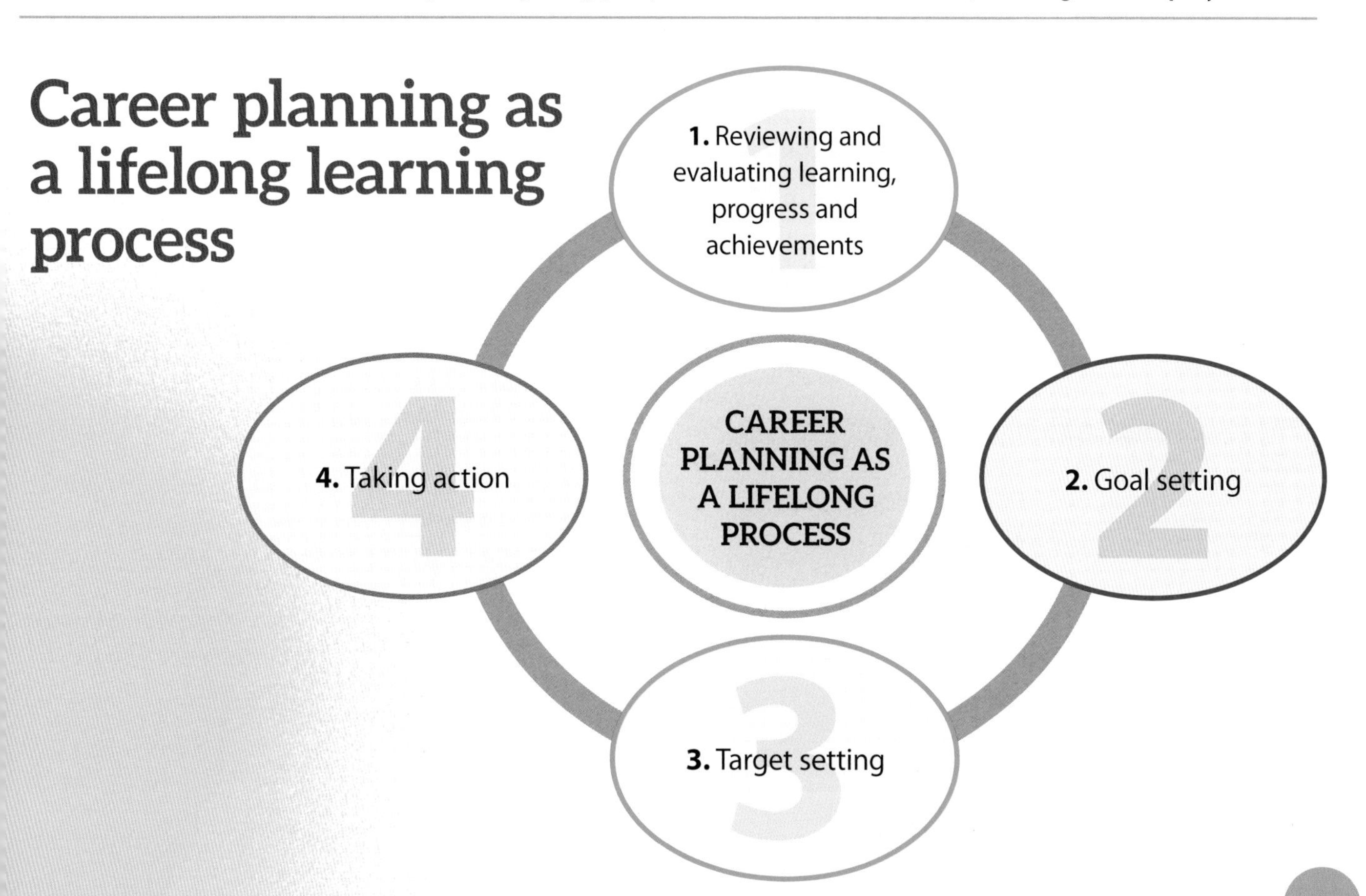

Reviewing and evaluating learning, progress and achievements

Lifelong career planning can put you in charge of your life and work, by helping you to decide how and when to make changes that will benefit you. It involves reviewing and evaluating progress, setting goals and targets, and taking action. Career planning involves self-reflection and asking yourself questions, such as: What do I want out of life? How do I get there? To do this, you must **review** where you are now: What are my interests and values? What are my strengths and skills? What are my achievements and qualifications? What has been less successful?

Next you need to **evaluate** your progress: How did I get here? How did I develop my interests and values? How did I gain my strengths, skills and achievements? What have I learned? How could I improve my performance? You might find it helpful to discuss these questions with a teacher, careers adviser or parent. Reviewing and evaluating your progress is a continual part of lifelong career planning. Remember that your plans may change over time, so it's important to be flexible.

Setting goals and targets

The next step is deciding where you want to go next and what you want to achieve – this is your goal. A goal is the final aim, the end result that you want to accomplish. Goals don't happen immediately or by themselves. You must do the things that enable them to happen, usually several things in several steps. These stages towards the goal are the targets. A goal will tend to be long term, while the targets to reach it will be medium or short term.

Both goals and targets take careful planning but first of all, you need to decide what your goal is. Perhaps you want to achieve good grades in your GCSEs, start an apprenticeship, study for A Levels, go to college or university, get a job, or own your own business – the list is endless depending on your ambitions and hopes for the future.

What is a SMART target?

Specific: A target should be straightforward and show clearly what you want to happen. It should also be something important to you or you will lack the motivation to achieve it.

Measurable: A successful target is one that is measurable. This means that you know how far away your target is and when it has been reached.

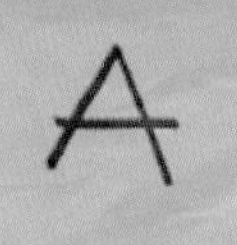

Attainable: A target should be realistic and achievable. If it is too difficult, it could easily result in failure, which is discouraging. A target needs to be a challenge, but not impossible.

Relevant: A target should be relevant to you. It needs to be worthwhile and in keeping with your wider targets.

Time based: There needs to be a time frame for the target to give you something to focus on – you need to start working towards your target now! However, make sure the time frame is realistic.

Taking action

The final step is to carefully plan how you will reach your goal, then put it into action. A series of appropriate short-term targets can help to work towards a long-term goal. Some people find that achieving goals and targets can be made manageable by working backwards. This means having a 'big picture' of what you want to do in life, then identifying the larger goals to help towards this. The next step is to break these down into smaller and smaller targets, which are short-term and achievable. Once you have your steps all planned out, it is time to put your plan into action.

Activity

John loves gaming and spends most of his free time online. He knows he is pretty unfit, but three of his friends have persuaded him to enter the Belfast Marathon with them as part of a relay team. The marathon is six months away.

Work out John's goal and set some targets to help him achieve this.

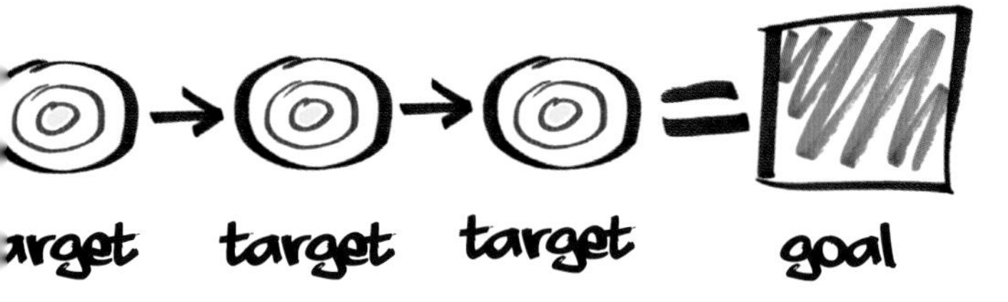

It is useful to regularly revisit your goals and targets. If you have achieved what you set out to do, then you need to consider the next stage. If you have partially met your targets, or been unsuccessful, then you need to give yourself something more realistic to work towards. It may be helpful to have someone to talk to and offer advice on your progress, such as a tutor in school.

Teamwork

Working in a group, discuss the following:

- What long-term and short-term goals do you have for your life?
- What targets do you have for getting there?

Activity

- Decide on a personal goal.
- Write down a series of targets that will help you achieve this goal.

The personal skills, qualities and attitudes required for a chosen career

In chapter 3B, you looked at the skills, qualities and attitudes required for a successful career (see pages 146–148). There are some employability skills that are universal. These include:

- Communication
- Teamwork
- Self-motivation
- Willingness to learn
- Loyalty and integrity
- Planning and organisation

However, specific careers will, of course, have their own requirements for skills, knowledge and personal competencies. This is why it's very important to make the right choices in your career planning, so what you achieve in now can equip you for the future.

Further thinking

Choose any three of the careers below.

- Using the Internet, research what skills, qualities and attitudes are needed for each.
- If you already have an idea of your chosen career, include this in your research.

Food scientist • Accountant • Electrician • Admin officer

Social worker • Game designer • Financial adviser

Insurance broker • Classroom assistant • Biochemist

Dancer • 3D designer • Sales adviser • IT technician

Editor • Human resources manager • HGV driver

Butcher • Radio presenter • Dog walker

Activity

Many employers choose to use the Internet to advertise their employment vacancies.

Look at the following examples. For each of the jobs advertised, describe the following:

- The skills and personal qualities the employer is looking for.
- Any additional skills that are not mentioned in the advertisement but you think would be an asset to the post.

Care assistant

Job duties: Deliver quality personal care to residents of the nursing home, supporting them with washing, dressing, eating and maintaining their hygiene, as well as ensuring they feel part of life in the home.

Experience: 1 year of care preferred. Training will be provided.

Hours: Full-time, shift pattern, including nights and weekends.

Nursery assistant

Job duties: Provide a stimulating, home-from-home environment for young children; assist with feeding and changing; plan activities; and liaise with parents.

Desirable skills: Genuine interest in children, good communication skills, flexibility, and good understanding of childcare and welfare issues.

Experience: A childcare qualification and experience in a similar role is preferred.

Hours: Full-time, 36 hours per week, worked over 4 days.

Sales assistant

Job duties: Assisting customers, operating tills, replenishing stock as required, maintaining high shop floor standards, meeting sales targets, and working as part of a team.

Experience: Experience within a retail environment is preferred.

Hours: Part-time, temporary, Christmas cover. Must be available for day, evening and weekend shifts.

Machine operator

Job duties: Operate production machinery in a busy factory, follow health and safety procedures, drive a forklift, work within a small team, and meet production targets and deadlines.

Experience: Production experience and a forklift licence is preferred.

Hours: Full-time, permanent, 36 hours per week, worked in 12-hour shifts. Includes weekend and night shifts.

The benefits of making informed career choices

Making informed choices is part of lifelong career planning. There are benefits in making informed choices at every stage along the way, whether you are making subject choices for GCSEs, deciding if further education is right for you, planning a career move or considering starting your own business.

The importance of careers advice

It is very important to take careers advice seriously. Careers advisers and careers teachers in school or college are knowledgeable about the current employment and further education situation. A careers teacher can help students to make decisions about their careers in some of the following ways:

- Students can discuss their likes and dislikes, and their personal capabilities. Based on this information, their careers teacher can then give advice on the jobs or courses that would suit them best.
- Careers teachers will be knowledgeable in all aspects of post-16 or post-18 courses and can suggest a course that is realistic. A teacher will be aware of what exams you are working towards and what you could aim for next.
- Careers teachers can give impartial advice to students so they are equipped to make their own decisions about their future.

Developing decision-making strategies

There are situations in life where there are important decisions to be made, which can have a lasting impact on future plans. Career planning is one of these. Having good decision-making strategies can be useful in helping you to select the right choice from a number of options. This might involve:

- **Gathering information** – When making a decision, it's important to be well-informed and know the facts.
- **Exploring the options** – Even if you think your mind is made up, consider all the different courses of action open to you.
- **Considering advantages and disadvantages** – It might be useful to make a list of the pros and cons.

- **Sharing your ideas** – Talk to a friend, family member or someone else who knows you well and get their opinion.
- **Evaluating your choice** – Weigh up all the information and advice then select the best course of action. Trust your judgement and stick to what you have decided.

Informed choices can help you to:

- make decisions that are right for you, that are realistic, and take into account your skills and abilities.
- do something you enjoy, rather than doing something because you have to.
- be mindful of your beliefs, morals and values when deciding on a career plan.
- work towards your long-term goals and ambitions for life and work.

External influences and their impact on young people's attitudes to education, training and employment

There are many external influences on a young person's attitude to education, training and employment, some of which can be positive and others which can be negative.

Family – Members of your family, such as a parent or older sibling, may try to influence you to choose the same career path as themselves – or try to put you off, if their experience has been negative. In some families, there is the expectation that children will be involved in the same line of work as their parents, perhaps even working for the family business. A family member might be a very positive role model, especially if they really enjoy their chosen career.

Friends – Friends can be good or poor role models. They can offer valuable advice, as they are often the people who know you best. However, some friends might want you to make the same choices as them, regardless of whether these choices are best for you. For example, a boyfriend or girlfriend may put pressure on you to study or get a job in the same town as them.

Teachers – Teachers and careers advisers may know your skills and capabilities very well and be in a good position to give help and advice. They can also offer up-to-date information on courses and employment opportunities, as well as arrange work experience.

Culture – Cultural influences on your career choices could come from your local area, ethnic group or social group. As with family, there may be expectations or limitations placed on you because of your background. Other cultural influences include how TV, films, social media and celebrities can influence career choices. Some successful and famous people might be good role models, while others may be linked with negative lifestyle choices.

Assessment for learning

1. Write down what the letter 'S' stands for in a SMART target. [1]
2. Name one skill that is important in the workplace. [1]
3. Describe two ways that a young person could achieve success in their GCSEs. [4]
4. Explain two influences on young people's career choices. [4]
5. Using the information in the Source and your own knowledge, analyse the importance of career planning. [6]
6. Evaluate the importance of professional advice when making decisions about careers and education. [10]

Source

Career planning is a lifelong process. A career plan can help you to identify your skills and interests, set career goals and take action to help you reach them. Having a career plan can help you check that your career is going in the right direction, as you gain the qualifications, skills and experience needed to move forward. Everyone can benefit from having a career plan, whether you are studying at school, ready to start work, or aiming for an important promotion.

Career planning puts you in charge of where your education and working life is heading. It is a road map to help you reach your career destination.

Glossary

Unit 1: Local and Global Citizenship

ASYLUM SEEKER: Someone whose claim for refugee status has not yet been determined. Not all asylum seekers are granted official refugee status.

BOYCOTT: A complete refusal to buy a product or take part in an activity as a way of registering a protest.

CIVIL SOCIETY: This term covers any organisation that isn't commercial or government, and includes independent organisations, such as NGOs, housing associations and religious groups. They help to look after people, protect their rights and improve health, education and living standards at home and overseas.

CONFLICT RESOLUTION: A range of methods for eliminating sources of conflict. It usually involves people talking to each other and working out a solution that is acceptable to everybody involved.

CULTURAL IDENTITY: The sense of belonging to a group. There are many different types of group that someone can relate to, including race, religion, nationality, language, gender, age and social class.

DEMOCRACY: A system of rule that should give equality and freedom to all citizens, and where everyone has equal access to power.

DEVOLVED GOVERNMENT (DEVOLUTION): A transfer of power from a higher level (such as the national government) to a lower level (such as the government of a particular region). Devolution can give greater responsibility to regional governments without the national government giving up its overall authority.

DISCRIMINATION: Being treated in a less favourable way than other people, usually because of culture, race, religion, gender, sexual orientation or disability.

EQUAL OPPORTUNITY: Everyone has the same chance as everyone else to receive an education or promotion at work. For example, a person should never be treated unfairly because of factors such as gender, age, race, religion or disability.

ETHNIC GROUP: Any group of people with a distinct cultural identity. Ethnicity can be defined by race, religion, language, food, music and traditions.

ETHNIC MINORITY: Any ethnic group who are relatively small in number in the area where they are living.

HUMAN TRAFFICKING: The trade of people, mostly for the purpose of sexual slavery, forced labour, prostitution or being forced to perform criminal acts.

IMMIGRANT: A person who comes to live in a foreign country.

IMMIGRATION: When people move into a country from another country.

LEGAL OBLIGATION: An action that must be carried out or a service that must be provided, as there is a law in place to make sure this happens.

LEGISLATION: Laws that have been made by the government.

LOBBYING: Bringing an issue to the attention of a local councillor, MLA or MP to encourage them to take action.

MARGINALISED: A person, or group of people, made to feel that they are excluded from society and therefore cannot play a full role.

MEDIA, THE: This term covers three main types of communication: print (newspapers and magazines), broadcasting (TV and radio) and the Internet.

MEDIATION: This involves a third party (the mediator) to help two or more people or groups to communicate on a difficult issue.

MIGRATION: The movement of people from one country to another. It can be permanent or temporary, and take place over long or short distances.

MULTICULTURALISM: When a community is made up of people from different cultural backgrounds

NON-GOVERNMENTAL ORGANISATION (NGO): A group that does not receive government funding and operates independently. Alternative names are 'Voluntary Organisation' or 'Charity'.

PREJUDICE: The word 'prejudice' means to 'pre-judge' someone without knowing anything about them. Prejudice is therefore a judgement based on ignorance.

PRESSURE GROUP: An organised group of people who aim to influence government policy, or the laws that they pass.

PROSTITUTION: A form of sexual exploitation that involves engaging in sexual activities in return for something beneficial, such as money, affection, drugs and alcohol, or somewhere to stay.

PUBLIC AUTHORITY: A group or organisation, such as a local council or Education Authority, that has been given official power to govern or administrate in the local community.

PUBLIC SERVICES: The services provided by the government to its citizens, such as education, healthcare, repairs to roads and collection of household waste.

RACISM: The belief that one race of people is superior or inferior to another. Racism can involve discrimination because of factors such as skin colour, language, nationality and culture.

SANCTION: An official action taken against a country to force it to obey international law. A sanction usually involves stopping trade, so the country cannot import any goods or sell its exports.

SCAPEGOAT: Someone who is blamed for the wrongs someone else has committed.

SECTARIANISM: The belief that one religious or political group (or sect) is superior or inferior to another (prejudice). It involves a dislike of the other group and discrimination against them.

SEXISM: Discrimination based on a person's gender.

SEXUAL EXPLOITATION: When an abuser uses their relationship or position of authority to take advantage of (exploit) someone and coerces them into taking part in sexual activities.

SOCIAL INEQUALITY: The unequal distribution of resources, opportunities and rights across society.

SOCIAL INJUSTICE: When individuals or groups are unfairly disadvantaged; this is often a consequence of social inequality.

STEREOTYPE: A crude mental picture that a person might have of someone from another culture. Stereotypes often assume that everyone from a particular group has the same characteristics.

REFUGEE: A person who has been forced to leave their country to escape war, persecution or natural disaster.

REFUGEE STATUS: This is a form of protection given to anyone who meets the definition of a refugee, including the right to remain in the country, and find employment or claim benefits.

THE TROUBLES: The three decades of political violence in Northern Ireland that took place towards the end of the last century.

Unit 2: Personal Development

ABSTINENCE: Making a positive decision not to do something, for example, drink alcohol or have sex.

ADOPTION: A legal procedure where all the responsibilities of a child's 'birth parents' are transferred to adoptive parent(s), who permanently raise the child as their own.

ANNUAL PERCENTAGE RATE (APR): The rate at which interest is charged on a loan.

ANOREXIA: An eating disorder where sufferers follow a strict diet, sometimes to the point of starvation.

ANXIETY: A feeling of unease, such as a worry or a fear about something.

ASEXUAL: A person with a lack of sexual attraction to any sex.

BALANCED DIET: A diet with the correct proportions of nutrients and food types to maintain good health.

BINGE EATING (or COMPULSIVE OVEREATING): This is a form of food addiction where the addict has no control over the amount of food consumed.

BISEXUAL: A person attracted to both males and females.

BLENDED FAMILY (or STEP-FAMILY): A family where one or both parents have children from a previous relationship, but they have combined to form a new family.

BODY IMAGE: This is how a person views their body and physical appearance; the feelings that arise from this can be positive or negative.

BUDGET: A plan for spending and saving, which balances expenses and the money that is available to spend.

BULIMIA: An eating disorder where sufferers make themselves vomit, or misuse laxatives, in an attempt to control their weight.

CHILD GROOMING: When someone establishes an emotional relationship with a child and gains their trust in preparation for sexual abuse or exploitation.

COMPULSIVE OVEREATING: This is a form of food addiction where the addict has no control over the amount of food consumed.

CREDIT CARD: A card that allows the card holder to borrow money in order to pay for goods and services.

CREDIT RATING: A calculation of a potential borrower's ability to pay back the money they wish to borrow. It is based on previous borrowing history, current financial situation and predicted future income.

DEBIT CARD: A card that gives direct access to a person's account; money is debited electronically when goods and services are paid for.

DEPRESSANT DRUG: A chemical substance that depresses the nervous system and which causes the body's reactions to slow down.

DEPRESSION: Persistent feelings of sadness, low mood or hopelessness for longer than a couple of weeks.

DOMESTIC ABUSE: Any type of controlling, threatening, violent or abusive behaviour between people in a relationship.

EXTENDED FAMILY: A family where there are more than two generations living together, for example, parents, children and grandparents.

FEMALE GENITAL MUTILATION (FGM): The cutting or altering of a girl's genitals for cultural reasons.

FOSTER FAMILY: Family care on a temporary basis for a child whose own parents are facing a crisis.

GENDER IDENTITY: This is the gender a person identifies with, regardless of the gender they were assigned at birth.

GRANDPARENT FAMILY: A family where the children are being raised by their grandparent(s) instead of their parent(s).

HALLUCINOGENIC DRUG: A chemical substance that causes the user to experience hallucinations; sometimes these can be very unpleasant.

HEALTH TRIANGLE: The combination of being in good physical, emotional and social health.

HETEROSEXUAL: A person who is attracted to someone of the opposite sex.

HOMOPHOBIA: A dislike or prejudice against anyone who is homosexual.

HOMOSEXUAL: A person who is attracted to someone of the same sex.

HUMAN TRAFFICKING: The trade of people, mostly for the purpose of sexual slavery, forced labour or being forced to perform criminal acts.

HYGIENE: Keeping hair and body clean through regular washing, bathing or showering.

IDENTITY THEFT: Stealing someone's personal or financial details with the intention of committing crime.

INTEREST ON A LOAN: The amount of extra money (in addition to the borrowed amount) that needs to be paid when repaying a loan.

MINDFULNESS: A person's awareness of their own feelings and what is going on in the world around them in the present moment.

MORTGAGE: A loan that is taken out over a long period of time and usually used to pay for property.

NON-BINARY: A person who does not identify with a specific gender.

NUCLEAR FAMILY: A family where two parents live with their biological children.

OBESITY: A medical condition where a person has become very overweight, which is having a negative effect on their health.

OPIATE DRUG: A chemical substance used to control severe pain. It blocks out feelings and makes the user appear cut off from the world.

PANSEXUAL: A person who is attracted to someone regardless of their sex or gender identity.

RESILIENCE: This is the ability to cope with difficulties in a positive way, avoiding any long-term negative impacts.

SELF-CONFIDENCE: A person's own opinion about their talents and abilities.

SELF-ESTEEM: The personal feelings that someone has about themselves.

SELF-WORTH: How a person rates their value in their relationships with other people.

SEXUAL ASSAULT: Any sexual act that a person does not consent to, or is forced into against their will.

SEXUAL EXPLOITATION: When an abuser uses their relationship or position of authority to take advantage of someone and persuades them to take part in sexual activity.

SEXUAL ORIENTATION: This term describes what sex or gender a person is attracted to.

SEXUALLY TRANSMITTED INFECTION (STI): An infection that is passed on through sexual activity or intimate touching.

SINGLE-PARENT FAMILY: A parent raising a child or children without a partner.

SOCIAL MEDIA: A collection of websites and apps that allow users to communicate, create and share information and images.

STEP-FAMILY (or BLENDED FAMILY): A family where one or both parents have children from a previous relationship, but they have combined to form a new family.

STIMULANT DRUG: A chemical substance that causes the body's functions to speed up.

STRESS: The degree to which a person feels overwhelmed or unable to cope as a result of unmanageable pressure.

TRANSGENDER: A person who identifies with a gender different to the sex (male or female) they were born with.

TRANSPHOBIA: A dislike or prejudice against anyone who is transgender.

VEGAN: A person who does not eat (or use) any products from animals.

VEGETARIAN: A person who does not eat meat.

WORK-LIFE BALANCE: Dividing time between work and personal life in a way that suits the individual.

Unit 3: Employability

ASSISTIVE TECHNOLOGY: New computer technology developed for the workplace to help employees who are disabled.

BUSINESS ETHICS: This involves businesses acting in a responsible way towards employees, the community and the environment.

CAREER PLAN: A road map that helps a person reach their destination in the world of work.

CODE OF CONDUCT: A document that sets out how an organisation expects everyone to behave in the workplace.

CURRICULUM VITAE (CV): A summary of a person's education and employment history, giving details of qualifications, training and experience.

DISCRIMINATION: Being treated in a less favourable way than other people, usually because of culture, race, religion, gender, sexual orientation or disability.

ECONOMY: The system of money and trade for a particular country, or area. It is concerned with the production of products and services and how they are distributed and consumed.

EMIGRATION: When people leave a country to live elsewhere.

EMPLOYABILITY: This means that a person is capable of finding work, making a success of their job and being able to change careers successfully if needed.

EMPLOYMENT CONTRACT: An agreement between the employer and employee, which is made as soon as a person accepts a job. An employee is entitled to a written contract within two months of starting work.

ENTREPRENEUR: A business person who is able to spot an opportunity and market it successfully, taking calculated risks along the way.

EQUALITY: Equal rights for everyone regardless of how they might be different to someone else. For example, a person should never be treated unfairly because of factors such as gender, age, race, religion or disability.

ESSENTIAL SKILLS: The basic skills needed for learning, life and work. Also known as key skills, these include literacy, numeracy and IT.

EXPORTS: The products, services and raw materials that a business or country sells abroad.

GLOBALISATION: The process of the world becoming more interconnected and interdependent, particularly in regard to trade and business.

IMMIGRATION: When people move into a country from another country.

IMPORTS: The products, services and raw materials that are brought into a country.

LIFELONG LEARNING: The idea that lifelong learning is a continual process. Once someone is in employment, the learning process will involve professional development and acquiring new work-related skills.

MIGRATION: The movement of people from one country to another, usually looking for more favourable conditions.

PRODUCT: An item that is bought by a customer.

SALARY: The payment received by an employee for the work completed for their employer.

SELF-EMPLOYMENT: When a person makes their own income by working for themselves, rather than working for someone else and being paid a wage.

SERVICE: An activity that is carried out for a customer.

SOCIAL RESPONSIBILITY: This is when the government, groups, businesses and individuals in society act in a way that benefits everyone.

SUSTAINABILITY: This means how much the use of resources impacts on their long-term availability. A sustainable business does not have a negative impact on the environment; the methods used in production and the end product will be environmentally friendly and renewable where possible.

TRADE UNION: A membership-based organisation made up mainly of workers. It protects the rights of employees in the workplace, ensuring that employers meet their legal obligations and responsibilities.

WORK EXPERIENCE: The opportunity for people to spend some time in a place of employment, discovering more about a career or job.

Index

Copyright information

CREDITS

Where information or data has been used, sources are cited within the body of the book.

The following photographs are included with the kind permission of the copyright holders. The numbers denote page numbers:

Cover image: iStockphoto

Belfast Pride Festival: 8 (bottom)

Colin Crowley: 49 (both)

iStockphoto: 9 (left), 10, 12, 14, 15, 17 (top two), 18 (both), 21, 22, 23, 24, 25, 28, 29, 30 (both), 32, 35, 39, 40 (both), 43, 44 (all), 45, 46, 47, 51 (both), 52, 53, 55, 56 (both), 58 (right), 59, 61 (top two), 63 (both), 64 (left two), 65, 66 (both), 68 (both), 70, 71 (left), 72 (top two), 73 (both), 74 (both), 75 (both), 77, 78, 79 (both), 80 (top), 81 (all), 82 (all), 83 (both), 84 (all), 85 (all), 86 (top), 87 (all), 88 (bottom right), 89 (top two), 90 (both), 91, 92 (both), 93, 95 (both), 96 (all), 97 (left and top right), 99 (both), 100 (top), 101, 102 (both), 103 (both), 104 (both), 105, 109, 110, 112, 113 (both), 115 (both), 116 (both), 117, 118 (all), 119, 120 (left), 121, 122 (left and bottom right), 123 (both), 124 (both), 125 (bottom), 126, 127, 128, 129 (both), 130, 132, 133, 134, 137, 138 (both), 140 (both), 141 (both), 142 (both), 143, 144 (all), 146, 147, 148 (both), 149 (both), 150 (both), 151 (both), 153, 154, 155, 157 (both), 158, 159, 160 (both), 161, 162, 163 (both), 164, 167 (left), 168 (both), 169, 170, 174 (left), 175 (top), 176 (right), 177

Liam Hughes: 8 (second from top)

National Archives and Records Administration, Records of the U.S. Information Agency, Record Group 306: 17 (second from bottom)

Police Ombudsman for Northern Ireland: 41 (logo)

Public Health England: 60

Robert Paul Young: 36

William Murphy: 8 (top)

LICENCES